The Mobile & Ohio Railroad in the Civil War

T0407374

ALSO BY DAN LEE
AND FROM MCFARLAND

The Civil War in the Jackson Purchase, 1861–1862:
The Pro-Confederate Struggle and Defeat
in Southwest Kentucky (2014)

Thomas J. Wood: A Biography of the Union
General in the Civil War (2012)

The L&N Railroad in the Civil War: A Vital North-South
Link and the Struggle to Control It (2011)

Kentuckian in Blue: A Biography of Major General
Lovell Harrison Rousseau (2010)

The Mobile & Ohio Railroad in the Civil War

The Struggle for Control of the Nation's Longest Railway

DAN LEE

McFarland & Company, Inc., Publishers
Jefferson, North Carolina

All photographs are from the Library
of Congress unless otherwise noted.

LIBRARY OF CONGRESS CATALOGUING-IN-PUBLICATION DATA

Names: Lee, Dan, 1954– author.
Title: The Mobile & Ohio Railroad in the Civil War :
the struggle for control of the nation's longest railway / Dan Lee.
Description: Jefferson, North Carolina : McFarland & Company, Inc., Publishers, 2022 |
Includes bibliographical references and index.
Identifiers: LCCN 2022029089 | ISBN 9781476689722 (paperback : acid free paper) ∞
ISBN 9781476647111 (ebook)
Subjects: LCSH: United States—History—Civil War,
1861-1865—Transportation. | Railroads and state—United States—
History—19th century. | Railroads—Military aspects—United States—
History—19th century. | United States. Army—Transportation—History—
19th century. | Confederate States of America. Army—Transportation. |
Industrial mobilization—United States—History—19th century. |
Mobile and Ohio Railroad Company. | United States—Politics
and government—1861-1865. | Confederate States of America—Politics
and government. | Railroads—United States—History—19th century.
| Railroads—Confederate States of America—History.
Classification: LCC E491 .L485 2022 | DDC 385.0973—dc23/eng/20220622
LC record available at https://lccn.loc.gov/2022029089

BRITISH LIBRARY CATALOGUING DATA ARE AVAILABLE

ISBN (print) 978-1-4766-8972-2
ISBN (ebook) 978-1-4766-4711-1

© 2022 Dan Lee. All rights reserved

No part of this book may be reproduced or transmitted in any form
or by any means, electronic or mechanical, including photocopying
or recording, or by any information storage and retrieval system,
without permission in writing from the publisher.

Front cover: Currier & Ives illustration of locomotive
(Library of Congress)

Printed in the United States of America

McFarland & Company, Inc., Publishers
Box 611, Jefferson, North Carolina 28640
www.mcfarlandpub.com

For Ezekiel

Acknowledgments

My sincere thanks to: Gordon Vernon, Citronelle Historical Preservation Society, Citronelle, Alabama; Lisa Schoblasky, Special Collections Services Librarian, The Newberry Library, Chicago, Illinois; Ken Barr, Reference Archivist, and Sarah McQueen, Program Assistant, Alabama Department of Archives and History; Jennifer Davis McDaid, Historical Archivist, Corporate Communications, Norfolk Southern Corporation; David L. Bright, csa-railroads.com.

Table of Contents

"In accepting war it should be pure and simple as applied to the belligerents. I would keep it so till all traces of war are effaced; till those who appealed to it are sick and tired of it, and come to the emblem of our nation and sue for peace. I would not coax them or even meet them half way, but make them so sick of war that generations would pass before they would again appeal to it."

—William T. Sherman to Henry W. Halleck,
September 17, 1863

Preface

On February 14, 1864, Major General William T. Sherman led four divisions into the important railroad village of Meridian, Mississippi. Two iron roads, the Southern and the Mobile & Ohio, crossed there, and the warehouses bulged with supplies for the Rebel army. Excepting only Mobile itself, Meridian was the most important M&O Railroad station remaining in Confederate hands.

No one sent to stop Sherman's march across Mississippi had succeeded. He advanced steadily from Vicksburg to Jackson, where eight months earlier he had conducted a brief campaign against General Joseph E. Johnston. When Johnston withdrew to the east, Sherman moved into Mississippi's capital city and put his men to work. They burned and looted and practiced railroad destruction with such thoroughness that one of his division commanders remarked, "Nothing was left but the roadbed," a phrase that accurately described the scene wherever Sherman visited. There was not much for Sherman to destroy in Jackson when he returned in the winter of '64, but he burned what there was, and then he continued east to Meridian.[1]

There is no evidence at all that Sherman ever studied Sun Tzu, who wrote in 5th century BC, "An army without its baggage train is lost; without provisions it is lost; without bases of supply it is lost," but the scruffy Ohioan grasped the principle fully, and he realized that in this new-style war railroads were the primary logistical tool which allowed his enemies the Confederates to remain in the field. Earl J. Hess writes that rail transportation "represented the only new element in military transportation by the 1860s," and he explains the importance of that new element, saying, "If a six-mule team could haul one and a half tons of freight in a wagon for 333 miles while consuming one ton of fodder, that amounted to '500 ton-miles of transport capacity' generated by that 'ton of mule forage.' A train could travel 35 miles on one ton of engine fuel, but haul up to 150 tons, amounting to 5,250 ton-miles." Sherman's theory regarding railroads was basic and uncomplicated: break them up and cripple the ability of his enemies to feed, clothe, and arm themselves.[2]

Sherman's men fell to their work with a demonic energy. Before they were done with Meridian they had destroyed the town and miles of track in every direction, not to mention dozens of bridges, trestles, water tanks, and depots. Meridian, said Sherman, "no longer exists." This was Sherman's new vision of war, perfected in Mississippi and pursued later with terrible effectiveness in Georgia and South Carolina. His "chief goal," as William G. Thomas says, was "to wipe a place from the map, to render it dead or worthless, to irrevocably alter the geographic connections that sustained the Confederacy." Uncle Billy embraced destruction and made it his trademark, and wherever he went his route was marked by scorched earth and "Sherman neckties."[3]

Sherman chose his target in February 1864 well. Former Secretary of War L.P. Walker said the Mobile & Ohio and the Memphis & Charleston constituted the "vertebrae of the Confederacy." Those two railroads, along with the Louisville & Nashville (and its Memphis Branch) and the East Tennessee & Virginia, were critical to the South's early wartime strategy in the Western Theatre. The Mobile & Ohio was unique among these for its length. The M&O ran 449 miles, from its northern terminus at Columbus, Kentucky, to its southern at Mobile, Alabama, and it was under almost constant attack from the spring of 1862 until the war's end three years later. Seen in its proper context, Sherman's strike against Meridian did not stand alone; it was the continuation of a series of skirmishes, raids, battles, and campaigns with the Mobile & Ohio Railroad as the strategic focus.[4]

The M&O crossed some of the richest land in the South and connected some of the major industrial cities of the region to one another and to the Gulf coast. Men and war materiel raced along its length at thirty miles an hour, often frustrating the Federals' plans and hardening their determination to put an end to it. And this they did. Moving from Columbus south, men like Sherman, U.S. Grant, Benjamin Grierson, and A.J. Smith wrenched control of the Mobile & Ohio from their opposite numbers, commanders like Nathan Bedford Forrest, Stephen D. Lee, P.G.T. Beauregard, and Joseph E. Johnston. By their conquest of forty miles here, thirty miles there, the Federals pinched close one of the life-giving arteries of the Confederacy. Then they made the necessary repairs and used it for themselves. After that, it was in the nature of war that the roles were reversed and the Rebels began raiding behind the lines to tear up and destroy what had become a Yankee railroad.

The state-of-the art railroad of 1861 ended the war in 1865 as many did, "run down, stripped of equipment, and without working capital." In places, to echo that Federal officer who witnessed the destruction of another railroad in and around Jackson in '63, there was nothing left but roadbed. The railroad that had been foreseen as a future blessing to the

South ended up bringing destruction and poverty to the region it served. The M&O RR became an irresistible prize, drawing contending armies who burned and killed along an accursed corridor that began in Kentucky and ended on the Gulf Coast of Alabama.[5]

What follows is the story of the Mobile & Ohio Railroad, 1861–1865, and the struggle between the men in blue and gray who fought for control of it.

Note: Railroads that appeared to be of greater length than the M&O did not operate under a single corporate banner. For example, what was called the Memphis & Charleston RR was actually a system of no fewer than five separate railroads.

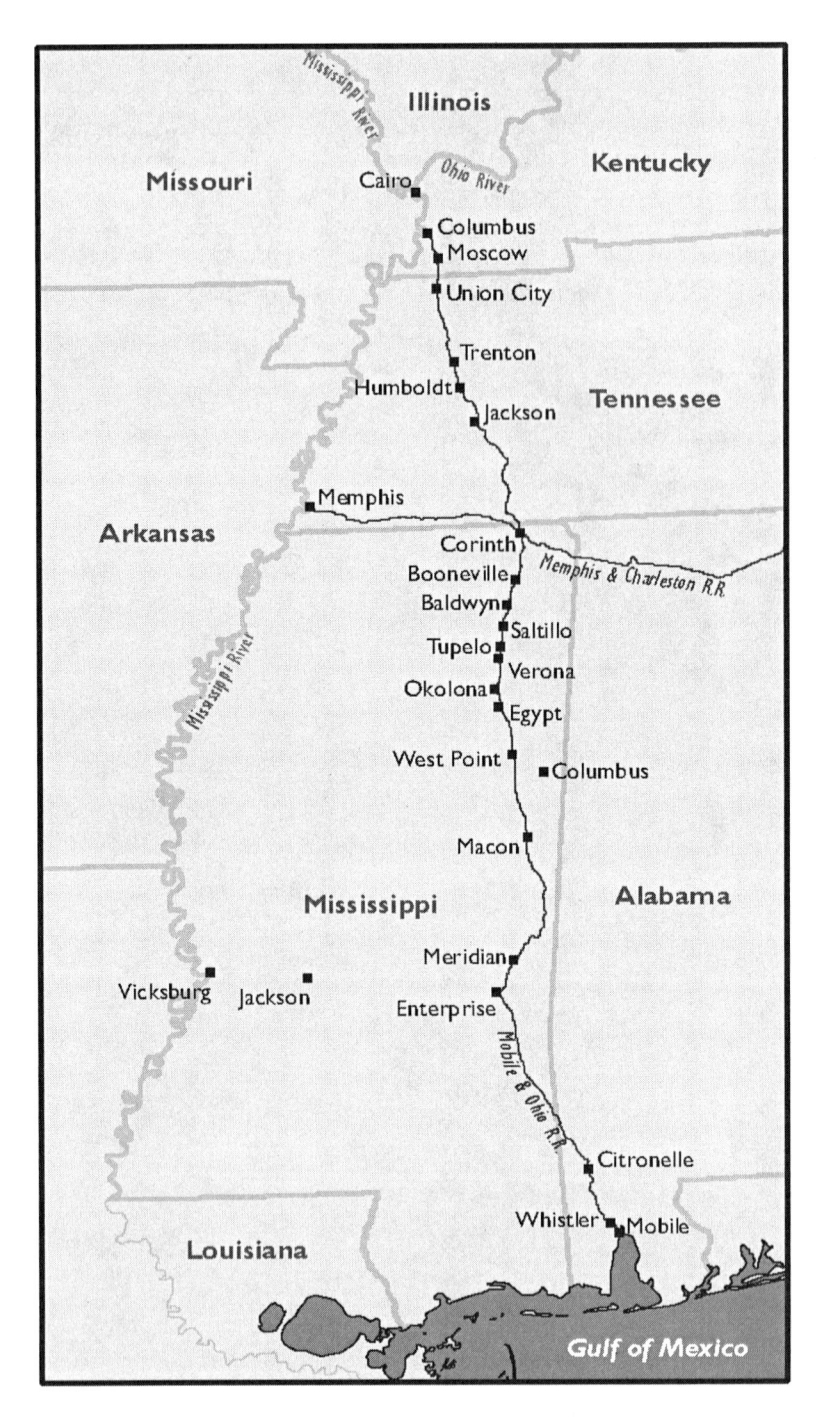

The Mobile & Ohio Railroad, 1861–1865 (map by Sasha Jovanovic).

CHAPTER ONE

The Politics of Secession

The final spike of the Mobile & Ohio Railroad was driven at Columbus, on April 22, 1861. The occasion was notable, but the joy that should have attended the completion of the nation's longest single rail line was absent. In an earlier time, newspapers throughout the Mississippi River Valley and north to Chicago would have devoted bold headlines and column inches to the event. Now coverage was reduced to a short paragraph: "Yesterday the last nail of the Mobile and Ohio was driven. The first train will soon pass over the entire road from Mobile, Ala., to Columbus, Ky." That was all. In the spring of 1861 the newspapers had no space to spare for such mundane news as the completion of a railroad, even one so impressive as the M&O. By the time this great steel unifier of regions was completed, the regions had begun tearing themselves apart.[1]

After the election of Abraham Lincoln in the presidential race of 1860, there was little doubt that Mississippi and Alabama would secede. Mississippi left the Union on January 9, 1861. On January 15, Governor John J. Pettus spoke to the state legislators of the new situation. He told the lawmakers that private business interests approved of and had promised to aid his efforts to defend the state. Pettus said, "The Mobile and Ohio Railroad Company have tendered me the free use of their road for the transportation of troops and munitions of war whenever the State may require it, placing at the disposal of the governor of the State extra trains, when required, free of charge." Many Mississippians learned of their state's decision to secede while traveling on the M&O Railroad. At depots all along the line, secession was announced by cannon fire, and "at those stations where cannon could not be procured, anvils were brought into requisition, and were managed with so much skill as to produce an equal uproar."[2]

Alabama followed Mississippi out of the Union on January 11. She was strongly conscious of the need to protect Mobile, her most vulnerable point. The city's U.S. Arsenal had been seized a week before secession, on January 4, "by four companies of volunteers from Mobile." Captain Jesse Reno of the U.S. Ordnance Department wrote his superiors, "I did not make, nor could I have made, any resistance, as they had scaled the walls and taken possession before I knew anything about the movement." He said that the governor's men now had "entire possession of the arsenal" and were demanding "all the public property."[3]

Governor A.B. Moore wrote to President James Buchanan that same eventful January 4 to officially inform him of the seizure of the arsenal, and also of the occupation of Fort Morgan and Fort Gaines at the entrance of Mobile Bay. By the seizure of these three installations, Alabama acquired not only the physical structures and the grounds, but also one hundred cannon, over twenty thousand stand of small arms, and 150,000 pounds of gunpowder. Governor Moore explained to the president that it was his duty to "make the secession peaceful, and prevent detriment to her [Alabama's] people." Believing that the United States Government was about to reinforce the forts "and put a guard over the arsenal," he had moved first in the interest of self-defense. Governor Moore said that his state would not be coerced and asserted that Alabama hoped "to avoid, not provoke hostilities."[4]

On January 12, the executive branch of Alabama authorized $10,000 for the defense of Mobile, and the citizens of the city, who had been so generous in their support of the M&O during its twelve years of construction, went down in their pockets again and promised to raise $100,000 more to lend. Governor Moore begged them to keep good records if they expected state reimbursements. He agreed that "Mobile must be defended at whatever cost," but he implored "every patriotic citizen" of Alabama "to husband every dollar of her resources by seeing that not a dollar is improperly expended."[5]

With the two southern-most states mobilizing for their defense, traffic on the Mobile & Ohio Railroad saw a marked increase. M&O cars carried construction material to Mobile for repairs on the forts and carried soldiers south to man them. The Selma *Morning Reporter* said, "The importance of the M&O RR [from] a military point of view has been recently thoroughly and practically established. Bodies of troops from North Alabama and Mississippi during the last week have been transported over it at the rate of several hundred per day with faculty and dispatch. A spokesman for the railroad said the M&O could transport twenty thousand troops per week, if necessary."[6]

While the militancy of Mississippi and Alabama was demonstrated early; the appetite for disunion in Tennessee and Kentucky remained in question. Both states had in their recent past unequivocal supporters of the Union; from Kentucky, Henry Clay, the Great Compromiser, and from Tennessee, Andrew Jackson, who, as President, had famously proclaimed, "The Union must be preserved," and who had threatened to personally hang the South Carolina leaders of the 1832 Nullification Movement. As winter turned into spring, neither state had made the fateful move. William J. Sykes of Tennessee had some pointed concerns of what a failure to secede would mean economically. He shared them with his fellow citizens in a letter to the Nashville *Union and American,* printed shortly after the presidential election. Sykes wrote, "If we decide to go with the North under Lincoln, what will become of our Memphis and Charleston Railroad, running through Alabama and Mississippi, what of the Mobile and Ohio, running through the same States, what of the railroad running from Nashville to Decatur? Where will our people sell their horses, mules, and other stock? Where will be the market for our negroes, if we have any to sell? Now nearly all our trade is with the South…. The Cotton States, as they are called, help to enrich us, and the Northern States to impoverish us."[7]

Hans L. Trefousse points out, "In the last analysis, whether Tennessee would really remain loyal depended upon national events … it was evident that Lincoln's actions concerning beleaguered Fort Sumter in Charleston Harbor, one of the few forts still in Federal hands and under siege by the Confederates, would have a great effect on the fortunes of the state." When Fort Sumter was fired upon and President Lincoln called for volunteers to quash the rebellion, the secessionist bloc in the Tennessee legislature followed the governor's wishes and guided through an ordinance of secession, subject to ratification by the voters. On June 8, the citizens voted in favor of separating from the Union by a vote of more than two to one. Military historian John Keegan explains that the action agreed upon was a bit more nuanced than mere secession. He says that Tennessee did not secede exactly, but passed a declaration of independence and "concluded an alliance with the Confederacy." He calls it a "transparently evasive measure."[8]

Tennessee had turned her back on her Unionist hero of earlier times. Kentucky would not. Of the four states traversed by the Mobile & Ohio Railroad, Kentucky's secession dilemma was the most interesting and the most perplexing. First was the matter of slavery. Slaves made up to twenty percent of Kentucky's population; they were, however, owned by twos and threes. E. Merton Coulter emphasizes that "no Kentuckian owned over 300 slaves; only seventy had over 50. The total number of slaveholders was 38,645. Slavery was, thus, widely dispersed over the state and entrenched with the average Kentuckian, the class that made up the backbone of the state's leadership." Coulter also says that the number of slaves in Kentucky had been decreasing in recent years. This was true in every region of the state except for the Jackson Purchase, the far western province of Kentucky, where the northern terminus of the Mobile & Ohio was found.[9]

Next came the question of blood relations. Kentucky was a state with deep ancestral roots in Virginia and the Carolinas. Her manners and social institutions were passed down from her Southern forebears of the frontier period. Pioneer families that came from the North soon adopted the culture and attitudes of their Southern neighbors. The Lyon family of Vermont is an example. Congressman Matthew Lyon led the family to Eddyville from Vermont in 1800. The first generation of Lyons, the emigrants, were shocked and offended at the slavery they saw around them when they made their home in Kentucky. Only a few years later, the second generation came to accept the peculiar institution and became prominent slave owners. The third generation not only owned slaves, but produced Brigadier General Hylan B. Lyon, who spent four years of his life fighting with unmatched determination for the perpetuation of slavery.

Still, settlers from the New England states were not common. Most Kentuckians traced family lines back to ancestors who came across the mountains from the old Southern states. Many of their *descendants*, however, had moved on, removing themselves to the North and West where they put down new roots. Kin fighting kin was a chilling prospect. Moreover, emigration flowed both ways. There were thousands from each of the three states across the Ohio River who were living in Kentucky. As a corollary to the matter of population make-up, one must also consider that Kentucky in 1860 had "nearly 60,000 foreigners, which was far more than any other Southern state possessed outside of Missouri." Many of these foreigners were the Germans living in Covington, Louisville, and Paducah, and they came out of a liberal tradition in Europe. They were pro–Union and anti-slavery. When the time came to choose sides, their influence would help hold Kentucky in the Union.[10]

Trade was equally as tangled. In the forty years before the Civil War, Kentucky maintained a "constant stream" of trade to the south in hogs, cattle, horses, and mules. Coulter says, "The Kentucky mule was as much a necessity on the Southern plantation as was the slave." Kentucky supplied a great many of the slaves, as well. In the three decades preceding the war, about 77,000 Kentucky-born slaves were sold into the Deep South. Kentucky hemp became the bagging for baled cotton and the ropes to bind it. With the advent of canals, steamboats, and railroads, though, Kentucky found new markets in the East and West for her agricultural and industrial products. "New York alone bought in 1860 more than 20,000 hogsheads of tobacco from Kentucky." In that same year, Kentucky had seventeen iron furnaces working, producing 42,500 pounds of pig iron, much of which went down the rivers to Evansville, Indiana, and beyond. The flow of Northern trade also ran the other way. Kentucky's heavy purchase of manufactured goods led George D. Prentice, editor of the Louisville *Daily Journal*, to warn his readers that secession would mean that Kentuckians would pay not only ruinous excise taxes, but high import duties, as well. R.E. Banta sums up Kentucky's situation by saying that, as a nexus of commerce between North and South, "friendship with both localities was vital."[11]

Finally, there was the certainty of military invasion if Kentucky went with the belligerent South. The Unionist Archibald Dixon warned, "In sixty days the North can pour an army of one hundred thousand men upon every part of us.... If we remain in the Union, we are safe; if we go out we will be overwhelmed." The supposed boundary of the Ohio River was not so much of an obstacle as it appeared at first glance. Coulter observes, "There were no less than twelve points on the Ohio River opposite Kentucky where railroads came down from the North; at only two points could connections be maintained with the South." He meant the Mobile & Ohio Railroad and the main stem of the Louisville & Nashville Railroad. Coulter overlooked the Memphis Branch of the L&N, which crossed the Tennessee line just below the little town of Guthrie, but his point is well taken. Kentucky was vulnerable along her northern border. If she seceded, the Federal armies would come and she would undoubtedly earn anew her ancient reputation as the Dark and Bloody Ground.[12]

Unionists and secessionists struggled through the early months of 1861 to gain the advantage. Meeting in special session in May 1861, the legislature took the unprecedented and constitutionally shaky step of declaring the state to be neutral in the contest between the North and South. The solution baffled some, angered others, and satisfied but very few. However, Kentucky's neutral stance did not last long. In the special election for Congress on June 20, 1861, Unionists won nine of Kentucky's ten seats. Only the 1st District, the Jackson Purchase, elected a secessionist. In August, in the elections for the state legislature, Unionists won seventy-six House seats to the secessionists' twenty-four, and in the Senate the figures were twenty-seven Unionists to eleven States' Rights men. The issue was settled. Three months of neutrality had ended; Kentucky had committed to the Union.

This might have put the Mobile & Ohio in a difficult position, considering that its northern terminus was in Columbus, Kentucky. Kentucky's other major railroad, the Louisville & Nashville, was in a similar situation, with its northern terminus in loyal Louisville and its southern terminus in Confederate Nashville. The difference was that Columbus was in the Jackson Purchase, the "Mad Dog District," the "South Carolina of Kentucky," where States' Rights fervor was so high that the region considered seceding from Kentucky, once it became clear that Kentucky would not secede from the Union. With such radical sentiments prevailing, the locals would present no threat to the M&O RR at its northern end.[13]

And what of the Mobile & Ohio Railroad? Like Kentucky, Tennessee, Mississippi, and Alabama, the M&O was an entity of its own that shared many of the characteristics of a state. It had defined boundaries, and it had its internal loyalties and its external alliances and rivalries (the Mobile & Ohio and the Memphis & Charleston were often bitterly competitive). The M&O had an executive and a legislative branch. It had a capital city (Mobile). It owned slaves and leased others, and it even had the power to issue and circulate money. In the state of Mississippi, at least, the M&O Railroad was among those authorized to issue up to $100,000 in "notes of any denomination not greater than three dollars nor less than one dollar." As was true between states, the principle of reciprocity applied; the railroads had to accept the notes of the other railroads in payment.[14]

Like the states through which it passed, the railroad was thrown into turmoil by the coming war, even as early as the fall and winter of 1860 and the spring of 1861. In his address to the thirteenth annual stockholders meeting of the M&O RR, held May 7, 1861, President Milton Brown was pleased to report that the line was, at last, fully operational. Then he alluded to the uncertainties of the war time situation. He said,

> In ordinary times, with our road finished, we might safely expect a large increase of income. And the time would seem appropriate to enter on a review of our financial condition, and make suggestions in regard to the future. But in the present uncertain condition of things, with a hostile army at Cairo, and a threatened, if not actual blockade of the Port of Mobile, and the whole country in arms, almost entirely breaking up commercial intercourse, and the ordinary business transactions of the country, it would be unsafe, at present, to make estimates of income or propose measures of future policy. This we leave until the development of events may throw additional light on the subject.[15]

The onset of war may have put immediate profits in doubt and frozen in place the development of long-range plans, but Brown was not leading a chorus of self-pity. He ended his address to the stockholders on a defiant note:

> Of one thing, however, we can speak with confidence and certainty—that your road, running through four States, will furnish in times of peace a great *artery* of commerce and in war a powerful *arm* of defence; and that in peace or in war its influence will be exerted in support of Southern Commerce and in the maintenance of Southern institutions.[16]

Next on the podium was L.J. Fleming, Chief Engineer and General Superintendent of the railroad. He reported that there had been no passenger injuries in the past fiscal year, a happy result of "the watchfulness and strict attention to duty of the officers, agents, and employees in every department." He reported earnings from the movement of passengers and freight of $1,402,858. The total of all expenses rising from repairs and machinery was $707,488. Interest payments, a separate outgo of funds, totaled $398,727. This left a black ink balance of $296,642. Fleming told the assembly that the earnings had increased "over the same period of the previous year," and would have reached $1,750,000 "but for the short crops and political agitation." He concluded,

> It was my intention on the completion of the road to review its history and present for your consideration the prospects of ultimate success as an investment of capital, but the Revolution of the Government, and the consequent destruction of business in every department of industry, and the uncertainty as to when commerce will resume its accustomed channels, destroys the value of all such speculations, and they are therefore omitted.[17]

Obviously, there was something else the Mobile & Ohio Railroad shared with the four states through which it ran. It was racing with irresistible momentum toward an uncertain future, and its fate was not entirely in its own hands.

CHAPTER TWO

The Two Gibraltars

In his message to the stockholders, President Brown alluded to threats at both the northern and the southern ends of the railroad. The danger to Mobile was from the Federal Navy blockade beyond the mouth of Mobile Bay. Neither the city itself nor the M&O RR terminus there were in immediate peril—the bay was thirty miles long—but an effective blockade would result in shortages that would cause suffering in the city and hamper the war effort throughout the Confederacy. Far worse than a simple blockade would be the loss of the bay, and the Confederates took early measures to strengthen their defenses there. Colonel William J. Hardee, commander of Fort Morgan, Fort Gaines, and the works at Grant's Pass, asked Major Danville Leadbetter of the engineering department to recommend improvements "to prevent the entrance of a hostile force into Mobile Bay." Leadbetter recommended "mounting a few guns in barbette" inside Fort Gaines and simultaneously arming each of the bastions "with one heavy pivot gun." By these improvements, said Leadbetter, "Fort Gaines will be defensible, and be made to exercise a strong influence on the defense of the channel west of the main ship channel."[1]

"At Fort Morgan," Leadbetter continued, "the citadel should be made bomb proof and receive a parapet of sand bags. These are the general dispositions urgently required for defense." This modest change, together with the exterior lines east of the fort, would make Fort Morgan "truly defensible." The mouth of the bay, which was more than three miles wide, continued to be of concern, however, because the forts "do not effectively command the middle of it." Leadbetter recommended the building of a floating battery to patrol the unprotected zone, saying "her fire combined with that of the forts would command the narrow channel effectually, and her locomotive powers would enable her to cruise with effect in the daytime."[2]

It was Mobile's good fortune in these early weeks of the war that the U.S. Navy concentrated more of its attention on New Orleans. Arthur W. Bergeron, Jr., says, despite Mobile's strategic position, the Crescent City "outranked Mobile as a port." It was only after the fall of New Orleans on May 1, 1862, that Mobile became "the leading port on the Gulf." Until then, the mouth of Mobile Bay was blockaded by only a ship or two at a time. The first was Lieutenant David D. Porter's *Powhatan*, which took up her post on May 26, 1861. Porter reported seeing on his arrival the U.S. flag flying upside down and below the Confederate flag from the main staff at Fort Morgan, a taunt flung at the blockader. Though ineffective in and of itself, the arrival of that first blockader was a sign of the future. At least some of the ships inside the bay took advantage of the Federals' offer to leave within the month "with their cargoes before a rigid blockade became effective." They warned that after May 31, "any vessel attempting to enter or leave Mobile Bay would be subject to seizure and the confiscation of her cargo by Federal authorities."[3]

To enforce the policy, the U.S. Navy kept a succession of ships on duty outside the bay. Following the *Powhatan*, the ships of the Gulf Blockading Squadron that kept vigil included the *Brooklyn*, the *Huntsville*, the *Cuyler*, the *Niagara*, the *Kanawha*, and the *South Carolina*. The Confederate blockade runners evaded them with skill, escaping the bay to make the three-day run to Havana loaded with bales of cotton, which they sold to British agents in Cuba, and returning with "military supplies and items for consumption by the civilian population" such as rum, medicine, and dry goods.[4]

As for the defenses on Mobile's land side, a veteran recalled that "there was a battery on every road leading into town and manned by the Alabama State Artillery. One of them, the Ladies Battery, was paid for by the women of the city who sold their jewelry to pay for it. It was on Bay Shell Road. The Home-Guard—men of fifty to seventy-five years—protected the city proper. They were armed with pikes and commanded by Captain Price Williams, Sr."[5]

It was not Mobile, but Columbus, on the other end of the Mobile & Ohio, that Confederate authorities considered to be at the most immediate risk. John Keegan writes, "The Mississippi—Ohio—Tennessee—Cumberland complex was of particular strategic importance since, in a Jeffersonian phrase, they interlocked, their interconnecting points or confluences, if held, conferring great advantage to the occupier." The most important of these rivers was the Mississippi, and the bluffs at Columbus dominated it. The Federals knew that they must have Columbus in order to proceed down the Mississippi, but they could not cross into neutral Kentucky to occupy it. Instead, they began massing troops at Cairo, Illinois. Cairo was at the confluence of the Ohio and Mississippi Rivers and only a few miles upstream from Columbus. The U.S. forces concentrating at Cairo did not lodge in the town itself, but at their cantonment a short distance below, Camp Defiance. By May 2, 1861, there were 5,250 troops at Cairo and Camp Defiance with plenty of ammunition stockpiled and thirty artillery pieces. The New York *Times* informed readers, "It is proper to be known that all the volunteers at Cairo have been regularly mustered into the United States service, and the encampment is regularly one of the United States Government."[6]

As miserable as it was with heat, humidity, mosquitoes, and rats, the delta at Cairo was the proper staging area for operations against the rivers. Cairo commanded the confluence and was also the southern terminus of the Illinois Central Railroad. It was the partner of Columbus and the Mobile & Ohio RR, the connecting point for the passengers, freight, and mail that traveled by river packet between the two railroads' terminals. It was for this reason that M&O President Milton Brown wrote on April 27 to Colonel Benjamin M. Prentiss, who was in charge of the Cairo troops. Brown told Prentiss that, in order "to allay all possible misapprehension," he wished to ask a few questions. They were:

> 1st. Can I safely say to persons desiring to ship freight through, or by Cairo, that they will be safe in doing so?
>
> 2d. Will boxes be shipped through, or by Cairo, be subject to examination of the contents by being opened?
>
> 3d. Can I say to all travelers that they will, in passing through Cairo, be protected in their persons and property?
>
> 4th. May I assure the public that the steamers running between the Illinois Central and the Mobile and Ohio Railroad will not be interfered with, and will be protected in a peaceful neutrality?[7]

Brown signed the letter "most respectfully yours" and awaited Prentiss's reply. The Federal commander's strangely punctuated letter came by return mail the same day. It said:

> To your first question I answer—Yes, Sir; provided said freight is not for army or equipping the enemies of the United States Government?
>
> To your second question I answer—they will not unless information has been previously received that they contain arms and munitions of war destructive to the United States Government?
>
> To your third question I answer—Yes; provided, however that said property be not munitions of war, destined to the enemies of the United States Government. We should be surprised to know that our civilized brethren, anywhere, have a doubt that we would protect persons passing through here, except the active enemies of the United States Government.[8]

Courtesy between the principal players was still the order of the day, but the newspapers could find no story in polite exchanges. Through the spring of '61, the Northern press ran stories of imminent attack from across the Ohio River. Well before the end of Kentucky neutrality, and while the poorly armed Confederate volunteers were still training in their Tennessee camps, the New York *Times* informed its readers, "The news from Cairo is still of an ominous character. Reports crowd the columns of all Western papers of forces collecting at Columbus, at Paducah, and other points in Kentucky, and on the Mississippi below, to attack the Illinois Volunteers now holding Cairo." On May 3, the New York *Times* told its readers, "that 1,700 stand of arms were landed at Columbus ... and that seven pieces of cannon were landed at Paducah yesterday." On May 28, readers learned that "The Secessionists in Paducah and Columbus are very noisy. They are backed by West Tennesseans, who intend suddenly to send thousands of troops by the Mobile & Ohio Railroad to Columbus, and by the Tennessee River to Paducah." According to the paper, the invaders' ultimate purpose was to provoke a fight with Colonel Prentiss at Cairo and force Kentucky to secede. If the whole state would not go out, they would at least separate and claim the Jackson Purchase.[9]

The policy of the Confederate government was to respect Kentucky neutrality, but some individuals living in the Purchase and points south held a different view. They had been calling for action since the start of hostilities in April. Only a few days after Fort Sumter, three citizens from Columbus wrote a long letter to President Jefferson Davis. They avowed their loyalty to the Confederate States, and they alerted him to the danger posed to the South if Cairo were occupied by "an abolition army." They said, "It will enable our enemies to cut off effectually all supplies from the above sources [Missouri and the Upper Mississippi] to the South." They also called Davis's attention to the strategic importance of their own town. They said,

> Columbus, too, is also a very important place, and should be garrisoned and fortified. The Mississippi here is very narrow, only half a mile wide, and to the north of the town are the iron banks—immense bluffs, which rise 200 feet above the river. An efficient battery planted there would effectually command the channel. Nothing could pass without our permission. It is the first high land below the mouth, which, added to the narrowness of the river here, makes it capable of being rendered an almost impregnable point.

They did not mention their brand new connection to the Deep South via the Mobile & Ohio, but Davis, being a Mississippian, would have known about it already.[10]

On May 10, William W. Lee of Noxubee County, Mississippi, wrote to Secretary of War L.P. Walker. He was alarmed at the concentration of Federal forces at Cairo, who were opposed down river by nothing more than "a few half-formed companies of volunteers and home guards, mostly without arms of any kind." Lee recommended that Columbus be fortified, saying, "there is no strategic point of half so much importance ... is should immediately occupied by a strong force notwithstanding the neutral position of Kentucky. Self-preservation demands it." He referenced the importance of the town as the terminus of the Mobile & Ohio, but pointed out that there was a secondary strategic depot on the M&O a few miles south. He said, "If the government should decide not to 'take and fortify Columbus,' then a strong force should be immediately sent to Union City, the intersection of the Mobile and Ohio with the Nashville and Northwestern Railroads."[11]

Secretary Walker received a similar letter the next day. Writing from Murray, Kentucky, A.P. Thompson told Walker that the people of the Jackson Purchase stood ready to "resist to the death," but "we are unarmed, comparatively speaking." He believed that President Lincoln's troops would undoubtedly try to take possession of certain points in Kentucky, "(to wit) the mouths of the Tennessee and Cumberland Rivers and the terminus of the Mobile and Ohio Railroad. The importance of these positions being held by friends of the South will be readily perceived by a glance at the map."[12]

Some military men, too, were urging their government to take action. Major Josiah Gorgas, commanding the Confederate Engineer Bureau, wrote to Walker that Columbus or Hickman should be seized, "lining the banks of the river with cannon and covering them with land works—an intrenched camp, capable of holding 30,000 men. With this the passage of the river could not be effected, and there would be no use in turning such a work, since nothing could be effected below it without a flotilla." No one, however, was more insistent on the importance of Columbus than General Gideon Pillow, commander of the Tennessee state troops (the "Provisional Army of Tennessee"). Pillow wrote to Governor Beriah Magoffin asking permission to occupy Columbus, and on May 13, he wrote Secretary of War Walker, "I must have support in assuming a position on the new line near Union City or at Columbus. Have applied for permission to occupy and fortify Columbus. No answer yet." The permission Pillow sought did not come.[13]

While the sound of the war drums increased, President Brown and other prominent Southerners continued to seek guarantees from General Prentiss that communications between North and South would remain open. In May, Brown and former Governor John J. McRae of Mississippi were part of a group that traveled to Cairo for an interview with Prentiss and "to learn in person the precise object of the concentration of troops at Cairo, and particularly to inquire whether any interruption of the running of the Mobile and Ohio railroad steamboat, connecting the Mobile and Ohio road with the Illinois Central, is meditated." Prentiss must have reassured them, presumably with the same conditions as he stated in his April reply to Brown's list of queries. On May 24, Captain W.A.R. Latimer of the *B.F. Chenney* ("which forms the medium of communication between the Mobile railroad at Columbus, and the Central Illinois at Cairo") placed an item in the papers stating that the riverboat "is still running regularly between Columbus and Cairo, and will run as long as travel continues on the road, and communication with the North and South is kept."[14]

The fact is that while both sides were nervous and both sides were massing troops on the edges of the Jackson Purchase, it was the North who made the most threatening moves during these first months of the war. It was to the South's advantage to respect Kentucky neutrality. As long as Kentucky remained neutral, she provided an effective shield to Tennessee. South of the state boundary, strung out along the route of the M&O Railroad, at Union City, Humboldt, Jackson, and Corinth, there were C.S.A. troops poised to make the short run north to Columbus, but they made no move to violate Kentucky neutrality.

The Federal troops from Cairo were more aggressive. They seized river boats mid-trip and searched their cargoes. They sent water-borne excursions down the Mississippi to intimidate Columbus. They sometimes fired their cannon when they pulled abreast of the town, and on one occasion, June 12, 1861, a detachment of the 8th Illinois came ashore to pull down a Confederate flag visible from the river. L.G. Faxon, editor of the Columbus *Crescent*, later said, "When the bow-legged, wooden-shoed, sour craut stinking, Bologna sausage eating, hen roost robbing, Dutch sons of _ _ _ _ _ _ _ had accomplished the brilliant feat of taking down the Secessionist flag on the river bank, they were pointed to another flag of the same sort which their guns did not cover ... and dared yea! Double big black dog-dared, as we used to say at school, to take that flag down—the cowardly pups, the thieving sheep dogs, the sneaking skunks dare not do so, because their twelve pieces of artillery were not bearing on it."[15]

The Federals set foot on Kentucky soil again that same June when a party of two hundred crossed from Cairo and tried to capture the Columbus Rangers, a militia group that was in the field on maneuvers. The Yankees were prepared to fire on the Rangers if they resisted. They came in the dark of night, alarmed the sleeping citizenry, and made a few arrests. They missed bagging the weekend soldiers of Columbus, but they had kindled a fresh blaze of fear and resentment. George Taylor of Columbus said, "It has never been the pleasure of any person connected with this flagrant infraction of Kentucky neutrality to allege any fault committed by a single individual of that party of Rangers. It was a wanton, unprovoked invasion of Kentucky soil to hunt down and murder Kentucky citizens."[16]

Federal contempt toward Kentucky neutrality having been convincingly demonstrated, General Simon Bolivar Buckner, commander of the

State Guard, ordered Colonel Lloyd Tilghman and six companies to move to Columbus. In civilian life, Tilghman was the chief construction engineer of the New Orleans & Ohio Railroad, a trunk line that connected Paducah with the M&O near Union City, Tennessee. It was a sign of growing Unionist sentiment in the other parts of the state, and consequently of the isolation of the Purchase in its Southern radicalism, that when Buckner ordered thirty tents and enough cooking utensils for Tilghman's men, the U.S. government agent at Louisville, W.P. Mellen, refused to let the inventory be shipped. Buckner wrote to Mellen in protest, "Am I to understand from this, that you claim the right to prevent the State of Kentucky from exercising the clear right of furnished her own militia with what is necessary for their equipment, and that you assume, as an agent of the United States Government, to supervise and veto the official acts of the constituted authorities of Kentucky, acting in accordance with existing laws?" Mellen did not reply directly to Buckner, but he did finally allow the items to be sent to Tilghman's camp at Columbus. Colonel Tilghman, disgusted with neutrality as a guiding principle, shortly afterward resigned from the State Guard and traveled to the Confederate training camp near Clarksville, Tennessee, where he helped organize and became the colonel of the 3rd Kentucky Infantry. Colonel Ben Hardin Helm, the brother-in-law of President Lincoln, succeeded Tilghman in command at Columbus. Helm, too, soon went south.[17]

Incidents like the seizure of boats, the flag-tearing episode at Columbus, and the attempted arrest of the Columbus Rangers continued through the summer. In the second week in August, Colonel Richard J. Oglesby, now commanding at Cairo, ordered the capture at Paducah of a civilian vessel called the *W.B. Terry*, which was suspected of running contraband tobacco into Tennessee. Oglesby said that he had "indisputable proof" that the *Terry* was guilty of smuggling, and he ordered her seizure "*without hesitating on the neutrality of Kentucky*" [Emphasis added]. After a group of armed Kentuckians seized a Federal mail packet in reprisal for the confiscation of the *Terry*, General Frémont said, "Events have transpired clearly indicating the complicity of citizens of Kentucky, with the rebel forces, and showing the impracticability of carrying on operations in that direction without *involving the Kentucky shore*" (Emphasis added). Subsequent to the events in Paducah, the U.S. Postal Department announced the shuttering of post offices in Paducah, Columbus, Hickman, "and all other post-offices in Kentucky west of the Tennessee River." It was another step that isolated and alienated the secessionist Jackson Purchase. The Federals in Cairo, always pleading that attack was imminent, patrolled the rivers and trespassed repeatedly on Kentucky's neutral soil. To the people of Columbus, Paducah, and the other towns of western-most Kentucky "Yankee power (the misuse of power in the view of most natives), was being felt more and more and had to be resisted. The Purchase was caught up in an unhealthy escalation that could lead but to one result. Events were about to take a very serious turn indeed."[18]

On September 2, 1861, Brigadier General U.S. Grant, commander of the District of Southeast Missouri, ordered Colonel Gustav Waagner to lead a force down the Mississippi and establish an outpost at Belmont, Missouri, across the Mississippi from Columbus. Grant's superior, General Frémont, had instructed him to "take possession of points threatened by the Confederates on the Missouri and Kentucky shores." Grant's move was the very type of threatening act that Major General Leonidas Polk had been expecting. Polk was commander of the Confederate Department No. 2, headquartered in Union City, Tennessee. He seems to have learned of Grant's move from a spy named Harris, who wrote him from Columbus, "Between 1500 and 2000. Loaded wagons, horses and artillery, light caliber; no fortifications yet.... The troops are camped in the woods opposite Columbus." Waagner stayed in Belmont only one night, but his expedition prodded Polk into action. Just the day before, he had written to Governor Magoffin, saying, "I think it of the greatest importance to the Southern cause in Kentucky or elsewhere that I should be ahead of the enemy in occupying Columbus and Paducah." Grant had made the first move, but he was not yet in Kentucky. There was still time. Polk ordered Brigadier General Gideon Pillow to steam across the Mississippi from New Madrid, Missouri, and land his troops in Kentucky. Pillow crossed the river on September 3, spent the night in Hickman, and the next day, September 4, led his men into to Columbus, where the civilians "welcomed them 'with the liveliest delight.'"[19]

General Polk's telegraph operator in Union City took down a September 4 wire from Tennessee Governor Harris, who called Pillow's move "unfortunate," and said, "the President and myself are pledged to respect the neutrality of Kentucky. I hope they [Pillow's troops] will be withdrawn instantly." And he coded and sent Polk's reply, "I regret that a movement so entirely acceptable to the people of Kentucky, and so essential to the security of western Tennessee, does not permit me ... to concur with your views. I had never received official information that the President and yourself had determined upon any particular course in reference to the State of Kentucky."[20]

The same day, Polk received a telegram from Secretary of War L.P. Walker, who was a little behind the curve of events. Walker said that he had just heard of Pillow's men in Hickman. "Order their prompt withdrawal from Kentucky," Walker ordered. On that same busy September 4, Polk sent a telegram to President Davis explaining that he thought the invasion was both timely and necessary to keep Columbus out of Union hands. "This demonstration on my part has had the desired effect," Polk said. "The enemy had withdrawn his forces even before I had fortified my position. It is my intention now to occupy and keep this position." Davis's answer led to a bit of chicanery on Polk's part. The general later claimed that President Davis replied, "The necessity justifies the action," which reads like unqualified approval. However, Polk's most recent biographer, Huston Horn, points out that when he submitted the transcripts of the wires to the C.S.A. War Department, Polk slightly altered the President's message by omitting one important word. It originally read, "The necessity must justify the action." That troublesome "must" can make the message read as an admonition to Polk for moving too soon, without sufficient justification. Polk's alteration leads one to believe that *he* realized the president was not completely supportive. Polk compounded his deceit, says Horn, in his message to Governor Beriah Magoffin. To the governor, he deliberately misquoted President Davis by changing the tense of the verb: "The necessity justified the action." It was all pretty shady for a Bishop of the Episcopal Church, but, in any case, his intentions were clear. His troops were in Columbus and there they were going to stay. Columbus had uninterrupted rail communications with Mobile on the Gulf, and Rebel guns would soon command the river and guarantee a secure connection with New Orleans.[21]

The people of the little town were ecstatic. On September 5, the day after Pillow's arrival, a group of citizens sent a long letter of appreciation to General Polk, who was still in Union City. It occupies more than three pages in the *Official Records*. The letter thanked Polk with "profound gratification" for saving them from the "tyrannical rules of the Northern Government." They reviewed at length the recent actions of the Federal troops, which began "from the first hour that Cairo became a military encampment." The letter spoke of the citizens' "sincere delight with which we hail the approach of the army under your command," and their "sense of restored confidence" that the Confederacy had not forgotten them. "It is from hearts filled with such emotions as these that the entire community extends to you and to your gallant army a cordial welcome," the citizens said.[22]

Polk's troops were in command of the town, but the general did not write Governor Beriah Magoffin until September 8. Two days earlier, General U.S. Grant's forces had occupied Paducah, and it may be that Polk had waited, anticipating such a Federal response, believing that it would lead Kentucky's political leaders to view his own invasion more favorably. Polk began his message to the Governor by stating once again his certainty that the Federals had been about to seize Columbus and threaten west Tennessee. He said, "My responsibility could not permit me quietly to lose to the command intrusted to me such an important a position." He said, however, that he would willingly leave Kentucky, "provided that she will agree that the troops of the Federal government be withdrawn simultaneously." Polk's arguments fell flat, and the legislature wasted no time in letting him know his troops were not welcome. The day after Polk's letter to the governor, Senator John M. Johnston, wrote to Polk on behalf of the people of Kentucky that he must withdraw his troops. Johnston said, "The people of Kentucky are profoundly astonished that such an act should have been committed by the Confederates, and especially that they should have been the first to do so with an equipped and regularly organized army ... in their name I ask you to withdraw your forces from the soil of Kentucky." Polk replied that the Confederates were in Columbus "not by chance, but by necessity" and repeated the offer he had made Magoffin. Two days later, the House and Senate of Kentucky passed a resolution instructing Governor Magoffin "to inform those concerned that Kentucky expects the Confederate or Tennessee troops to be withdrawn from her soil unconditionally." They made no such demand of the Federals in Paducah, only the Confederates in Columbus. Magoffin vetoed the resolution. The legislature quickly overrode the veto and went further by providing for a special expulsion force to be led by Brigadier General Robert Anderson and calling for the state militia to be mobilized under Brigadier General Thomas L. Crittenden. With no option left, Magoffin submitted to the legislature's will and issued a proclamation against the Confederate occupiers of Columbus.[23]

General Leonidas Polk.

General Polk stoutly defended his decision to invade in a September 14 letter to Jefferson Davis, saying, "I believe, if we could have found a respectable pretext, it would have been better to have seized this place some months ago, as I am convinced we had more friends then in Kentucky than we have had since." Polk also asked for reinforcements so that he could drive Grant away from Paducah "before he has time to fortify." General Albert Sidney Johnston supported General Polk. Johnston wrote to President Davis, "The troops *will not* be withdrawn." (emphasis Johnston's) and announced his own invasion of the state. He said, "I design to-morrow (which is the earliest practicable moment) to take possession of Bowling Green with 5000 troops." He justified it, as Polk had done, by calling it "self-defense."[24]

General Polk had packed his Union City headquarters aboard the cars and moved up the railroad to Columbus on September 6 and got his first look at the town that had been the object of so much concern and conversation in recent weeks. Columbus was a town of about one thousand people, more quaint than substantial. It had only four brick buildings, but Columbus was on its way. The Mississippi River carried the wealth of the North, the Midwest, and the South past its wharf, and the newly laid rails of the M&O RR gleamed like a sterling promise of prosperity. However, it was not its choice location as a rail and riverine crossroads so much as its potential as a transportation choke point that made Columbus of immediate military importance.

A two-hundred foot high ridge rose steeply behind the town. "The Chalk Bluffs just below town and the Iron Banks, as the bluffs just north of town were called, constituted the most dominating military position in the whole stretch of the Mississippi from Cairo to Memphis." It was these bluffs that Polk intended to transform into the impregnable "Gibraltar of the West."[25]

To begin, Polk ordered three tiers of batteries. "First, fifteen feet above the water's edge, they built a water battery [10-inch Columbiads and 11-inch howitzers]. Midway up the bluffs, came other batteries. At the top bristled cannon from a string of earthen forts." In all, Polk counted 142 cannon, one of which was a rifled Dahlgren called the Lady Polk. It was said to be "the biggest gun in the Confederacy." Some of Polk's guns pointed east, inland, covering the roads from Paducah. The Fighting Bishop ordered the roads to be well picketed, and cavalry patrols went out to watch for the approach of Grant's bluecoats. As for the river, Polk placed some mines ("torpedoes," in the parlance of the day) in the channel, but that experiment failed. The mines would not detonate and, anyway, the current kept sweeping them away. A second experiment was the initiative of General Pillow. He wanted to plant gigantic anchors on each shore and stretch a heavy chain between them to impede Federal boats trying to descend the Mississippi. This, too, was a failure. When it was tried a few weeks later, the chain broke from the current of the river. The big chain was called "Pillow's Folly." Polk had hopes that he would receive two new ironclads, and he was encouraged to learn in October that two had been begun at Memphis in October, but they would not be completed in time to help defend Columbus. He had to make do with a small fleet of river steamers, which were unimpressive at first glance, but which would go on to do good service. Completing his defenses, Polk established across the river, near Belmont, an observation post named Camp Johnston. It was manned by one regiment of Arkansas infantry, a battalion of Mississippi cavalry, and a field battery.[26]

The works on the bluffs were most impressive. Called Fort De Russey, they consisted of five interconnected forts with an ingenious fresh water system. Powerful pumps sent the water up from the river through a system of cast iron pipes. Some clever craftsmen used leftover pipes to make speaking tubes, "an intercommunication system between command posts in the trenches." The amount of earth moved and logs cut to make the works represented an incredible feat of labor by the young soldiers, and yet it constituted only a part of their duties. When not at work on the forts, they drilled and drilled some more. They drilled constantly. Sam Watkins was not at Columbus, but his experience as a young Tennessee volunteer could not have been much different from that of his comrades at Fort De Russey. Watkins said, "Companies were made up, regiments organized, left, left, left was heard from morning till night. By the right flank, file left, march, were familiar sounds." As distasteful as the endless drilling was to young recruits, John Keegan observes, "The obsessive repetition of drill movements, taught from books by officers or sergeants who were themselves only a page ahead of their pupils was ... exactly the correct way of preparing the innocents for battle." It included the essential task of learning to handle their firearms. Keegan continues, saying that there "was a great deal of practice in the seventeen separate movements necessary to load and level the rifle, extracting the paper cartridge from the pouch, tearing it with the teeth, pouring the powder down the barrel [etc.]. Speed and dexterity in loading did not, however, exhaust the requirements of the drill master. It was also necessary to mass the effects of discharge, by training the soldiers to stand shoulder to shoulder and perform the drill movements simultaneously; otherwise the impact of the volley was diminished."[27]

Henry M. Stanley, who was at Columbus as a volunteer in Co. E, 6th Arkansas Infantry, took the rigors of the soldier's life hard. He said, "We had condemned ourselves to a servitude more slavish than that of black plantation hands.... Any of [the officers] might strike me, and I should have to submit. They could make us march where they pleased, stand sentry throughout the night, do fatigue-duty until I dropped, load my back as they would a mule, ride me on a rail, make a target of me if I took a quiet nap at my post; and there was no possible way out of it."[28]

Many of the young officers, too, were new to the work, just learning their duties, and some of them were no doubt puffed up with the bars and oak leaves on their uniforms. The punishments they inflicted were sometimes sudden, arbitrary, and out of all proportion to the offense. Huston Horn tells of an incident involving Lieutenant William Orten Williams that proved the fundamental accuracy of what Stanley had to say about the young soldiers' helpless plight. Williams was a young Virginian, a kinsman of Mrs. Robert E. Lee and a suitor of one of the Lee daughters. One day at Columbus, "Williams encountered a fledgling sentry whom Williams killed on the spot for the recruit's failure to salute him properly. Williams's written report explained: 'For his ignorance, I pitied him; for his insolence, I forgave him; for his insubordination, I slew him.'" Williams went unpunished, though he was thereafter "a bit of a pariah." He subsequently left Columbus for another assignment. Sometimes the young soldiers were not killed at the whim of a sadistic officer but because of simple inexperience. One young sentry sat down on the M&O track to take a rest, fell asleep, and was killed by an incoming train.[29]

Still, in spite of the hardships and dangers, many of the volunteers did enjoy camp life at Columbus. John Milton Hubbard (7th Tennessee Cavalry), recollected, "We were in 'hog and hominy' country, and the soldiering was of the holiday kind. We made long marches through the Purchase and saw many evidences of Southern sympathy. Indeed, the whole population seemed to be friendly to us, as even those with Northern sympathies prudently kept quiet." A soldier whose letter appeared in the Memphis *Appeal* called the civilian population "generous, kind and hospitable" and said of them, "They bend no knee to the Baal of Lincolnism … a more generous, brave, and noble people do not hie than the Southern Kentuckians."[30]

In some ways, the hardest working man at Columbus was Major General Polk. He was asked to clothe, feed, house, organize, and train the new soldiers, and more of them kept coming. One new outfit was the 7th Kentucky Infantry, which was organized in Hickman County about the same time as Polk entered Kentucky. The 7th was posted at Camp Burnett, eight miles from Columbus. The boys came to war armed with flintlocks, "but they were all soon furnished with a musket that had been changed from a flint-lock to a percussion, and a very destructive gun." Their other individual weapon was a "big knife from eight inches to two feet long, made from big files, buggy or wagon springs or tires; these were the instruments of warfare [the converted muskets and the big knives] with which they intended to prosecute the war against the Federal armies in the event they could not get [better] arms."[31]

Getting better arms for the volunteers was a major challenge Polk faced, and not just for the volunteers at and in the vicinity of Columbus. On September 21, 1861, his assignment was shifted from commanding Department No. 2, which was now the responsibility of General Albert Sidney Johnston, to being the commander of the 1st Division in that department. From that day on, Polk was continually harassed to supply men and weapons to Forts Henry, Donelson, and Pillow in Tennessee, Fort Heiman in Calloway County, Kentucky, and a new outpost called Camp Beauregard which was "a sort of way station between Fort Henry and Columbus," on the New Orleans & Ohio Railroad near Feliciana in Graves County. All the while, he was expected to maintain the all-important position at Columbus and its outpost across the river, Camp Johnston.[32]

The rations, weapons, and various kinds of equipment came in by river and by railroad, but the Mobile & Ohio was beginning to experience shortages that hindered its performance. On September 21, 1861, Secretary of War Judah P. Benjamin wrote to the Quartermaster General to inform him that, since the rolling stock on the East Tennessee & Virginia Railroad was inadequate, he was going to have to make up the deficit by getting engines and cars from other lines, either by contracting for them or, failing that, by requisitioning them. The Western & Atlantic and the Mobile & Ohio had enough machinery to supply the need, said Benjamin; he ordered the quartermaster department to get the necessary locomotives and rolling stock by whatever means. Ultimately, the government took a total of seven locomotives and seventy cars for use on the ET&V RR, and Polk's supply line from Mobile was rendered a little less efficient. There were also instances of friction between the army and the corporation arising from the individual needs of each and the general demands of war. The Mobile & Ohio had missed a semi-annual interest payment of almost $34,000 on its loans from the state of Tennessee, and it did not help the bottom line of the already-stressed railroad that it had agreed to carry men and materiel for the government at half price. It appeared that Polk overestimated the railroad's generosity when he issued a vaguely worded order having to do with passenger passes on the M&O. President Brown wrote Polk on September 23, saying that he had seen the order, and wondered who, exactly, was authorized to issue the passes. If they were not proper in every way, the government would not reimburse the railroad when the vouchers were submitted.

President Brown was expected to do too much with too little by a board of directors, uncomprehending civilian and military customers, and high-hatted government officials. General Polk faced similar problems, plus the question of life and death which depended to a great extent on the unknowable plans of his enemies across the rivers. Brown struggled on, but the burden was too heavy for Polk. On November 6, 1861, he composed an official letter asking to be relieved of command.

That evening, General U.S. Grant steamed south from Cairo with two brigades of infantry on six river steamers. He had two companies of cavalry and the Chicago Light Battery, and the added firepower of two gunboats, the *Lexington* and the *Tyler*. His objective was Camp Johnston, Polk's outpost at Belmont.

General U.S. Grant.

CHAPTER THREE

Columbus Is Ours

About dawn, November 7, 1861, Major Henry Winslow awoke General Polk with news that the pickets had spotted a Federal flotilla a short distance upstream. That in itself was not particularly alarming. Federal gunboats from Cairo were a common sight on the river; they were always watching, and sometimes they fired their guns at the men as they labored on the works. This was different, though; these boats had stopped at Lucas Bend on the Missouri shore and long lines of men were coming down the gangplanks. They evidently intended some action against Camp Johnston.

There was much to do and not much time. Colonel James C. Tappan, commander of Camp Johnston, had spent the night in Columbus. General Polk got him up and across the river to his post. General Pillow and five thousand men had left Columbus earlier that morning on an overland march to Clarksville and Fort Donelson. Polk sent a courier pelting after them in the pre-dawn murk with the news that the Yankees were landing; Pillow and his men must return at once. Brigadier General Benjamin F. Cheatham's men of the Second Division were awakened and sent to their places in the barricades guarding the approaches from Paducah, and the gunners of the shore batteries were gotten up and told to prepare for action. Since Brigadier General John P. McCown's Third Division was nearest the point of the Federal debarkation, Polk went in person to inspect McCown's preparations. He found that McCown had not waited for orders; he had already advanced the "long range guns" of Captain Robert A. Stewart's Pointe Coupée Battery (supported by Lieutenant Colonel J.B. Kennedy and the 21st Louisiana Battalion), and the big siege guns of Captain S.D.H. Hamilton's Tennessee Battery were ready for battle. Soon, the guns on the bluffs began to fire, sending shells toward the Federals disembarking from their transports on the Missouri side upstream.

General Pillow and his men arrived back in Columbus, and since they were already supplied for action, Polk ordered them down the bluff to the wharf where the steamboats *Prince* and *H.R.W. Hill* had raised steam and were waiting. They began ferrying the Rebels across. General Pillow went with the first wave of four regiments: the 12th, 13th, 21st, and 22nd Tennessee.

Polk believed that the activity on the far bank was a diversion. Shelby Foote says an attack on Belmont "made no sense, as far as he [Polk] could see," for it was "a place not only worthless in its own right, but obviously untenable, even if taken, under the frown of the batteries on the bluff across the river." The real attack, he thought, was coming from the direction of Paducah. Pillow had not been able to take his entire division across the river, so Polk sent the balance to augment the firepower of General B.F. Cheatham's men in the land-side barricades overlooking the Paducah road. When he came to examine the works, he found that "all was in defensive readiness, the trenches occupied."[1]

In the meantime, on the Missouri shore, Colonel Tappan had placed his infantry lines and arrayed his artillery to cover the roads that the Yankees must come down. He sent some cavalry forward to observe the enemy. His pickets had already fired a few shots at them as they disembarked, and a small firefight erupted before the Confederate riflemen faded back through the trees in the direction of their camp. The Federal infantry continued to come off the transports, the scene enlivened by the Confederate shells dropping around them, and by 8:30, they were all ashore. While they formed up to march, their field pieces were rolled down the gangplanks. At 10:00, the Yankee skirmishers advanced, "across the slough, and into the 'labyrinth of wild wood,' and over gullies."[2]

Pillow arrived twenty minutes after Tappan's deployment was made. He took command of the Confederates and began readjusting Tappan's lines from a superior position to an inferior one that left most of the line in an open field. He rearranged the artillery, as well. The four regiments of Tennesseans Pillow had brought across the river fell into line alongside Tappan's men. Colonel Thomas J. Freeman of the 22nd Tennessee examined with a critical eye the arrangement ordered by Pillow and told General Polk in the aftermath of the battle, "No worse arrangement of our forces could have been made." Freeman said there was better ground immediately behind the line, where there was a small rise crossed by a rail fence; behind the rise was a ravine where his men could have taken cover while the enemy approached across several hundred yards of open field. But Pillow did not take advantage of the terrain. He later explained, "Had I been less pressed for time to make the necessary dispositions of my small force, my imperfect knowledge of the surroundings of the field would of itself have embarrassed me; but I had no choice of position, nor time to make any reconnaissance, nor even satisfactory disposition for occupying the field left me." The question, of course, is, if he did not know the terrain, why did he not trust Tappan, who did? Further, why could he not see, as Colonel Freeman did, the better ground for deployment just in his rear? Whatever the reasons, Pillow's orders stood. The men realigned according to instructions and waited in the November sun for the Federals to appear.[3]

Before the infantry engaged, a duel broke out between the Kentucky shore batteries and the two Union gunboats. Commander Henry Walke of the U.S.N. said, "I attacked the Confederate batteries, at the request of General Grant, as a diversion, which was done with some effect. But the superiority of the enemy's batteries on the bluffs at Columbus, both in number and the quality of his guns was so great that it would have been hazardous to have remained long under his fire with such frail vessels as the *Tyler* and the *Lexington*." After thirty minutes the gunboats disengaged and returned to safety upstream. They would return, but for the moment the threat they posed was neutralized. Those who consider the battle of November 7, 1861, to be strictly a Missouri battle should consider Walke's comments and the testimony of others as to the importance of the Confederate batteries firing from the Kentucky shore on that bloody day.[4]

On the Missouri side, in that river bottom woodland, the ground was so soft and the trees so thick that it took some time for the Federals to make their way through. The Rebel skirmishers annoyed them, but could not stop them entirely, and they finally emerged from the trees about 10:30. Now the soldiers, equally green on both sides, began to learn a new and frightening lesson in soldiering. The fighting men of both armies conducted themselves well; the mistakes this day belonged to the officers. The Federals formed their ranks and delivered into the Rebel right wing "a most furious fire." The Confederates fired back, but Don Singletary, a soldier in Colonel R.M. Russell's regiment, the 12th Tennessee, said they found themselves outgunned. "We had muzzle loading guns and had been on picket duty so often that we were all nearly out of ammunition," he said, "and in our rush and haste no ammunition was given us or brought over the river. I had only seven cartridges." Colonel John V. Wright's 13th Tennessee and Colonel Thomas J. Freeman's 22nd Tennessee also began to run low on cartridges. Of those who had come over with Pillow, only Colonel Ed Pickett's 21st Tennessee did not expend their ammunition. They were the farthest from the fighting, and, discovering after seven or eight rounds that their fire was ineffective, Pickett ordered the men to quit firing.[5]

The different colonels sent word to General Pillow that their ammunition was almost gone, and his answer was to order a bayonet charge. Colonel Tappan said, "I thought that there was evidently a mistake as to the order, but on seeing Colonel Russell's regiment preparing to move, I ordered my regiment to charge." The Confederates crossed seventy yards of open ground, about halfway to the enemy's position, before the charge faltered. They were still seventy-five yards from the trees where the Yankee line stood. That was the distance according to Colonel Tappan, who added, "To have advanced father in the charge, we would have been in danger from our battery on our left and of being flanked by the enemy, who were in force on our right." Colonel Freeman agreed with Tappan's estimate of the distance and said, "My regiment did not reach the position of the enemy nearer than this, as an order was shouted along the line, coming from the left to 'Retire!' Retire!' Whether the order came from General Pillow I do not know." Freeman, who was critical of Pillow's choice of ground, also found fault in the order to make a charge with the cold steel. He said, "I think the charge was ill-judged and almost impossible to have been executed with success against an enemy in such numbers ... and he at the same time enjoying the protection of the heavy timber for his men."[6]

At least one regiment made it into the trees. Braving the enemy's fire and obviously not hearing the order from the left to retire. Colonel Pickett and his 21st Tennessee reached the woods where they came under "a tremendous fire of musketry" from "a very short distance." Soon realizing that he was unsupported on his flanks, but that it was also too dangerous to retrace his steps, he ordered his men to kneel and fire. They held their place for forty-five minutes before dwindling ammunition left them with no option but to withdraw.[7]

If Lieutenant Colonel Daniel Beltzhoover's battery of guns had been better placed, the Confederates might have been able to drive the Federals back, but Pillow had shifted the guns before the fighting began. Freeman said that "the field artillery we had was placed so far on our left, and in such position that I do not think five of the enemy were touched by a shot from it." The guns had been firing steadily through the first phase of the battle, though, and even before charge began, Beltzhoover saw that he was running out of ordnance. Now, the guns could not cover the infantry as they fell back from their failed charge, but the artillerists on the Kentucky shore observed what was happening and decided that " it was upon their shoulders to save the day.... They opened up with everything they had. It was a terrible storm of Confederate iron, but it flew too high." The rounds from the Kentucky gunners shivered the tree tops and rained splintered boughs and limbs on the Yankees, but it did not stop them. They emerged from the trees and the Confederate line began falling back. Tappan said that they retired "in good order, without any confusion," even as the Federals kept firing. They were headed back to Camp Johnston and its surrounding abatis. There they planned to make their stand, but they soon discovered that they were in danger from a new direction, and once again the crisis stemmed from one of Pillow's decisions at the beginning of the day. When Pillow took command he removed a section of field pieces from the lower road and grouped them with the other guns on the left. Uncovering the lower road was a critical mistake. Tappan said, "I would here state that it was in direction of said road that a regiment of the enemy came into the rear of our troops and took possession of my camp." The attackers were the 27th Illinois Infantry under Brigadier General Napoleon B. Buford and a company of cavalry belonging to Captain J.J. Dollins. The Yankees moved into Camp Johnston to rest and scrounge for food while the Rebels, deprived of their preferred fallback position, retreated toward the river. Nathaniel Cheairs Hughes and Roy P. Stonesifer say in their fine book about the battle, "Pillow shouted and begged his men to stand and fight, but nothing seemed to avail. They sought the shelter of the high riverbank," and this is where Captain W.L. Trask of the *Charm* found them.[8]

The C.S.A. steamers had been crossing the Mississippi between Columbus and Belmont while the fight was going on. The *Charm* ferried medical staff over to the Missouri shore, along with about 150 Tennesseans who had been shaken loose from their regiments and missed their ride when Pillow crossed. It carried the wounded from the battle on its return trip to Columbus. There, it took aboard some ammunition, Colonel Samuel F. Marks and the 11th Louisiana Infantry, and one company of Lieutenant Colonel Thomas H. Logwood's battalion of Tennessee Cavalry, and pushed off again for Missouri. En route, it met the *Prince* on the way to Kentucky. The *Prince* had also been busy. It returned to Columbus in the morning after depositing Pillow's four regiments on the Missouri shore, had loaded up a cargo of ammunition, and hurried back to Belmont. After that, Captain B.J. Butler kept his boat on the Missouri bank, until about 11:30 or 12:00 when he steamed back to Columbus with a message for General Polk: send more ammunition. Crossing to Kentucky, Butler observed the *Charm* and the *H.R.W. Hill* racing back toward Missouri with reinforcements. Butler delivered Pillow's message and crates of cartridges were quickly carried aboard. He said, "I suppose I was not kept waiting for the ammunition more than ten minutes." Loaded up, he headed back. By that time, the Federals had taken Camp Johnston and had planted a battery aimed toward Columbus.[9]

The *Charm* with its load of reinforcements was taking "heavy fire from the enemy's cannon." Captain Trask steered it through without damage and approached his landing spot, only to find it "obstructed by our disorganized forces, who endeavored to board and take possession of our boat, and at the same time crying: 'Don't land!' 'Don't land!' 'We are whipped!' 'Go back!' etc." Captain Trask managed to get six companies of Marks's infantry ashore before the whipped and panicked men from the earlier fighting rushed the *Charm*, forcing him to back the boat away from its mooring and return to deeper water. Trask took the steamer upstream about two hundred yards to land Marks's four remaining companies and Logwood's cavalry. The infantry leaped ashore when the boat drew near the bank, but the cavalry mounts could not disembark that way and Trask discovered that he had no gang planks on board. He said, "I now concluded to recross the river to the Columbus side and allow the cavalry to embark on some other boat or borrow state planks from some other steamer. I succeeded in doing the latter through the kindness of Captain [Preston] Lodwick, of the steamer *Kentucky*." His human and equine passengers deposited at last, Trask returned under fire to the Bluegrass shore. The *Charm* sustained some damage and one man was injured when a solid shot tore through the boiler deck, but she made it safely to the Kentucky bank, where she picked up reinforcements and turned back toward Belmont.[10]

While the Union artillery on the riverbank fired at the town of Columbus and its batteries and at the brave little tea kettles crossing and recrossing the Mississippi, the two Federal gunboats reappeared. They began by firing long-range at the Confederate boats, and they moved closer to attack the "frowning battlements" on the Columbus heights. It took some moments for the Confederate gunners to find their range; then, said Commander Henry Walke, "their shot and shell began to have a telling effect." When a solid shot crashed through the *Tyler*, wounding several men and beheading another, Walke was persuaded that it was time to pull back. The gunboats retired, firing, upstream to their starting point. Now the Rebels turned their attention to the Union guns across the river. General McCown ordered Captain Smith P. Bankhead's Tennessee battery forward to silence the artillery on the Missouri shore, but General Polk had already ordered Captain Melancthon Smith's battery of Mississippi guns and "the rifled gun in the fort" into action, and it was they who forced the Yankee gunners back from the riverbank. At the same time, the shore batteries became engaged again with the enemy gunboats. They came "low enough down the river to throw shells into the works," but after an hour's fight, they retired once more upstream and out of range.[11]

The contest had reached a turning point. About 12:30, General Polk ordered his Second Division commander, General B.F. Cheatham "to take the nearest steamer and to move promptly across the river to rally and take command of the portions of regiments within sight on the shore." Polk instructed him to take one of his brigades along. He chose the First Brigade under Colonel Preston Smith. While Smith's brigade was preparing, Cheatham went ahead and crossed aboard the *Prince*. Before he departed, he sent an order to Captain Melancthon Smith to move his battery down near the river and shell occupied Camp Johnston. Cheatham said, "the order was executed in the most gallant and effective manner, and contributed not a little to the general success of the day."

It was told to Mark Twain by one of his riverboat friends that just before the *Prince* landed Cheatham leaped ashore, still mounted, and shouted to the men, "Now follow me to hell or victory!" The spirit of the happy warrior was contagious; even General Pillow admitted, "The brave General Cheatham, now having reached that part of the field, by his presence added new vigor to the pursuit." To his credit, Pillow had remained with the men, trying to restore order, and when Colonel S.F. Marks and the 11th Louisiana Infantry appeared, he directed them to move through the woods and attack the enemy's rear. Their fight was still going on when Cheatham arrived.[12]

Now, the men cowering beneath the brow of the riverbank took off their coats and formed once again to go to work. General Cheatham said in his report that he led them "in the direction of the enemy's transports and gunboats, intending, if possible, to take them in flank." The First Brigade was not yet up, but Cheatham did not wait.[13]

The Federals had been enjoying their victory over the Confederates in Camp Johnston. They had hoisted the American flag and were listening to music and General John A. McClernand's impromptu stump speech. They were looting the tents for plunder and gorging on Rebel grub. Grant had lost control of his men to an embarrassing degree and only began to restore order when he ordered the tent city burned. Someone—Grant claimed it was himself, but it may have been another—noticed two C.S.A. riverboats crossing to the Missouri shore "with soldiers from boiler deck to roof," and their heading would put them between the Federals in Camp Johnston and their transports. General McClernand moved out, followed by Colonel Henry Dougherty. Colonel Marks was attacking them as they retreated; they were not expecting to receive a flank attack, as well.[14]

General Cheatham and his patchwork brigade had moved north only a short distance when they encountered a detachment of Illinois cavalry and the 7th Iowa of Colonel Dougherty's brigade and the 31st Illinois of General McClernand's. Cheatham formed his men for battle in the cover of a shallow ravine, and the "at once opened upon the enemy a most terrific fire." The Federals responded, "but under the rapid and galling fire of our columns the enemy soon wavered and were charged upon with the bayonet and completely routed." With only a moment to read the ground and assess the situation, Cheatham had done what Pillow had failed to do—to take advantage of natural cover in order to catch the enemy by surprise and then to rout them at bayonet point. Cheatham added that his men slaughtered fleeing Federals "from that point to within a few hundred yards of their gunboats," a distance of over two miles.[15]

Cheatham said that his men had regained "several pieces of artillery," killed and captured many of the enemy, and captured some forty more.

He now returned to the river landing to get his own brigade under Colonel Preston Smith. General Pillow was there and General Polk had come over from the Kentucky side. Polk had steamed across only when "satisfied the [land] attack on Columbus for some reason had failed." They all returned toward the front, taking particular notice of the number of dead and wounded and the amount of discarded knapsacks, cartridge boxes, canteens, and even weapons. At the cabin the Federals had used as a field hospital, they picked up Colonel Marks and the 11th Louisiana Infantry, fresh from their fight, and together they continued to the U.S. transports. Coming within sight of them, the Confederates took position in the woods and in an adjacent cornfield. They opened a "heavy fire" upon the boats and the men boarding them. Pillow said the Rebels' fire was "so hot and destructive that the troops on the boats rushed to the opposite side of the boats and had to be forced back by the bayonet to prevent capsizing." Some of the bluecoat infantry answered with musketry, but it was the gunboats whose fire was the most daunting to the Confederates. The Federals cut their hawser lines and the transports began pulling away. The gunboats, in deeper water, blasted salvos in the direction of the hidden Confederates, pounding them with "grape, canister, and shell." The boats soon steamed out of musket range. As the sun went down, the Battle of Columbus-Belmont came to an end.[16]

Pillow had lost the fight in the morning, but Grant had allowed victory to slip away in the afternoon. He tried in the following days to put the best face on it, though there was no denying that he left Camp Johnston under the bombardment of the C.S.A. artillery on the Kentucky side of the river and because the Rebels at Belmont were receiving infantry reinforcements. He had been chased by Colonel Marks and General Cheatham back to his transports and then steamed away, still under fire, surrendering the field, having accomplished nothing. The truth was, Grant was whipped.

In his report, General Polk thanked everyone, beginning with God, as was befitting a pillar of the Episcopal Church, and then came down considerably in the universal hierarchy to thank General Pillow for his "persistent energy and gallantry, courageously supporting and encouraging his troops by cheering words and personal example." He thanked General McCown "for the manner in which he controlled the movements of the gunboats by the judicious management" of the guns on the Kentucky shore. Polk's biographer expands further the commanding general's opinion of the decisive role played by the Kentucky guns. He says, "The barrage, in Polk's view, was instrumental in 'turning the fortunes of the day.' His chief of artillery, Maj. Alexander P. Stewart, thought the battle 'was really won by the big gun[s].'" Polk went on to thank General Cheatham, "who, at a later hour, by this promptitude and gallantry rallied the broken fragments of our column and directed them with such resistless energy against the enemy's flank" and he thanked others, too, before concluding that "to recite in detail all the instances of skill and courage displayed by individual commander and their several commands would be to run well through the list of those who were engaged." He felt invigorated enough by his own performance to write his department commander, General Albert Sidney Johnston, on November 28, "I have waived my resignation, as [President] Davis seems very much opposed to it, and shall endeavor to do my duty." Polk estimated his losses at Columbus-Belmont at 641 in killed, wounded and missing and believed the Federals had lost upwards of 1500.[17]

The victory made Polk a Southern hero. Sheet music for new songs like "The Belmont Quickstep" and "The Lady Polka" began to appear. Southern leaders understood at once the effect that Polk's defeat of the Federals would *potentially* have internationally. The telegram of victory Polk sent to President Davis was shared verbatim with the Confederate envoys in England "as diplomatic ammunition that might help swing Great Britain toward recognizing the Southern government. 'It was gratifying to receive the official contradiction of the Northern account of the battle,' an English diplomat wrote Secretary of State Robert M.T. Hunter."[18]

The Confederacy nearly lost its newest hero four days after the battle. Polk was wandering among the gun emplacements atop the Columbus bluffs when he stopped to congratulate Captain William Keiter, whose crew had worked the Lady Polk. Throwing her enormous shells ("lamp-posts"), among the Yankees, she had contributed much to the victory of November 7. The bluecoats had fled Camp Johnston in such haste that Keiter's young gunners left an unfired round in the big gun's breech. Polk now asked Captain Keiter to fire the gun upstream in a demonstration of its power and range. Keiter agreed. No one seemed to consider that the tube of the cannon, hot to the touch in action, had cooled and constricted around the shell inside. The lanyard was pulled, and the cannon barrel exploded and detonated the nearby magazine. The explosion wounded or killed an undetermined number of men—perhaps as many as twenty-eight. William D. Pickett, General Polk's chief of engineers, wrote of the accident in 1904 and said, "The gun was found in four pieces," not scattered, but all "in the direction indicated by the explosion of the magazine." The powerful detonation of the magazine, causing the fragments of cannon to fly laterally, probably saved Polk's life. He and several others were standing directly behind the Lady Polk and were therefore spared the full force of the sideways blast. However, Polk was knocked over by the explosion and incapacitated for three weeks.[19]

During General Polk's recovery, General Pillow assumed command at Columbus. He had been envious of Polk from the beginning and wanted the top spot for himself. Hughes and Stonesifer cite his "jealousy and painful awareness of status," and quote an observer who said, "Pillow openly expressed himself as being better suited for command than his superior." Now he was in charge. What President Brown of the Mobile & Ohio thought about the ascension of Pillow is not known, but President Sam Tate of the sister railroad, the Memphis & Charleston, said from Memphis, "No one here has the slightest confidence in Pillow's judgment or ability, and if the important command of defending this river is to be left to him, we feel perfectly in the enemy's power." Luckily for Tate's peace of mind and that of other thoughtful observers, Pillow's tenure was brief. Polk resumed command on December 4. Polk resigned shortly afterward and returned to Tennessee to await reassignment.[20]

For several weeks after the battle, Columbus was quiet, but significant events were happening on other fronts. On January 19, 1862, on the opposite end of the Confederate line in Kentucky, at Logan's Crossroads in Pulaski County, Confederate General Felix Zollicoffer was defeated by General George H. Thomas. Zollicoffer was killed. That same month, General Don Carlos Buell was preparing to lead his army from its base on the Green River down the L&N Railroad to threaten the Confederate center at Bowling Green. In support of this movement, General Henry W. Halleck (General Frémont's successor) ordered Grant to make a two-pronged reconnaissance in force, a demonstration to confuse the Rebels as to the Federals' real objective. General John A. McClernand would move from Paducah in the direction of Columbus while General C.F. Smith would march down the bank of the Tennessee River toward Fort Henry, and its satellite across the river on the Kentucky bank, Fort Heiman. A gunboat flotilla under Flag Officer Andrew H. Foote would steam up the Tennessee on Smith's left flank.

McClernand set out on January 11 with 5200 men drawn from Paducah and the smaller outposts of Cairo, Illinois; Fort Holt, Kentucky; and Bird's Point, Missouri. The weather was bad and the expedition moved slowly. They lived off the land, meaning that McClernand "took and appropriated" as he saw fit, and their creeping pace was very bad indeed for the farmers who were made to support them with corn, potatoes, pork, and poultry all along their route. General Grant joined the column at Milburn, thirteen miles east of Columbus. Beyond there, as McClernand reported, "I maneuvered my forces so as to leave the enemy in doubt whether my purpose was to attack Columbus … or destroy the railroad leading from Columbus to Union City, and to awaken apprehension for the safety of each." General Polk at Columbus was not fooled. He saw McClernand's march "as an attempt to draw his forces out of Fort De Russey [and] the fighting bishop was too canny to fall for it." Polk wired General Johnston that he was going to keep cavalry patrols out to watch McClernand's movements and do nothing beyond that but wait inside his works. If McClernand wanted a fight, he could find it at Columbus. Since Polk would not come out, and McClernand would not attack the Gibraltar of the West, the Federal column proceeded on its expedition unmolested, and by the end of the day on January 21, all the troops were back at their starting point.[21]

General Smith's and Flag Officer Foote's excursion up the Tennessee was no more eventful than McClernand's, but it was more important in the long run. Nearing Fort Henry, General Smith boarded one of the gunboats and steamed close to the unfinished Confederate works. He could see their pronounced vulnerability, and he returned to Paducah eager for battle. He convinced Grant who, together with Foote, persuaded a much less amenable Halleck. Finally, on January 20, "Old Brains" approved an amphibious expedition, not too different from the one against Columbus-Belmont in November, except in strength, and this one was a success. Fort Henry and Fort Heiman fell on February 6, 1862. Their surrender doomed the Confederate line in western Kentucky. Cities and towns on the Mississippi below Columbus were startled at the turn of fortune. The New York *Times* reprinted an article from the New Orleans *Delta* that asked the question: "Should Columbus fall, what is to prevent the enemy from sweeping down the river with the immense fleet of gunboats and floating batteries which he has been so long preparing at St. Louis and Cairo, and with a hundred thousand men under Halleck, while an expedition striking us from the sea would attack us on the other?" The *Delta* said Columbus was "the Northern key to the Mississippi delta" and advocated strengthening it by an additional five thousand men. The Memphis *Daily Appeal* added its voice for the preservation of Columbus as a Southern bulwark: "Columbus and New Orleans are now by far the two most important points in the Confederate States ... let the control of the Mississippi river and the mighty valley it drains fall into the hand of the enemy and there is no calculating how long the bloody drama may be protracted."[22]

Yet, Columbus could not be saved. The Confederates' northern defensive line was coming apart, and General Johnston saw no alternative but to begin the withdrawal from Kentucky. He ordered that Bowling Green be evacuated and that Fort Donelson on the Cumberland be strengthened to cover his flank until his army could safely reach Nashville. Fort Donelson turned out to be a much harder contest than Fort Henry, but its fate was the same. The combined firepower of the U.S. Army and Navy, along with the mistakes of the fort's principal commanders, General John Floyd and his second in command General Gideon Pillow, finished Fort Donelson. It fell on the 16th of February.

Polk's position at Columbus was left isolated and vulnerable on both flanks. Confederate Adjutant General Inspector Samuel Cooper decided that Columbus must be abandoned and sent the order to the Western Department on February 19. The work began immediately. To prevent a surprise, Polk ordered "the track of the Mobile and Ohio Railroad should be torn up," which required the commissary and quartermaster stores and the ordnance to be transported by wagon a distance of three miles to the new railhead. It was reported, "Every man coming into Columbus is impressed, even farmers with their teams." President Brown of the M&O "placed fourteen locomotives and two hundred cars at the disposal of General Polk." Evacuation of the men began on February 25, with the sick and wounded. On the 27th, McCown's men left on transports for Island No. 10; many of the heavy guns went with them. Next was A.P. Stewart's brigade, which traveled by water to New Madrid. McCown's and Stewart's men were luckier than Cheatham's; his brigades had to march over muddy winter roads to their new assignment, Union City, although at least some of the men in Polk's command went south by rail. Henry George of the 7th Kentucky said that the troops moved south to Jordan and State Line Station and "embarked on cars of the Mobile & Ohio Railroad." Only the cavalry and Polk and his staff remained of the twenty-two regiments (seventeen thousand fighting men) that had defended Columbus so well. March 2 was Polk's last day in the Gibraltar of the West. He wrote to Secretary of War Benjamin that day, "The work is done. Self and staff move in half an hour. Everything secured." After they left, the cavalry moved among the camp's buildings with torches and turned them "into a roaring conflagration." They spared the M&O depot in Columbus, but, as they rode south, they destroyed two railroad culverts below Moscow, Kentucky, to discourage pursuit.[23]

The next day, March 3, Flag Officer Foote led a flotilla down from Cairo to investigate rumors that Columbus had been abandoned, but the rain, fog, and low lying smoke from the smoldering camp defeated his purpose. He said the haze "prevented us from ascertaining whether or not the water battery had been removed." He returned upriver. Later that day, four companies of the 2nd Illinois Cavalry under Lieutenant Colonel Henry Hogg approached Columbus from the land side. All was quiet. They rode into Columbus and pitched camp.[24]

The next morning, Foote returned with a stronger force of thirteen vessels and all or parts of four regiments commanded by Brigadier General William T. Sherman. They spotted Hogg's cavalry in the bluff-top ruins. Brigadier General G.W. Cullum said, "Satisfied that our troops had possession, they landed, ascended to the summit of the bluff, and together planted the stars and stripes amid the heartiest cheers of our brave tars and soldiers." He was pleased to report, "Columbus, the Gibraltar of the West, is ours."[25]

General Polk and his staff joined General Cheatham in Union City. They remained only a few days. On March 8, 1862, General P.G.T. Beauregard at Jackson wired Polk, "I believe it would be well to establish your headquarters at once at Humboldt, for the present." Polk followed his general's suggestion and moved his headquarters down the M&O to Humboldt, leaving behind Colonel Edward Pickett with the 21st Tennessee Infantry and Colonel T.H. Logwood's cavalry to garrison Union City. Federal troops under Colonel Napoleon Buford surprised the Confederates on the morning of March 31, 1862, and routed them. Union City was lost; the Confederates' northernmost outpost was now Humboldt. At the intersection of the Memphis Branch of the L&N Railroad and the Mobile & Ohio, it was a prime strategic location. The New York *Times* said the Humboldt line was "a naturally good one, and, if properly strengthened, would prevent all approaches to Memphis from the Northeast."[26]

There was no getting around the fact that the first three months of 1862 had been disastrous for the Confederates. They had lost the territory north of Humboldt to all the way to Columbus. They had lost the mouths and long stretches upstream of the Tennessee and Cumberland Rivers, and they had lost control of the Mississippi River down to Island No. 10. And the Mobile & Ohio Railroad had lost the northernmost seventy-five miles of its line.

CHAPTER FOUR

Corinth

It was not just the loss of territory, it was the loss of trade that had to be taken into account by the officers of the M&O, a railroad already facing some harsh financial realities. The year 1861 had been difficult, with profits of only about $58,000; "half a million less that they would have been in times of peace." Chief Engineer and General Superintendent L.J. Fleming identified several causes, including the Federals' control of Cairo and their blockade of Mobile, which prevented the export of the cotton crop, which in turn left the planters unable "to make the usual fall purchases." In addition, said Fleming, the railroad could not import supplies and the rails, spikes, machine parts, and other materials needed for repairs. They had to pay a premium price for the materials available, and repairs consumed "the stock of supplies then on hand." Receipts down, expenses up—the railroad's final tally showed the disappointing results.[1]

There were other losses. It was reported that "a new and beautiful sleeping car from the Philadelphia car works, originally destined for the Mobile and Ohio Railroad," could not be delivered. It was sold to the Pittsburg & Fort Wayne Railroad instead, and whatever money the M&O had paid up front was lost. Likewise, the M&O could not make deliveries. The Washington, D.C. *National Republican* said, "There is but little money there [in Mississippi].... Stations along the Ohio and Mobile railroad are packed with freight, much of which has been there for months, those to whom it is consigned being too poor to pay the charges. The Railroad Company, to protect itself, has been obliged to adopt the rule to receive no more freight for towns in Mississippi unless the charges are prepaid."[2]

At least, the wartime government remained a lucrative source of revenue. In October 1861, a committee of executives of the Mobile & Ohio and the East Tennessee & Virginia railroads met to establish the "classification and rates" charges for transporting government freight. For the 1st Class, percussion caps and ammunition, the rate was 45¢ per cwt. per one hundred miles. For the 2nd Class, all other freights except livestock and fodder, the rate was 20¢ per cwt. per one hundred miles. For the 3rd Class, livestock, the rate was $20 per car load per one hundred miles, and for the 4th Class, fodder, the rate was $15 per carload per one hundred miles. The committee agreed to accept "Treasury Notes or Bonds of the Confederate States" in payment. In the first year of the war, government receipts helped the railroad weather what most Southerners believed would be a short storm. On October 30, 1861, two weeks after the new railroad rates went into effect, the M&O delivered twenty-three tons of railroad iron to Fort Morgan at Mobile. Captain Samuel H. Lockett handed over $759 in full payment. Two weeks later, after delivering 112 more tons of railroad iron and forty kegs of railroad spikes to Fort Morgan, the railroad was paid $4116. The problem was, as the war went on, the government sometimes did not pay at all.[3]

Even in 1861, when the government in Richmond paid its bills, the income was not sufficient to make up for the railroad's shortfalls. On July 1, 1861, the Mobile & Ohio missed paying the semi-annual interest on its Tennessee bonds. The sum due was $34,000. The M&O was not alone in its default; other railroads that failed to meet the deadline included the East Tennessee & Virginia and the Nashville & Chattanooga. By law, the governor of Tennessee had the right to place the railroads in receivership. Governor Isham Harris refused to do so. When Harris addressed the legislature on October 7, he said, "Believing, as I do, that their failure to pay resulted from no want of inclination on their part, nor from bad or improper management on the part of their officers and employees, but from the fact of the general prostration of trade and commerce, almost their entire business for the last six months having been the transportation of troops and munitions of war, which they have done with the utmost promptitude and upon the most accommodating terms, I have felt neither the security of the State nor the interest of the companies would be promoted by placing them in the hands of receivers, and I have therefore declined appointing such receivers."[4]

Other states sought different solutions for the difficulties railroads were facing. The Mississippi legislature granted several railroads—the New Orleans, Jackson & Great Northern, the Mississippi Central, and the Mississippi & Tennessee, as well as the Mobile & Ohio—to issue their own money, up to a total of $150,000 each and only in denominations of one, two, and three dollar notes. It was hoped this would "supply the want of change so seriously felt in all parts of the State."[5]

The one true remedy for the general prostration of business on the Southern railroads, of course, was a quick end to the war, and the officers of the M&O felt confident that the brilliant officers and gallant soldiers of the Confederate States army would bring the hostilities to a timely close and business would recover. They went ahead with plans to enlarge the machine shop at Jackson, Tennessee. With an anticipated work force of between three and four hundred men employed at the shop, the railroad would "do all their own work there, even their locomotives." It was an ambitious plan that showed a decided optimism toward the future. However, the year 1862 would prove, even more than the previous year had done, that the military was distressingly unable to drive the Yankees from Southern soil. There was no end to the war in sight.[6]

The Confederate troops were gathering at Corinth, Mississippi, and General Albert Sidney Johnston hoped to reverse the recent Confederate setbacks from there. From the Gulf Coast came Major General Braxton Bragg, commander of the Department of Alabama and West Florida. His orders, dated February 18, instructed him to "hasten to the defense of the Tennessee line," but to leave "an effective garrison in the forts in Mobile Harbor and provide an ample supply of food for them." The government was serious about Mobile; the next month the Confederate Congress would appropriate an additional $1,200,000 for its defense and the defense of the Alabama River. Bragg left nearly 4800 men in Mobile and departed for Corinth on February 28.[7]

Others were coming. All the troops that could spared from Louisiana, from east and middle Tennessee, and from South Carolina converged on Corinth. And by rail from Columbus, via Union City and Humboldt, came General Leonidas Polk. Polk had a new assignment as of March 6, 1862. He assumed command of the I Corps, all the troops of the Army of the Mississippi "north of Jackson, Tenn., and along the Mississippi River north of Memphis." General Bragg was assigned to command of the II Corps, which was everything south of Polk's sector, i.e., all the troops in northern Mississippi and south of Jackson, Tennessee. It was a sign of the confidence the Confederacy had in Bragg at this time that he simultaneously retained command of his own department in Alabama and Florida, and was also named General Johnston's chief-of-staff. General Hardee was given command of the III Corps, which consisted of the same division he had brought from Tennessee. In all, discounting the sick and wounded, Johnston had an effective force of about 41,000.[8]

General Bragg of the II Corps took a particular interest in the railroads. Much of the Mobile & Ohio and the important rail junction of Corinth were in his territory. On March 5, 1862, calling the railroads within his command "absolutely necessary for military purposes," Bragg ordered: "To suppress disorders, arrest all persons traveling without proper authority, and prevent undue interference by unauthorized persons on the Memphis and Charleston and Mobile and Ohio railroads, General [Daniel] Ruggles will make the necessary details from his command to send a guard of one commissioned officer and five men with each passenger train on these roads."[9]

The train guards were among the lucky ones, for their assignment enabled them to get away from Corinth. Corinth was on land that had belonged to the Chickasaw Indians until the Pontotoc Treaty of 1832. The town was founded in 1856 at the intersection of the M&C and the M&O railroads. Peter Cozzens says, "The railroads increased the town's growth. By 1861, only five years after the first building went up, Corinth boasted a population of 2800 people, many fine homes, and an institution of higher learning called Corona Female College." The town had a number of churches "and three hotels, the most notable being the imposing three-story Tishomingo Hotel located near the intersection of the railroads." Most of the citizens had opposed secession; prosperity made them fearful of the destructive effects of disunion. Yet, disunion had come, and the soldiers had moved in. They discovered at once that, for all its military advantages and social amenities, Corinth lacked one necessity: good drinking water. One soldier said the well water was reminiscent of "coal-tar, dish water, and soap suds mixed." Another said it had a "bluish color and greasy taste." It made him think of castor oil. Rain was collected in barrels as a source of potable water, but the spring showers created another problem; the runoff pooled in an area that was swampy to begin with, and it buoyed to the surface the bodily waste of thousands of soldiers in bivouac. McPherson says that Corinth was an "ecological trap." The atmosphere was nothing short of poisonous. Soldiers fell sick by the thousands.[10]

The cavalry was lucky, too, to be able to escape the miasma of Corinth and the hard labor of erecting earthworks from mud. Colonel Nathan Bedford Forrest was one of the cavalry leaders, and it was he who brought the news to headquarters that General Don Carlos Buell and the Army of the Ohio were "rapidly approaching Grant's base at Savannah." Almost simultaneously, Major General Benjamin F. Cheatham sent a dispatch from his observation post at Bethel (about twenty miles north of Corinth on the M&O), "to General Polk saying that part of the Union army was advancing" toward his position. All incoming reports went first to General Beauregard, second in command, who passed the intelligence on to General Johnston along with his opinion that the moment was now, while Buell and Grant were separated, "to advance, and strike the enemy at Pittsburg Landing." Johnston agreed. He had given up Kentucky and Tennessee and knew that he needed a victory to restore the nation's trust in him. He wired President Davis that he was going to march with forty thousand men from Corinth and the various outposts "to offer battle near Pittsburg." He added, "Hope engagement before Buell can form junction."[11]

Johnston's orders went out as soon as they could be printed. To corps commanders Polk, Bragg, and Hardee: "Hold your command in hand ready to advance upon the enemy in the morning [April 3] by 6 a.m., with three days' cooked rations in haversacks, 100 rounds of ammunition for small arms and 200 for field pieces. Carry two days' cooked subsistence in wagons and two tents to the company." O. Edward Cunningham says, "It was General Beauregard's idea, and General Johnston undoubtedly supported it, to cover most of the twenty-two mile march on Thursday and assault General Grant on Friday, April 4." The young soldiers marched out of Corinth on the morning of April 3, armed with weapons ranging from modern Enfield rifles to steel-pointed pikes and confident in the manner of youth that they would whip the Army of the Tennessee.[12]

They marched back to Corinth a few days later, looking not so young and almost eleven thousand fewer in number. About 1700 had been killed; General Johnston was one of the dead. The rest were wounded or missing. They returned to a town that had become one vast hospital. While the army was gone, "hospital flags (yellow) were run up at most of the private residences and all public buildings, churches, and hotels. Physicians, Sisters of Charity, Sisters of Mercy, and nurses from Memphis, New Orleans, Mobile, and other points had been assigned to those places ready to receive the wounded." As the doctors and nurses treated wounds, they learned in more detail what had happened to the soldiers who had marched out so gallantly only a few days before. A critical situation had developed at the very beginning of their short campaign when it took longer than expected to concentrate the men from the various outposts. Johnston's time table was knocked galley west. The importance of that change in schedule was not realized on the first day at Shiloh, April 6, when the Confederates surprised Major General Grant and shoved his forces back to the Tennessee River, but it became apparent that night when the Army of the Ohio under Major General Buell began to arrive. The next day, April 7, the combined Federal armies attacked with renewed vigor and broke the Confederates under General Beauregard, successor to the late General Johnston, who had bled to death of a relatively minor wound on the first day. The survivors slumped back to Corinth, enriched only in experience and the thousands of weapons they had captured and picked up on the battlefield.[13]

Defeated and dispirited though his army might be, Beauregard knew that they must save this essential rail intersection. Brigadier General L.P. Walker, former Secretary of War, had said that "the Memphis and Charleston Railroad and the Mobile and Ohio Railroad, which intersects the Memphis and Charleston at Corinth … constitute the vertebrae of the Confederacy." General Beauregard ordered his men to expand the works for the attack imminently expected. Under the direction of General Bragg, the men nearly doubled them in length, and, as Cozzens observes, they "had done well, constructing the works on ridges whenever possible and anchoring them in forests or creek bottoms. Heavy siege guns, protected by earthwork epaulements, were mounted at vulnerable points." Beauregard would soon have enough men to occupy the enlarged trenches. Major Generals Earl Van Dorn and Sterling Price arrived from the Trans-Mississippi during the second week in April, "as well as a few [other] scattered regiments." Unfortunately, the spring weather continued inclement, and the Southerners in Corinth consequently continued to fall ill in shocking numbers from pneumonia, ailments of the bowels, and typhoid fever; this in addition to the hundreds of wounded that required care. Nearly one-fourth of Beauregard's men were down, and more died as the days went on. An estimated "eight out of ten amputees died, victims of erysipelas, tetanus, and shock."[14]

General P.G.T. Beauregard.

Beauregard's effectives tented all around the town. Mrs. Ella Palmer remembered, "The hills around were covered with camps. At night a vast area was ablaze with camp fires; and if one would go out and listen, the voices of a thousand soldiers singing or cheering could be heard. The Confederate soldiers were great singers as well as brave fighters; they sang at all times and at all seasons. The harder their luck, the more they sang." Certainly, the Confederacy's luck had been hard, and it seemed to get only harder. The men learned while they sang at Corinth that New Orleans had fallen on May 1 when General Benjamin Butler and five thousand Federals moved in.[15]

And the death toll in Beauregard's camps kept rising. Mrs. Palmer continued, "The women and girls of Corinth, besides making bandages and lint, knitting socks for the soldiers, etc., made small bouquets to be place on the breast of every man who died in the hospitals and whose remains were shipped away or were buried at Corinth."[16]

Beauregard had fewer than half the number of General Henry W. Halleck at Pittsburg Landing, but the spies the Creole sent out to be captured were feeding the Federal commander wildly inflated estimates of the number of Confederates waiting in Corinth. Beauregard also organized diversions. A cavalry squadron that went out spread the rumor "that they were riding point for Van Dorn's army, which was on its way to seize the mouth of the Tennessee River and then cut off Halleck's retreat when Beauregard struck him in front with superior numbers." All of Beauregard's ruses played on Halleck's natural caution, but he finally set out on the thirty-mile march to Corinth on April 30. He had three columns, each one an army. Major General John Pope's Army of the Mississippi was on the left wing. They were fresh from their victory at Island No. 10 on April 8. Major General Don Carlos Buell and the Army of the Ohio, who had saved the Federals on the second day at Shiloh, made up the center, and Major General George H. Thomas's Army of the Tennessee was on the right. The Army of the Tennessee had been Grant's, but he had been surprised and nearly beaten on the first day at Shiloh, and when Halleck arrived to assume overall command of operations, he removed Grant and put Thomas in his place. Grant was named second in command to Halleck, which meant that he had no influence at all.[17]

Halleck's army has been said to have "crawled," "slithered," and "crept" toward Corinth. There is hardly a word left to describe the slowness of Halleck's forward progress. It was barely progress at all, measuring it day by day. Road construction was one time consuming duty. The bluecoats not only corduroyed the main roads but also built lateral roads "so that in case of necessity troops marching by different routes could reinforce each other." Retarding progress further was Halleck's constant expectation that his men build field works. William T. Sherman said, "We fortified almost every camp at night." Grant said, "The National armies were intrenched all the way from the Tennessee River to Corinth." The Federals advanced only twelve hundred yards per day, but they kept coming.[18]

As alarming as the Federal advance toward Corinth was, it not the only front that demanded Beauregard's attention during these days of mid–April. Memphis, too, was in peril. When Island No. 10 fell, the Mississippi River was open all the way to Fort Pillow, and Memphis was suddenly at risk. The officials there began to remove their military stores to Corinth on the cars of the Memphis & Charleston Railroad. From there, they continued south toward Columbus, Mississippi, on the Mobile & Ohio. The M&O was expected to cooperate with the M&C, but that soon became a contentious arrangement.

On April 18, W.J. Ross, General Superintendent of the Memphis & Charleston complained to Beauregard that his railroad was transporting large amounts of various stores from Memphis to Corinth for shipment to "Columbus, Miss. and other points on the Mobile & Ohio Rail Road. In order to prevent our Road at this place from being blocked it is absolutely necessary the Mobile & Ohio should remove freight on arrival." Superintendent Fleming had informed Ross that he could only take fifteen carloads per day, but Ross did not believe him. Beauregard referred the matter to Major Robert B. Hurt, the Military Superintendent of Railroads. The next day, April 19, Hurt wrote Beauregard that he had sent Superintendent Fleming a note saying, "It is of the utmost importance that the Army stores destined for Columbus, Miss., be forwarded at once." But he added, "Old feuds exist between the officers of the two Roads connecting at this place, and I fear that many of the recent annoyances and delays, may find their origins in this fact." However, Fleming pleaded that the failure to perform up to demands stemmed not from any ancient rivalry but because M&O was being asked to do too much. Fleming said in his reply to Major Hurt, "I beg to say that the conveniences and arrangements for transporting Freight on the Columbus Branch are entirely inadequate to the demands made by the several departments." He said that the Columbus Branch of the Mobile & Ohio had been built to handle local traffic only; it was difficult to run such a volume of "imperfect" machinery from other companies over it "without some of the cars leaving the Track." He said, "If the Freight coming forward now is to be sent down the Road as fast as delivered by the Memphis & Charleston Rail Road it will inevitably result in a blockade, which will lock up & render useless a large part of the Machinery of the Mobile & Ohio Rail Road." Three weeks later, Superintendent Fleming was still working to resolve the problem. On May 7, Fleming wrote to Colonel Hypolite Oladowski, chief of ordnance, "I have sent an engine down the road this morning to take down any guns, ordnance stores, or other Government property which may be left at stations by reason of the failure of cars. The very hard service to which the machinery has been subjected here [Corinth], without the necessary shops here, or time to send it to Mobile for repairs is having the inevitable effect." Because of the imperative need to save everything possible from the Yankees, the railroad was hiring black men at $1 per day to transfer ammunition from broken down cars to others that were still able to roll.[19]

Saving everything possible from the Yankees was of increasing urgency, for they were certainly on their way, and sharper clashes were erupting as the bluecoats drew near Corinth. Pope, on the Federal left wing, was proving to be a particular problem for Beauregard—and for Halleck. Grant said, "General Halleck kept his headquarters generally, if not all the time, with the right wing [Thomas]. Pope being on the extreme left did not see so much of his chief, and consequently got loose as it were at times. On the 3d of May he ... threw forward a division to Farmington within four miles of Corinth." Halleck had ordered his commanders "not to bring on an engagement," but Pope, nevertheless, initiated "quite a little engagement at Farmington that day." Brigadier General James D. Morgan's division was advancing through the swamp east of Seven-Mile Creek when they met Beauregard's skirmishers. They fought briefly, before the Rebels retired. The Federals followed, only to be stopped by felled timber in the road and a burned bridge. After a two hours' delay, the Federals continued down the road to Farmington. They found the Rebels in a "strong position in front of the town." An artillery duel broke out. The Union artillery silenced the Confederates' four guns and then the infantry charged. The forty-five hundred defenders of Farmington turned and ran two miles, littering the road with clothing, caps, canteen, arms, and accouterments as they went. The Federals followed and ended their pursuit only when General Pope, remembering Halleck's instructions, recalled his troops. They returned to camp east of Seven-Mile Creek. That night, Halleck ordered Pope to fall back and "conform with the general line." Pope's Federals maintained pickets in the area, though, and Cunningham says another fight "broke out again on the following day." For the next few days, Pope's pickets traded sporadic fire with Beauregard's across a narrow no man's land.[20]

The attack of May 3 had stung the Confederates, and Beauregard watched for a chance to repay the bluecoats. He thought he saw an opportunity as Pope's men lingered in the Farmington area. Cunningham says, "Farmington was only about four miles from Corinth, and the swamp area around the little town meant that the hero of Island No. 10 was virtually isolated from the rest of the army." On May 9, Pope made another strong reconnaissance, still operating under Halleck's admonition to "avoid any general engagement," but Beauregard had other plans. He ordered Brigadier General Daniel Ruggles's division of Bragg's corps to "distract Pope's attention with a frontal assault while Van Dorn attacked the Union left."[21]

Ruggles's men advanced in the morning, scattered some Federal cavalry with artillery fire, and took possession of Farmington before pushing on. Ruggles saw "masses of the enemy apparently in line of battle some distance in front," and opened on them with three sections of artillery, "awaiting in the mean time the advance of General Van Dorn's division on my right." He ordered his three batteries to "sweep the forest [where the enemy was] and the more elevated ground beyond," arrayed his men in battle formation and advanced across an open field. Ruggles said, "The contest of our infantry with the enemy was for the space of half an hour sharp and spirited, until we drove them before us to another skirt of timber and underbrush." The Confederates charged again and drove the Federals across Seven Mile Creek, "where the pursuit was called off and the bridge burned." The Confederate attack was vigorous, but with an entire army behind him, Pope could surely have handled Ruggles's division, perhaps even fought his way into Corinth and bagged Beauregard's army. Halleck's instructions had been clear, however, and after two hours of fighting Pope recalled his men. Ruggles's success on May 9 was not entirely a victory of Confederate arms; it was largely a result of Pope's decision to disengage in deference to Halleck's instructions.[22]

The attack on Pope would have damaged the Federals considerably more if General Van Dorn had carried out his assignment. His attack on the Union flank was supposed to be the main Confederate effort of the morning, but Ruggles had carried on the fight alone; Van Dorn never appeared. Special Inspector Colonel William Preston Johnston, ordered to review the late operations in Department No. 2, concluded in his July report to President Davis that Van Dorn was not solely to blame for the failure to attack. Colonel Johnston wrote, "General Hardee, who was with General Van Dorn, informs me that the troops were brought to the point designated in the plan of battle, but that the approaches to the enemy's position were not as contemplated by General Beauregard." The country was not open, as Beauregard had thought. It was swampy and heavily timbered, and there was only a single road by which to advance. Johnston said, "The plan of battle was a very good plan of battle, but the topography of the country in which it was to be fought would not permit its execution."[23]

After the Federals retired from the fight, Brigadier General J. Patton Anderson ordered Lieutenant Colonel Franklin H. Clack to detail an officer and some men to collect from the field the useful equipment the Federals had discarded. Clack selected Lieutenant R.H. Browne and Co. B of the Florida and Confederate Guards Battalion. Following the Federal line of retreat, Browne's company had collected a large quantity of items when General Anderson came up and ordered Browne to save only "the most valuable, such as blankets, etc." The rest was to be destroyed. They had no wagons to carry everything back to Corinth. Browne said, "I proceeded forthwith to execute the order, gathering about 150 blankets in one pile and a like number each of oil-cloths, knapsacks, overcoats, etc. These latter were set on fire." The promiscuous wastefulness of war and of young men at war is sublime, a sign of the alien moral code of an extreme state of being that would not be tolerated in more normal times. On this occasion, the waste was curtailed because conveyances were located. Browne said, "General Bragg came up with a detail of wagons and ordered me to extinguish the fire, which was done at once. He then informed me that he had a sufficient detail of men to take charge of the articles," and they were delivered to the quartermaster in Corinth.[24]

A few days later, the Federals moved into Farmington, "threw up strong earthworks," and placed their guns. For the next twenty days, "Beauregard kept his forces in line of battle, and skirmishing between the armies became commonplace." Some of them grew into something larger. There was a "sharp affair" of an hour's duration near the cabin of a man named Russell, and another spirited fight at Serratt's Hill, but in the opinion of some, it was the ultimate Confederate failure to hold on to Farmington that sealed Beauregard's fate at Corinth. Colonel William Preston Johnston reported to President Davis that, in retrospect, it seemed evident "that Corinth could only be held by beating the enemy, and that, so soon as he was allowed to take position at Farmington in such manner that we could not compel him to fight, Corinth was no longer tenable."[25]

During those last twenty days in May, every fight represented nothing more than a waste of life. The Confederates could make no impression on the enemy, and Halleck would not give his Federals the freedom to attempt a breakthrough. Still, the Rebels could never relax their guard. Beauregard's "orders stated that each regiment should camp 400–800 yards to the rear of its place in the line of defense, and each regiment would be responsible for building a good road from camp to the front [in order] to accommodate the movement of artillery.... Each division should have a brigade in reserve 400 yards to the rear." As for the flanks, "any roads approaching the left and right flanks of the army should be blocked in all swampy places." This was vital on the left because there the "obstructions would force the Yankees to move toward the Mobile & Ohio Railroad" and General Polk's artillery.[26]

By May 28, the Federal infantry was dug in on high ground from which they "could look over the parapets of the rebel works in Corinth and hear their drum and bugle calls." They brought up the artillery the next day. The end was near. Beauregard, painfully aware of the Yankee artillery and the infantry's disposition, had already ordered the withdrawal from Corinth. After a May 25 council of war, "he began working on the particulars of the evacuation" and on May 29 "the retreat got under way in earnest." Michael Ballard continues, "While wagon trains moved south, a band walked around town playing retreat, tattoo, and taps, while drummers beat out reveille.... One empty train ran back and forth a short distance on the Memphis & Charleston rail line. Each time the train got close to town, the Rebels cheered as welcoming reinforcements. They also cheered when supply trains returned from the south on the Mobile & Ohio to reload." The ruse also included sending "deserters" into the enemy's lines, "talking about a major attack in the morning and saying they wanted no part of it."[27]

The wisdom of putting the defensive barricades well out of town was fully appreciated now, for though the Federals could "look over the parapets," as Sherman claimed, they could not see the bustle and commotion in the town, which would have given the game away. Mrs. Ella

Palmer remembered that when Beauregard began to evacuate, amputations were ongoing at the hospital in the Baptist church where she nursed. "The wounded were sent away as fast as they were able to travel," she said, "About one o'clock in the morning General Price had a mortar fired as a signal for the remaining soldiers to spike the guns of the batteries and evacuate the trenches." Mrs. Palmer, the hospital staff, and the remaining patients (those who could travel) got on one of the last two trains out of Corinth. Mrs. Palmer said, "The train was packed. Aisles, platforms, and steps were crowded. The tops of the cars were so loaded with men that there was danger of the roofs breaking in. No one was allowed to take any baggage except carpetbags and lunches." As she looked out, Mrs. Palmer could see the civilians of Corinth fleeing. She said, "All along the railroad for miles could be seen men, women, and children trying to get away."[28]

Until about five o'clock that morning, Beauregard's deceptions had worked almost perfectly. John Pope had reported the arrival of enemy reinforcements in Corinth on the 29th and apprehended an attack against his lines at dawn on the 30th. While he braced for the attack that never came, the last Confederates moved through Corinth, setting fires "to destroy all the provisions and army stores, and to blow up the arsenal." Sam Watkins said, "The town was a blaze of fire and the arsenal was roaring and popping and bellowing like pandemonium turned loose." As the last troopers left, they set fire to the bridges behind them and took down the road signs. In a few moments, the arsenal blew up, and that was the end of Corinth for the Confederates. Few regretted their departure. Watkins said that to the Confederate soldier Corinth "was but one vast graveyard that entombed the life and spirit of once brave and chivalrous men. We left it to the tender mercies of the Yankees without one trace of sorrow or regret."[29]

Upon hearing the explosion, the Yankees sent forward skirmishers to probe the outer lines. They were deserted but for logs painted black, the famous "Quaker guns," and crews of mannequin scarecrows. The scouts returned to report their findings, and brigades, divisions, whole armies began to move forward, hardly believing that Corinth was theirs. The town was empty, except for a few families and the sick soldiers who had been too ill to travel. Everyone else had left with Beauregard. The Mobile & Ohio had been of double benefit to the Confederates in the final days; it had deceived and intimidated the Federals by its comings and goings, and it had carried Beauregard's army to safety.

The Creole had made a clean escape, but he did not know that days earlier General Pope had sent a brigade of cavalry under Colonel Washington L. Elliott to make a wide loop east through Iuka before doubling back west to strike the M&O at Booneville, thirty miles south of Corinth. The horse soldiers left Farmington on the night of the 27th. At Booneville on the morning of the 30th, the very day of the Rebels' final departure from Corinth, Elliott found a mixed force of infantry and cavalry guarding the railroad and about two thousand sick and convalescent evacuees from Beauregard's army. Near the Mobile & Ohio depot was a greater prize, a train "consisting of 1 locomotive and 26 cars; 5 loaded with ammunition for artillery and for small arms; 1 platform car, with 1 brass and 2 iron field pieces of artillery; the balance of the train loaded with officers' baggage, clothing, provisions, and quartermaster's stores." Furthermore, the depot was loaded "with ammunition, subsistence, and quartermaster's stores."[30]

Elliott dispatched Lieutenant Colonel Edward Hatch and the 2nd Iowa Cavalry to occupy the Rebel cavalry north of town. The Iowans pushed the graybacks out of the way and went to work, cutting the telegraph line north [not knowing that Halleck had moved into Corinth] and tearing up track. Colonel Philip Sheridan and the 2nd Michigan Cavalry rode south of Booneville and, finding no infantry near enough to threaten them, began "to destroy the road, by tearing up the track, bending the rails, and burning the crossties. This was done in four different places by both officers and men."[31]

While the work of destruction was going on north and south of Booneville, Elliott had the rail cars rolled nearer the M&O station "and had them fired, both depot and cars, first causing the sick of the enemy to be removed beyond danger from the explosion of powder and shell." The Confederates did manage to save a few cars. Captain Frederick Ingate, Assistant Quartermaster of the Army of the Mississippi, reported an act of exceptional courage on the part of a civilian quartermaster clerk named E.L. Elliott. Elliott dashed out as the enemy fell back a safe distance from the impending explosions and "detached three cars from the burning train … & thereby saved two carloads of ammunition and one of Enfield rifles." He also saved the lives of "several sick soldiers who were unable to get out of the way." Elliott did this under the eyes of the Federals and was "repeatedly ordered by the enemy to desist," but he persisted and became a momentary hero.[32]

Colonel Elliott said that he and his men listened to the explosions from the rail cars and the depot for "two or three hours." The next morning, May 31, they began the return march to Farmington. Outside of Booneville, they exchanged shots with Colonel W.R. Bradfute and four hundred Rebel cavalry, who could do nothing more than pester a brigade. Colonel Elliott and his men continued north and west unimpeded and arrived back at Farmington on the evening of May 31. He reported the value of C.S.A. property he had destroyed "at from one-fourth to one-half millions of dollars."[33]

Pope's infantry was following the cavalry, making what turned out to be a short pursuit of Beauregard. Along the way they saw quantities of army paraphernalia discarded by the retreating Confederates, and when they passed through Booneville they looked in awe at the amount of damage Elliott and his men had done. Such burnings had not yet become commonplace. A diarist from the 63rd Ohio took particular interest in the ruined cargo of the rail cars. He said the "musket barrels lay in heaps, smelted together by the heat."[34]

Halleck had won at Corinth what amounted to an empty gourd, but he did have control of an important railroad intersection and staging area for future operations, and he had driven Beauregard's army a considerable distance to the south. The administration in Washington was delighted. On July 11, 1862, the War Department relieved Halleck of command of the Department of the Mississippi in order to promote him to general-in-chief of the armies.

Halleck's southern counterpart, General Beauregard, was also relieved of his duties after Corinth, but for a different reason and in different circumstances. He announced in a brief wire to Richmond on June 3, 1862, that he had evacuated Corinth, and in his after action report he said, "I feel authorized to say by the evacuation the plan of campaign of the enemy was utterly foiled—his delay of seven weeks and vast expenditures were of little value, and he has reached Corinth to find it a barren locality, which he must abandon as wholly worthless for his purposes." On June 15, Beauregard went off to a resort near Mobile to restore his health. He had doctors' affidavits proving that he needed a rest, but President Davis was not particularly sympathetic to the Creole's real or imagined ills. On June 20, the president removed Beauregard from command and installed in his place General Braxton Bragg, a "quick tempered martinet" who nevertheless brought some order to a dispirited army. A veteran of these days, Lieutenant Philip B. Spence of the regular Confederate States army, later remembered that, under Bragg's "stern, strict" discipline, "the morale and spirits of the men were as cheerful as before our disastrous defeat on the second day's battle of Shiloh." Spence added, "Officers and men at this time had the utmost confidence in Gen. Bragg as commander of the Army of [the] Mississippi."[35]

Richmond, however, still wanted answers. President Davis sent Colonel William Preston Johnston to Mississippi to determine, among other things, why there had been so much sickness at Corinth and the "circumstances and purposes" of the retreat from Corinth. Davis wanted to know the losses of "troops, stores, or arms" during the retreat, the condition of the troops, and finally the plan of future operations. Colonel Johnston's report has already been alluded to.[36]

Johnston stepped down from the train at the unimpressive hamlet of Tupelo. Thirty years earlier it had been a Chickasaw village, and it had never grown very much larger. A correspondent described the town as "a very small place … it contains scarcely more than houses enough for railroad purposes." The ridges outside of town made a good campsite, however, and Colonel Johnston found Bragg's army there. He described the position as "healthy, pleasant, and capable of defense." He found their wells, kitchens, and sinks to be arranged in the best sanitary manner, and he, like Lieutenant Spence, observed that the men's spirits were high. "The discipline of the army seems excellent," Johnston said. He reported an evident regard for private property and said, "In the vicinity of the camps composing the Army of the Mississippi the fences are unharmed and the fields unwasted. In the Army of the West, also, respect is shown to the rights of private property."[37]

The complete figures for the loss of stores and arms in the aftermath of Corinth were not available for Johnston's review. He did collect and submit "a list of ordnance and ordnance stores destroyed by the Federals at Booneville," and he referenced "the vast number of stragglers who deserted the line of retreat [who], weakened by disease and discouraged, abandoned their fire-arms, which it is feared are irretrievably lost." He added, "The loss of small-arms is large."[38]

As for the necessity and wisdom of abandoning of Corinth, Johnston found that Beauregard's subordinates "fully sustain his view as to the necessity of the evacuation of Corinth at the time it was performed. Another day's delay might have proved fatal to the army." While in Corinth, the army was brought to a low state of effectiveness by "bad food, neglect of police duty [that is to say, an accumulation of filth], inaction, and labor, and especially the water, insufficient and charged with magnesia and rotten limestone." He said that Beauregard's efforts to solve the problem of potable water by boring artesian wells had proven a failure. The statistics were revealing: "With an aggregate 112,092 the effective total had wasted way to 52,706 men. The sick and absent numbered 49,590, including officers." All these conditions considered, Johnston concluded, "Not only does the retreat of General Beauregard appear to have been at the time a necessity, but also that it might have been made with propriety a month earlier."[39]

A week after he assumed command of Department No. 2, General Bragg issued a declaration to the men at Tupelo, announcing that their sojourn was about to end. He said, "A few more days of needful preparation and organization and I will give your banners to the breeze—shall lead you to emulate the soldiers of the Confederacy in the East." But, at the time of Johnston's inspection tour he had made no move to go on the offensive. Peter Cozzens says, "A lack of transportation and the summer drought ruled out extended marches across northern Mississippi, and the nearest possible objective, Corinth, was too well fortified to attack." Colonel Johnston reported that Bragg "had not determined his plan of action." He thought that he might "avail himself of the railroad to advance immediately 22 miles to Baldwyn. He deliberated between attacking at Corinth and leaving that army behind to cross into Tennessee and attack Buell." In the end, Bragg decided on the latter; he would take thirty thousand men south on the M&O to Mobile, cross the bay, and continue by rail on the other side to Chattanooga. General Don Carlos Buell and the Army of the Ohio were approaching Chattanooga from the west, along the line of the M&C Railroad, and they must be kept from that important gateway city. Furthermore, from Chattanooga, Bragg could easily co-ordinate with Major General Edmund Kirby Smith, commanding the Department of East Tennessee from his headquarters in Knoxville.[40]

Bragg left sixteen thousand men at Tupelo under General Sterling Price. Van Dorn, who had gone off to Vicksburg, had about the same number of men, "and could perhaps work with Price if necessary." A grand plan was taking shape. Ballard says, "Bragg envisioned Van Dorn and Price invading western Tennessee, while he and [Edmund Kirby] Smith cut Buell's supply line." If the broad summer offensive was successful, the Confederacy would regain everything that was lost and more; the Confederates of the West would control everything north to the Ohio River.[41]

CHAPTER FIVE

Iuka and Second Corinth

As uncomfortable as it sometimes was, the railroads and the military were joined in an unbreakable relationship. Each was dependent on the other and each, to a large degree, bore responsibility for the success or failure of the other. In the aftermath of Beauregard's retreat, the Mobile & Ohio Railroad's performance became central to the investigation of a special court convened to examine "the conduct of the quartermaster's department of the Army of the Mississippi" during the siege and evacuation of Corinth. The court made its findings public in June 1863. Among its conclusions: the railroads serving Corinth had been insufficient "for the transportation of a full supply of forage for the army at Corinth, and at the same time to supply the army at Corinth, and at the same time to supply that army with all other quartermaster's commissary, and ordnance stores required, and at the same time meet the sudden and unexpected demands for the transportation of large numbers of troops, the sick, etc." The railroads were worked to their "utmost capacity," but competition for their use often meant that loaded trains were shunted off onto spurs or side tracks and "thus detained or delayed in arriving at their place of distribution."[1]

The court found that "the transportation operations on the occasion of the evacuation of Corinth were expeditiously and successfully conducted by energetic and competent officers of the quartermaster's department," who saw to it that "there was no public property left in Corinth upon the evacuation of the place, except a few tents and broken wagons, some old harness and some [damaged or condemned] ordnance stores ... not worth the cost of transportation." The court of inquiry excused the quartermaster department for the destruction of the train at Booneville and wrapped up its investigation, saying that "the evacuation of Corinth, so far as the quartermaster's department was concerned, was a complete military success."[2]

While the Southerners reviewed their efforts after the abandonment of Corinth, the Federals consolidated their hold and repaired the damages to the 211 miles of M&O Railroad they now controlled, Columbus to Corinth.

This was *their* railroad, part of the logistical equation of future offensives, and they lashed back the Confederate raiding parties who tried to injure it anew. On Halleck's orders, the Federals had moved the "Columbiads and rifled guns, with carriages and ammunition" from Fort Donelson to Columbus and mounted them "in position best for iron-clad gunboats." In addition, several more of the big guns were on their way down the Ohio River from Pittsburg to Cairo, and they, too, would be forwarded to Columbus.[3]

Details were posted to salvage wrecked trains and to rebuild damaged bridges and tracks. The Federal force on the Mobile & Ohio south of Corinth was sixty thousand, according to Halleck, and many of them were engaged in railroad repair. The line was restored in June. The vast needs of the occupying army compelled Halleck to request that 184 cars and six locomotives be sent from Louisville to Columbus for service on the M&O RR. General Halleck also had his men adding to the Corinth works, which he had already described as "exceedingly strong."[4]

Occupying the formerly Confederate-held towns was difficult in more ways than one. Aside from the sweaty work of strengthening fortifications and rebuilding the railroads, of standing on picket duty and going on patrols through the hinterland, there was the Federal soldiers' knowledge that the local people despised them. They lived in the midst of an antagonistic population that Andrew F. Lang describes as "civilian enemies who did not wear a Confederate uniform." Lang writes that "Union soldiers learned that a surreptitious Southern army stalked Federal armies, employing any means necessary to repel the invaders." He adds, "An unrestrained war unfolded within the more sanctioned conflict waged by otherwise civilized belligerents.... This conflict waged far beyond the front lines, had few rules and perpetuated chaotic violence."[5]

There were little acts of espionage and vandalism against the Yankees. Sometimes, civilian spies became telegraph operators, as in the case of a man who was a telegrapher on the "exceedingly important" line between Corinth and Memphis. The line was subject to being cut along unguarded lengths, but in the summer of 1862, vandals had suddenly "refrained from cutting the wires." The reason for their "unusual amiability" was soon discovered. Operators in Memphis had been noticing something unusual "in the working of the instruments, and surmised that some outsider was sharing their telegraphic secrets." When the eavesdropper made the mistake of sending a message, they caught him. The Memphis *Daily Appeal* explained, "Individuality shows itself as well in telegraphing as in the footsteps, or in handwriting." The spy was found to be a man named Ed Saville, and as soon as his identity was known, one of the Memphis telegraphers messaged him, "Ed Saville, if you don't want to be hung you had better leave! Our cavalry is closing in on both sides of you!"[6]

Saville expressed surprise that they had found him out, but he said, "I've been here four days and learned all we want to know. As this is becoming rather a tight place, I think I will leave. You'll see me again when you least expect it. Good bye, boys!" He cut the wire and took the pocket telegraph key he had been using and made good his escape. Saville's interception of communications about troop numbers and locations probably did not do the Federals any great harm, but it did reveal, once again, the need for constant vigilance against mischief in the midst of a hostile population.[7]

A more serious threat was the number of civilians who operated as scouts and guides for the guerrillas and took action themselves as bridge burners. The same month that Mr. Saville's espionage was revealed, the newspapers carried details of a raid against Humboldt by a gang of two hundred guerrillas, an attack so unexpected, "Our cavalry ignomiously fled without firing a shot." The Southerners overpowered the guard of fifty men, killing some of them and taking others prisoner, and one humorist among the raiders took the telegraph key and sent a wire north to Columbus, Kentucky, that said, "Hurrah for Jeff Davis." The surprised Federal operator who took the message replied, "Get out, you rebel son of a bitch." The newspapers reported that "a conversational sparing match then took place, but no information of importance was elicited." The raiders found and burned the M&O bridge south of town, "piloted" there by citizens of Jackson who had cynically taken the loyalty oath. The co-conspirators returned home and pretended innocence, but "Gen. [John A.] Logan learning of their duplicity, caused the arrest of fifteen of them. In their homes were found the muskets and accoutrements of three soldiers who were killed." Logan ordered those homes where the evidence was discovered be burned to the ground. One of the men who was arrested, a Mr. Whipple, "a wealthy and influential man, was tried and found guilty. He was sentenced to be hanged at the bridge.... Gen. Logan approved the sentence, and yesterday [July 30] at three o'clock, it was carried into execution. Two others under arrest will undoubtedly be convicted and executed." The item concluded, "Bridge-burners in Logan's command will undoubtedly hang." To try to put pressure on the home folks to bring outrages against the M&O and its bridges to an end, an order was issued that required all white male residents "living within ten miles of the Mobile & Ohio railroad, who have not already taken the oath of allegiance, to do so within five days after the promulgation of this order. Persons reached by this order can report to the nearest post commandant. Their failure to report will involve their arrest, and a persistent refusal, after arrest, to take the oath, will be punished by expulsion south of the Federal lines." There is little evidence that the Southerners took the oath seriously. It is doubtful that decree had much effect.[8]

The occasionally violent acts of the most militant citizens in the local population were the most terrifying. To the young soldier on picket duty or the lonely courier, death could come out of the darkness at any moment. The people were watched, but no one could tell at a glance who was a dangerous enemy and who was merely resentful. Lang says, "The uncertain and often confusing dynamics of military occupation exposed the Union soldiers to a unique kind of warfare far beyond the front lines, one that few volunteers imagined when they enlisted."[9]

Keeping what had been won was the duty of the soldiers, but the weight of it fell more heavily on the officers, for their responsibilities were not individual but comprehensive, and they knew that no place was safe from the Rebels then in Tupelo or their civilian allies. They collected every scrap of intelligence and watched events nervously. Brigadier General Frank C. Armstrong's Confederate cavalry was roaming west Tennessee and northern Mississippi, and the Federals believed that something was afoot. On August 29, Brigadier General Grenville M. Dodge at Trenton wired headquarters in Columbus, Kentucky, "From all the information I can obtain there is some movement in contemplation in West Tennessee by the rebels. They are massing all their cavalry; have drawn in all their guerrilla bands, and everything is very quiet. General Grant telegraphed me last night that they had massed 6000 cavalry and intended to attack our lines at some point." No point was more important than Corinth. Since at least early August, Brigadier (soon to be Major) General William S. Rosecrans had made his headquarters there. He had succeeded General Pope as commander of the Army of the Mississippi after the spring campaign, when Pope was called east. Rosecrans was under his friend U.S. Grant, who now commanded the District of West Tennessee.[10]

Confederate officers hoped to win back what had been lost, but in the fall of 1862 there was also the larger strategy to consider. General Bragg had gone off with a sizeable portion of the C.S.A. Army of the Mississippi to Chattanooga. Before he left, Bragg had reconfigured Confederate Department No. 2 into three districts. Brigadier General John Forney was given command of the District of the Gulf. The all-important city of Mobile was in Forney's district. Alabama Governor John G. Shorter felt that its defense was in good hands. He had confidence in the abilities of General Forney, "a most valuable and efficient officer" who had "effected as much as any other man could and perhaps more" for the protection of Mobile, and its protection was vital. A conquered Mobile would mean the railroads would "pass into the possession of the enemy," the public property, including vital foundries and workshops would be lost, and the Trans-Mississippi would be "cut off by a belt of country as wide as the State of Mississippi and one-half of Alabama." More intimately terrifying was the prospect of thousands of liberated slaves rising in rebellion to murder and plunder. Shorter hoped that if Mobile were ever about to fall, "that orders will be given that not one stone be left upon another. Let the enemy find nothing but smoking and smoldering ruins to gloat over." The state legislators, safe in Montgomery, passed a resolution that Mobile "shall never be desecrated by the polluting tread of our abolition foes … that is should be defended from street to street, from house to house, and inch by inch until, if taken, the victor's spoils should be alone a heap of ashes."[11]

By General Bragg's order, General Sterling Price was given command of the District of Tennessee, and General Earl Van Dorn was given command of the District of the Mississippi. The framework of command looked fine on paper, but Bragg "failed to give clear and precise orders to his district commanders or to leave one of them in charge." He did tell Van Dorn that if he and Price united their forces, Van Dorn's rank would put him in charge. Then Bragg took his leave. In East Tennessee, he and Edmund Kirby Smith planned a campaign against General Don Carlos Buell, expecting to draw him away from Chattanooga by threatening Nashville and, ultimately, Louisville. It was imperative that General Rosecrans at Corinth not break away to effect a juncture with Buell. General Price was expected to keep Rosecrans occupied, and his partner in the effort was to be General Van Dorn. Van Dorn was not on the scene. After the departure of Bragg from Tupelo, Van Dorn had led his army to Vicksburg. Through late July and into August, Price repeatedly asked Van Dorn to come join him for an attack on Rosecrans; Van Dorn kept refusing. In the end, he suggested that Price move south from Tupelo and join *him*. As Price understood his orders, this was contrary to what Bragg wanted, so he decided he must move alone to attack Rosecrans and let Van Dorn explain himself. Price rumbled north on the Mobile & Ohio, and made his headquarters at Guntown. He launched his campaign from there on the eleventh of September.[12]

W.P. Helm of the 3rd Texas Cavalry remembered that as the Confederates advanced, "the Northern forces retreated, and the tales of horror, of insults to women, and indignities shown the men by the Yankee army were such as to get us wrought up almost to frenzy." The retreating forces belonged to General Rosecrans. He had moved east from Corinth, in the direction of Iuka, but, when Price approached, "Old Rosy" fell back, leaving only Colonel Robert C. Murphy's brigade to defend the town. Price's cavalry, under Colonel Frank Armstrong, attacked Murphy at Iuka on the morning of September 13. Murphy held on all day and into the night, hoping for reinforcements from Rosecrans. None came, and Murphy slipped away in the small hours of September 14. Price moved into Iuka later that day. The Federals had escaped, but they had "left behind $30,000 worth of commissary and quartermaster stores, a long train of railroad cars laden with supplies, and dozens of well-stocked sutlers' shops." Still, Price's object of holding Old Rosey had not been accomplished. Rosecrans could simply cross the Tennessee River further west and proceed into Middle Tennessee to join Buell. Price knew "the only sure way of preventing Rosecrans from slipping into Middle Tennessee … was to attack him at Corinth." He tried again to interest Van Dorn in a joint operation. Van Dorn politely refused, suggested once more that Price come join him, and then tried to force the issue by writing to Richmond demanding that he be given authority over Price "that there may be a concert of action." The matter went all the way up to Jefferson Davis, whose view of the matter gratified Van Dorn. President Davis said, "The troops must co-operate and can do so only by having one head. Your rank makes you the commander." On September 16, Van Dorn (now that he was assured by presidential decree that he would be in charge) wrote Price that he was ready to join in an attack on Corinth. He ordered Price to march to meet him at Pocahontas. The order came too late. Price answered on September 19, "I will move my army as quickly as I can in the direction proposed by you. I am, however, expecting an attack today … they are concentrating their forces against me."[13]

Price was quite right. Grant and Rosecrans had developed a plan, and their soldiers were on the move. From Grant's command post at Burnsville, Major General Edward O.C. Ord was advancing east with two divisions on the north side of the Memphis & Charleston to attack Iuka from the northwest. Rosecrans was moving with two divisions on the south side of the M&C to attack Price from the southwest. Together, they had an aggregate of about seventeen thousand men. The odds were about even; Price had fifteen thousand men.

That is, the odds would have been about even had Price not gained the advantage by a delay in one of the Federal columns. Grant's surrogate, General Ord,

General William S. Rosecrans.

attacked first in mid-afternoon, September 19, and pushed to within striking distance of Iuka. He paused there to wait for Rosecrans, as Grant had instructed him. Rosecrans was not yet in position because the day before one of his divisions had been misled by a local guide. The timetable was thrown off by hours and could not be corrected in time for Rosecrans to meet Ord as planned. It was not until after four o'clock, more than two hours behind schedule, that Rosecrans was up and ready. He pitched in, expecting help from Ord at any moment. Ord's officers could see the smoke rising from Rosecrans's fight, but, in one of those inexplicable auditory phenomena that occurred throughout the war, they could not *hear* the sound of battle. They thought the Rebels were abandoning Iuka and burning the stockpile of Yankee stores. Grant had said "to await sounds of an engagement between Rosecrans and the enemy before engaging the latter," and they could hear nothing. Ord's men remained in place, and Rosecrans fought Price alone.[14]

Even though they were fighting only half of the enemy forces present at Iuka, the battle was the fiercest that many of Price's men had ever seen, and it was terrible on the officers, an attrition that left many Confederates on the field without leadership. Surviving officers were unexpectedly called upon to take charge. The lines of command became confused, and uncertainty reigned in the smoky dusk. The fighting ended at 8:00 p.m.

Through the night, pickets traded fire at the slightest noise or glimmer of light. Fires were forbidden along the lines; in places, no more than seventy yards separated the combatants. The wounded left on the field of battle cried for water, but the alert pickets on both sides prevented any would-be angels of mercy from offering succor to the men who suffered.

The weary Confederate officers got no sleep that night. Very early on the morning of September 20, after an informal conference among themselves, Price's subordinates went to the home where the general was sleeping and awakened him to say that they had discussed their situation and all agreed: the army must retreat. Price had to be convinced. He later reported, "I had proposed to renew the battle in the morning and had made my dispositions accordingly," but in the end he came around to their point of view that he was facing "a greatly superior force," and that "my position was such that a battle would endanger the safety of my trains." He ordered the wagons to begin rolling at 3:00 a.m. with an escort of one brigade out of General Dabney Maury's division. His other two brigades would "take up blocking positions on a ridge east of town." General Louis Hébert's division would follow the wagons, and General Frank Armstrong's horse soldiers would be the rear guard.[15]

In the last hours before dawn, Rosecrans heard the sound of Price moving, but he could not interpret it: was the enemy "changing positions to take him in the flank," or was he escaping? To meet either eventuality, he dispatched orders for the army to be ready to attack at dawn. He intended to return to the original battle plan; Ord would advance first against the Confederate right, followed by his own attack against the Confederate left, but the rising sun showed that Price had slipped away down an unguarded road. Rosecrans pursued. Colonel Edward Hatch and the 2nd Iowa Cavalry were in the lead. Hatch reported, "The enemy's trains and flankers were so heavily guarded that I could find no practicable point to attack them." About eight miles out, he caught up with the rear guard, but was surprised when he came upon "a masked battery, with support of two regiments of infantry and a strong reserve of cavalry." General Maury had prepared an ambush for him. Maury said, "They received the fire of the Second Texas Sharpshooters and Captain [Hiram] Bledsoe's battery at short range, and were charged by [Robert] McCulloch's cavalry and utterly routed." The pursuit was called off and not renewed. Price got away with his army intact and his wagons filled with captured Yankee loot.[16]

In the fight of September 19, the Federals had suffered about 750 casualties; the Confederates 700. September 20 dawned with nearly the same odds as the day before, but Price had been persuaded by his officers that retreat was the wise thing to do. The men felt bitter and betrayed as they fell down the road to Baldwyn. W.P. Helm of the dismounted 3rd Texas Cavalry shared the feeling of many in the ranks that they had been let down by their officers. Helm said, "Victory perched on our banners, but it was won at a terrible price.... The next day we retreated, and victory was reversed." The soldiers acted out their resentment in plundering against the rural people, and when they stopped in Baldwyn on the 23rd, they were so demoralized that they did not even bother "to lay out a regular camp, and the men bivouacked as they pleased in the woods outside town."[17]

Neither side had exactly pinned the others' ears back, but Price claimed victory, admitting at the same time that it came at a horrendous cost in blood, some of it from his best officers. He did not mention in his report that he was at the head of an army disillusioned and disgusted that their hard-won victory had been given away. General Grant, too, claimed victory at Iuka. He wrote, "If it was the object of the enemy to make their way into Kentucky, they were defeated in that; if to hold their position until Van Dorn could come up on the southwest of Corinth and make a simultaneous attack, they were defeated in that. Our only defeat was in not capturing the entire army or in destroying it, as I had hoped to do." Afterward, resentment simmered in the Federal army. Rosecrans found it incredulous that he had had to fight the Confederates alone. He asked both Grant and Ord why they had not attacked. Their answers did not satisfy him, and the long standing friendship between Rosecrans and Grant suffered the first injury of the several that finally ended their mutual affection.[18]

After the Battle of Iuka, Grant retired up the railroad to Jackson, Tennessee, where he made his headquarters. Rosecrans returned to his post at Corinth and prepared to defend it. He pulled back from the Beauregard line and put a small army of black laborers to work strengthening the Halleck line, which was "about a mile and a half from the town, extending from the Memphis and Charleston railway on the west around southerly to cover the Union front in that direction." However, Rosecrans wanted protection for the railroad depots to be closer still, so he ordered a new line of works to be built only one-half mile out. Key to his defenses was a string of lunettes, beginning with Battery Powell north of Corinth and curving around the west side of the city until it terminated with Battery Lathrop on the south. In the center, only about two hundred yards from the intersection of the Mobile & Ohio and the Memphis & Charleston was Battery Robinett. On September 28, Rosecrans learned that the Confederates were again on the move.[19]

Price and Van Dorn had met at Ripley on September 25, where, according to a witness, their armies, "lay encamped [for] two days, sweeping everything that was to eat, that could be bought for love or money. Cornfields and cribs, potato patches and gardens, meat houses and pantries suffered to the last point of endurance." While the soldiers raided the truck patches and pantries, Van Dorn explained to Price and the division commanders his plan of attack. From Ripley, the combined army of about 22,000 men would march toward Pocahontas, Tennessee, as if to strike the railroad at Bolivar, but they would execute a sharp turn to the southeast at Pocahontas and catch Rosecrans napping at Corinth, the "linchpin of the Federal defenses in North Mississippi." Van Dorn believed that once he eliminated Rosecrans, he could move freely in any direction he wanted, perhaps west toward Memphis, or, perhaps, as Bragg expected and wanted, north through Tennessee and western Kentucky to the Ohio River. General Mansfield Lovell's division of Van Dorn's army set out on the afternoon of September 29, augmented by William H. Jackson's cavalry who had come down from the vicinity of Bolivar and Jackson, where they had been destroying sections of the M&O RR to deprive the garrison at Corinth of supplies. The divisions of Hébert and Maury moved out for Pocahontas the next day. General Bragg was aware of Van Dorn's plan and his shortcomings as a leader, and he expressed his concerns in a letter to Jefferson Davis. Bragg said Van Dorn "is most true to our cause and gallant to a fault, but he is self willed, rather weak minded and totally deficient in organization and system. He never knows the state of his command, and wields it only in fragments." Whether these flaws of character and leadership style would prove fatal to the campaign remained to be seen.[20]

Van Dorn masked his true intention to move on Corinth by having his men begin repairing a bridge over the Tuscumbia River as if they planned to attack Major General Stephen A. Hurlbut at Bolivar, but by October 2, the Rebel infantry was across the Hatchie River and moving en masse down the road to Corinth. The 1st Mississippi Cavalry led the Confederate column. They encountered a Yankee cavalry detachment, which did not stand to fight but fell back under fire. Frank A. Montgomery said, "We kept up a running fight with them for two or three miles, without any loss on either side so far as I know." The Rebels nabbed a few of the Federals; the rest escaped to report the news that the enemy was near and closing in.[21]

General Earl Van Dorn.

The Confederates came in sight of the Federal field works about two miles from the town. Many of the butternuts had built works for Beauregard in the spring, but what they saw before them now was something much stronger than what they had left behind and much better manned. While the men and their officers considered the hard task before them, Van Dorn deployed them for battle. Lovell's division was on the C.S.A. right, on the south side of the Memphis & Charleston Railroad. Just beyond the end of his line, on the extreme right, was Colonel William H. Jackson's cavalry. Stretching toward the northeast across the wedge of land between the railroads were the divisions of Maury and Hébert, with the latter's flank resting on the Mobile & Ohio. Brigadier General Frank Armstrong's cavalry was beyond Hébert's left; his men were breaking up the M&O to prevent the arrival of any reinforcements from the north. That was it; Van Dorn kept no reserve. As they moved forward the three divisions would be compressed into a spear point they hoped would pierce the heart of the Union defense at Corinth.

In the works across the field the Federals waited. Van Dorn had believed that Rosecrans had only fifteen thousand men, but the Federal commander had called in two outlying divisions, thinking that he might have to dispatch them to Hurlbut. He had not sent them off before the Rebels turned in his direction, and now he had an aggregate of about 23,000—a thousand more than Van Dorn—inside his works. On the Federal right was Brigadier General Charles S. Hamilton's division. The M&O

Railroad divided him from the command on his left, Brigadier General Thomas A. Davies's division. Holding the Federal left flank was Brigadier General T.J. McKean's division. Far off to the left rear was the reserve division, that of Brigadier General David S. Stanley.

Lovell's Confederate division opened the attack. At 10:00 they stepped off against General McKean. The Federal gunners greeted them with long range artillery fire, but when the Confederates crossed the M&C tracks, they switched to canister rounds. Cozzens says, "the carnage was terrific." The attackers' charge failed. They reformed and charged ahead a second time with the Rebel yell. Yankee led stopped them. They re-formed, and charged again. This time they pushed forward through the storm, braving the enemy fire, captured one of the cannon that had been punishing them so, and continued after the fleeing Federals. They forced the Northerners back another half mile, after which Lovell ended his attack. He let his men "collect and bury the dead, carry off the wounded, and begin repairs on the damaged [cannon] Lady Richardson." Meanwhile, General Maury was in a hard fight, over to the left.[22]

Just a bit after Lovell launched his assault, Maury threw his division against General Davies. Davies's men had come out from their camp at five o'clock with three days' rations, forty rounds in their cartridge boxes, and 160 more per man in the wagons. In heavy columns, the Rebels boiled out of the woods at the wide end of the triangle formed by the M&C and the M&O railroads. They charged headlong into devastating cannon fire. The Federal artillerists "fired from 15 to 21 rounds" and "mowed lanes" through them, but the butternut infantry kept coming. They pushed back Davies's left and entered the Union works after only a quarter hour of fighting. Davies's right remained on the line, fighting for its life and fighting hard. The Confederates faced shattering salvos of grape and canister, but they kept charging. The Union line began to waver, and then it melted away. The defenders fell back half a mile to regroup.[23]

The Rebels were not done with General Davies. It was 2:00 p.m., plenty of daylight left, and Van Dorn "insisted the attack be pressed." Price resisted, but finally agreed to continue after a half-hour recess for his men to rest. The mercury had reached nearly 100°and the men were desperate for a breather, but at 2:30 the fight *would* go on.[24]

In fact, it did not. It always took longer than expected to get men in position, and at 2:30 they were not quite up. It was three o'clock before they were ready, and the delay was costly. The Federal artillery opened on them. The Rebels advanced some guns of their own, the Missouri batteries of Captain John Landis and Captain Henry Guibor. They engaged two batteries of the Federal 1st Missouri Light Artillery, under Major George H. Stone. Stone said, "Here for one and a half hours one of the most fierce artillery duels on record raged with all the fury of desperation." Twice Stone's caissons ran empty and a re-supply had to be brought up from the rear in limbers pulled by six-mule teams. The third time the gunners ran low of ammunition, the batteries retired. General Davies wrote, "The artillery had fired, of all calibers, over 1,500 rounds of artillery ammunition, and still no reinforcements had arrived and no attack made on the right and left flanks and rear of the enemy to support me." He had asked Rosecrans for reinforcements, but whether they would come or not was academic, for when the artillery fell back, the Confederates charged, "in steady line, firing as they advanced." Davies's men returned fire. The Rebels "fell like the leaves of autumn, staggered for a moment, closed up their openings, and advanced again." They fought on in the awful heat, back and forth; several officers reported that the rifle barrels became so hot they blistered the men's hands and the cartridges exploded in the barrels before the men could tamp them in; they detonated and blew the men's hands apart or fired ramrods through them. Men fell out of the fight, wounded by their own weapons. Colonel Augustus L. Chetlain of the 12th Illinois said, "Again and again the attack was renewed and maintained with great obstinacy.... One after another Davies lost his three brigade commanders—General Hackelman was killed, General Oglesby was desperately wounded, and Colonel Baldwin was wounded and disabled for the time." The situation was critical. Then, to Davies's relief, General Joseph A. Mower brought up his brigade and formed on the left of the battle line. Davies's relief was short lived, for before Mower's men "could be deployed into line they became panic-stricken and broke in confusion." It seemed that Davies was on his own again, but now the momentum shifted to the Federals.[25]

General Hamilton's division was on the U.S. right flank, beyond the M&O RR and so far from the fighting that it had not yet been engaged. The retreat of McKean's and Davies's divisions left General Hamilton's division about a half-mile (some say as much as a mile) in front of the new Federal line. Hamilton had seen the fight of Davies's division on his left, and he adjusted his battle line in response. Hamilton wrote, "The enemy approaching in force between the Memphis and Charleston and Mobile and Ohio Railways forced Davies by successive attacks back to the vicinity of the town. My front was gradually changed to meet the advance of the enemy.... The division had swung around on the center as a pivot." His division had performed a quarter turn, counterclockwise, so that instead of facing north as it had when the day started, it now faced west in a straight line behind the M&O. When the Confederates advanced to the attack against Davies about 2:00 p.m., Hamilton advanced his 1st and 2nd Brigades to hit the charging Rebels in their left flank. Moving across the uneven, forested ground, the Union 1st Brigade, under General Napoleon Buford, drifted too far to the right. Buford got tangled up with a Confederate skirmish line and never joined the attack as Hamilton had planned. The other brigade, under General Jeremiah C. Sullivan, also had hard going, but it reached its objective. Sullivan wrote, "Between my position and the enemy lay a swamp, covered with a dense growth of underbrush, vines, and fallen trees, through the center of which runs the dry bed of a creek." He negotiated these, cautioning his men to be silent as they advanced, and attacked. He said, "Our advance was so entirely unexpected by the enemy that, had we been supported as intended, I may be pardoned for stating that in my opinion the fight of the succeeding day would not have occurred." The startled Confederates fell back, leaving between eighty and one hundred men captured, and Sullivan called a halt only because of a lack of support. The Rebel artillery opened on them with two batteries, and the 2nd Brigade retired. Division commander Hamilton was well pleased. He said that Sullivan's action brought about "the most happy result of the movement," because it kept the Rebels from rolling over the retreating Davies and occupying the town.[26]

The Federal infantry had finished its day's work; that of the surgeons continued. Archibald B. Campbell, medical director of Rosecrans's army, had selected in the morning the new commissary depot in Corinth as his hospital, "and everything was prepared (medicines, instruments, cots, and buckets of water ready) some time before the first wounded man was brought in." By late morning, it was plain that the depot was inadequate. Dr. Campbell took over the Tishomingo Hotel, and then the Corinth House. The pleasant railroad hostelries of 1860 were transformed into scenes of horror. Soldiers from the camps who came to check on their friends felt sick at what they found. Corporal Samuel H.M. Byers of the 5th Iowa said in his memoirs, "Never will I forget the horrible scenes of that night.... In one large room of the Tishomingo House surgeons worked all the night, cutting off arms and legs.... I saw the floors, tables, and chairs covered with amputated limbs, some white, broken, and bleeding. There were simply bushels of them, and the floor was running blood. It was a strange, horrible sight—but it was war." The amputations were still going on at 2:00 a.m., when "all lights were ordered out." An hour later, according to Dr. Campbell, orders came from Rosecrans "to remove the wounded to Camp Corral." The hospital itself was under fire. Dr. Horace Wardner of the 12th Illinois Infantry was tending Brigadier General Richard J. Oglesby, who had been shot in the side in late afternoon, during the Davies fight. Wardner said that as Oglesby was being removed out the east end of the Tishomingo, "a shell came through the walls of the west end, but fortunately did not explode." The surgeons and stretcher bearers with their burden of wounded emerged from the hotel to find the outside just as terrifying. Shells were falling all around as the stewards loaded the wounded into ambulances for the agonizing ride to the new hospital site farther back. When the wounded were unloaded, safe beyond the range of Yankee shells, the ambulances returned to the front to be ready to bring back the grisly harvest of the new day, October 4, 1862.[27]

Through the night, U.S. water wagons went around to the parched troops at the front, and Rosecrans rode the lines to encourage the men and to give his division commander their assignments. McKean's division was posted on the left flank, then Stanley, Davies, and finally Hamilton on the right. The night was nearly gone when Rosecrans returned to his quarters for a couple of hours' rest. Only thirty minutes later, the Confederates began firing. These were the same guns that forced the evacuation of the hospital. The new day's battle had begun, but the Confederates were firing too high, which was good fortune for the frontline troops; they rather enjoyed watching the shells trace their fiery trails above. The Rebel fire continued unanswered for an hour. The Union artillery replied a little after 5:00 a.m., when the pre-dawn light was enough that they could be sure of their targets. They quieted the C.S.A. guns in half an hour, and then the U.S. infantry and sharpshooters killed the Confederate draft horses. The Rebs had to leave a gun and a caisson to be captured. General David S. Stanley, speaking in 1897, called the early morning barrage a "rude reveille," and said, "To this day it is a puzzle what the foolish [Confederate] captain of artillery expected to do by crawling his battery in the dark near to our picket line, and then firing his shells into a town at random."[28]

General Earl Van Dorn had left his forces in line as the day before: Lovell on the right, Maury and Hébert of Price's corps in the center and on the left, respectively. Hébert was given the assignment of opening the attack at dawn. Dawn came at six o'clock, but Hébert's charge did not. The staff officers Van Dorn sent to learn the reason could not find him. An hour after the time he was supposed to send his division into battle, the procrastinating Hébert appeared at Van Dorn's headquarters. Pleading illness, he asked to be excused from leading the attack. Van Dorn agreed to do so, and the responsibility went to Brigadier General Martin Green. Green was found in a retired position near the Mobile & Ohio Railroad where his men sat eating breakfast. No one had briefed him on the plan to attack at dawn; now he learned he was expected to lead it. He turned command of his brigade over to Colonel William H. Moore and tried to absorb as quickly as he could both the situation and what needed to be done in order to execute a plan that he barely understood because he had only just learned about it. Time was passing.

Van Dorn later reported that, in the interval between Hébert's being excused and his successor Green's attack, General Maury's left wing "became engaged with the enemy's sharpshooters and the battle was brought on and extended along the whole center and left wing; and I regretted to observe that my whole plan of attack was by this unfortunate delay disarranged. One brigade after another went gallantly into action." Brigadier General John C. Moore, who commanded a brigade in Maury's division, said, "We had gone not 100 yards before the enemy seemed to discover our design and at once operated on us, and kept up the severest fire I ever imagined possible to concentrate on one point in front of a fortification." On went the men of Maury's division, through the abatis and across the open ground to the works. General Rosecrans was watching. He said they came in "overpowering force."[29]

Van Dorn's plan had been turned inside out by Maury's attack on the Federal skirmishers. Green's (now Hébert's) men had been expected to attack first, to cross the railroad and perform a right wheel to hit Davies's right wing (that is to say, the center right of the Union line) at Battery Powell. But Maury had gone first, drawn into an attack closer to the center of the Union line. The Confederates' élan won the admiration of the Federals officers watching. General Stanley, who was on Davies's left, said the Rebel formation was "splendid," a "grand and powerful assault." But the steady fire of the Federals was a terror to the attackers. And Van Dorn's plan was ruined.[30]

The advantage seemed to be all with the defenders. From the protection of their works, they were simply slaughtering the Rebels. Then, as occasionally happened even in the most seasoned of troops, some of the men on the Union line unaccountably lost their nerve. Stanley's right flank broke and ran, along with the limbers and caissons of Dillon's battery (of Hamilton's division). They careened through the two reserve regiments— the 12th Illinois and the 81st Ohio—injuring twenty-one men "and throwing the two regiments into confusion. This communicated a stampede in the ammunition wagons ... and they too started on a run to the rear." The enemy had captured Dillon's field pieces and were rushing the others. The crews abandoned their guns and escaped on the limbers and caissons. Only one battery, Green's, retreated in good order. The retreat of the artillery "had a very demoralizing effect upon the stability of the infantry line." The front line was streaming toward the rear. Major Leonidas Horney of the 10th Missouri said the infantry regiments supporting the guns gave up and fell back "in perfect disorder and rout [and] it was only by fixing bayonets and threatening to bayonet those who attempted to force through the lines that we were able to prevent being overborne and trampled underfoot by horses, infantry, and artillery in their flight." The enemy was over the barricades and in the works. They began to shred Sweeny's brigade on the left with enfilading fire, and they retired, "firing as they went." At this, the Rebels "took possession of the earthwork, captured the seven guns in it, and held our whole line."[31]

Several regiments of Arkansans and Mississippians fought their way past Battery Powell and made it into Corinth. They had chased the 7th and 50th Illinois into town. General Moore said his troops "penetrated to the very heart of Corinth, driving the enemy from house to house and frequently firing at the windows and driving them out." They raced by Rosecrans's headquarters. Cozzens says, "Rosecrans hurled obscene epithets and threats their way, but no one paid him the slightest attention." The Rebels made it to the Tishomingo Hotel before the Federals began to resist. The fighting was brutal and sanguinary. General Van Dorn wrote, "A hand-to-hand contest was being enacted in the very yard of General Rosecrans headquarters and in the streets of the town." Colonel John V. Du Bois led the Federal counter attack with his 3rd Brigade of General Davies's division. It only failed when it was broken up by the "blind fire" of Battery B, 2nd Illinois Light Artillery. The battery's commander, Lieutenant Fletcher H. Chapman, believed that he was firing into a group of Rebs, but it killed and wounded "several men and officers" in blue, and the brigade gave away for the second time that morning. Considering the danger from friendly fire coming from behind, Colonel Du Bois said, "For the second break I do not blame the men." Shaken loose from their commands, the men fought on desperately as "small squads." Defeat seemed imminent. Suddenly, the 17th Iowa came up. Their brigade commander, Colonel Samuel A. Holmes, had led the Hawkeyes to a vantage point on the north of Corinth and they were shooting down the Confederates below like target practice. Then they fixed bayonets and charged. Cozzens says, "They struck the rear of the Rebel mass before they could recover from Du Bois's counterpunch and the death of their commander. What remained of unit integrity disappeared." General Moore said humorously that his Rebels "brought off two or three horses which they found hitched in the streets near the Corinth House, their owners being absent." The rest ran, and many surrendered. Another group of Confederates was driven from the town square by the 5th Minnesota. Other Federal units piled in. Resistance was of no use. The Rebels in Corinth were the forlorn hope of the day's fighting, and as they streamed back in disorder they may have been surprised to see that the Federals had driven their comrades out of Battery Powell, as well, and had regained their guns. The Yankees, even though they had fallen back when the Rebels rushed them, had steadied and shot down the Rebels moving among their field pieces and siege guns. They prevented the guns' removal, and then they charged to drive the enemy from their works.[32]

The Federal right flank was also intact. General Green's attack against Hamilton stepped off about ten o'clock. Maury's attack on Davies had come straight on, but the forces attacking Hamilton "moved over the ridge to the eastward, and changing direction to the right deployed under cover of skirmishers and came directly down on my front from the north." Though one of his batteries, Dillon's, had been caught up in the rout of Davies's division, Hamilton's infantry and his remaining artillerymen held steady, "and as soon as the enemy came in sight, my reserve batteries … opened with guns double-shotted with canister and sweeping over the whole front with their storm of iron." Hamilton ordered his infantry to charge. "The regiments opened fire, and, advancing with cheers and volleys, their banners streaming to the winds, they moved to the onset. It was too much for even rebel courage." The artillery fire had checked the Confederates' charge; the infantry racing toward them reversed it. They turned and ran, the Yankees on their heels. With Battery Powell back in Union hands and General Hamilton's division chasing Green's Confederates from the field, Rosecrans judged correctly that "The battle was over on the right." General Stanley said, "Should God spare me to see many battles I never expect to see a more grand sight than the battlefield presented at this moment. The enemy had commenced falling back from the town and batteries before our advancing infantry. The roll of musketry and the flash of artillery was incessant as the enemy tried in vain to form line under fire. As the smoke cleared up I can safely say I could see every fighting man on the field; but we were not long left spectators of the fight." The butternut brigades of General C.W. Phifer and General John C. Moore were advancing to attack General Stanley and Battery Robinett.[33]

Captain George A. Williams of the 1st U.S. Infantry said, "During the time the enemy was being repulsed from the town my attention was drawn to the left side of the battery by the firing from Battery Robinett, where I saw a column advancing to storm it." The Federal artillery from Battery Robinett and Battery Williams (to the left and a little behind; just south of the M&C) began firing grape and canister into the attackers, but they continued to within fifty yards "when the Ohio brigade arose and gave them a murderous fire of musketry, before which they reeled and fell back to the woods." Cozzens says, "The slaughter stunned the Federals" and quotes Colonel John Sprague as saying that when the smoke cleared he saw "apparently ten yards square a mass of struggling bodies and butternut clothes." It was a veritable carpet of Confederate dead and wounded, men blasted to rags, horrible to witness, terrible to contemplate, yet the Rebels regrouped to come again. Fifteen minutes later they surged forward at the double quick. Captain Williams of the 1st U.S. said they stormed the redoubt and reached the ditch before being repulsed. The carnage was as immense as before, and some of the Rebs found that they could take no more. Williams recalled, "During the charge eight of the enemy, having placed a handkerchief on a bayonet and calling to the men in the battery not to shoot them, surrendered, and were allowed to come into the fort."[34]

After the charge failed, the Confederate sharpshooters kept busy by peppering the Federals. They targeted officers. Colonel John W. Fuller's Ohio Brigade lost nine of its thirteen field officers. Behind the Rebel snipers, the infantry was forming for a third try at Battery Robinett. They came at a run, taking terrible losses, but they reached the outside of the works. The men inside began lobbing grenades at them; the Rebels hurriedly snatched them up and tossed them back. Some began to clamber up the face of the wall. At the top, they suffered "ghastly consequences." Lieutenant Charles R. Labruzan said, "Oh God! I have never seen the like.... I saw men running at full speed, stop suddenly and fall on their faces, with their brains scattered all around; others with legs and arms cut off, shrieking with agony." Labruzan was beside one of his 42nd Alabama infantrymen who "put his head up to shoot into the fort, but he suddenly dropped his musket and his brains were dashed in a stream over my fine coat, which I had on my arm, and on my shirt sleeves." At any moment of normal life, such a gruesome event would haunt a man's dreams forever, but this was battle and they were all moving through a nightmare world, and similar eruptions and splashes of gore could be seen in any direction one looked. The men of the 1st U.S. Infantry "were firing from the inside of the embrasures at the enemy on the outside, a distance of about 10 feet intervening," yet the Rebels kept coming. One of the most conspicuous attackers was Colonel William P. Rogers of the 2nd Texas Infantry. He was mounted, firing his pistol with one hand and, at one point, carrying the regimental colors in the other. His regiment was leading the attack on the north face of the redoubt. Some got over the parapet and into the fort. Captain Williams said the defenders "fell back into the angle of the fort as they had been directed to do in such an emergency." The Federal artillerymen were being killed, their pieces falling silent. But, Williams continued, "Two shells were thrown from Battery Williams into Battery Robinett, one bursting on top of it and the other near the right edge." None of the Rebels who got into the fort came out alive. Outside the walls, the 11th Missouri Infantry was on the attack. They fired two volleys into the attacking Texans and then they waded into them with the bayonet. Cozzens says, "The charge of the Eleventh Missouri broke the momentum of the Texans' attack." The killing went on, even as the boys from the Lone Star State tried to disengage. One of the casualties was Colonel Rogers, whose name appears in almost every report, although the accounts of his death vary widely in the telling.[35]

What seems to have happened was that Colonel Rogers was trying to fall back, found himself in a pocket from which he could not escape, had tied a white piece of cloth around a ramrod as a flag of personal surrender, and, in the smoke and confusion of battle, was shot by a volley (fired, Cozzens thinks, by the 63rd Ohio), and fell several yards from the wall. One witness says that Rogers's body was found forty feet from the wall. All agree that Rogers was the personification of courage. J.H. McClay of the 47th Illinois Infantry, said, "In all my service, covering a period of nearly five years in the front, I have never witnessed such notable bravery as was displayed by Colonel Rogers." Decades later, after Stones River, even after Chickamauga, Rosecrans considered this third assault on October 4 to be "about as good fighting on the part of the Confederates as I ever saw." Bravery did not carry the day, though; the third and final attempt to reduce Battery Robinett was over.[36]

The Confederates had "swept over the ditch and into the fort like a human hurricane," at Battery Robinett, but even a hurricane blows itself out. While the Confederates attacking Battery Robinett struggled bravely and failed, Lovell's division had not engaged, although General John S. Bowen, in army parlance, "felt" the Yankees at Battery Phillips. He sent forward a detail of sharpshooters and four field pieces. A dozen Federal cannon responded and Bowen's battery was destroyed. Satisfied that no gains were possible on that front, Bowen pulled his brigade back to a protected spot. They were still there when the bloodied, tattered remnants came tumbling back from Corinth and Battery Robinett. It was midday, and the Battle of Corinth was over. Cozzens says, "Van Dorn could not have rallied the men if he tried. Lovell's division excepted, the army was wrecked." The Confederates began to withdraw. Van Dorn said, "Exhausted from loss of sleep, wearied from hard marching and fighting, companies and regiments without officers, our troops—let no one censure them—gave way. The day was lost." When he sent Lovell the order to have his division fall in to cover the retreat from Corinth, the division commander was astonished. Lovell had been expecting to receive an order to attack. He "said to Colonel James Gordon, 'I don't understand this, Colonel. I've got a position here, and I can whip anything that can come out of Corinth or hell, and by God, I don't want to leave it!'" However, when Gordon pointed out that "the other parts of the line had been cut to pieces," Lovell reluctantly prepared to carry out Van Dorn's orders. Brigadier General John Villepigues's brigade moved into position to shield the battered Confederates from attack.[37]

When he saw the Confederates withdrawing, Rosecrans said, he "rode along the lines of the commands, told them that, having been moving and fighting for three days and two nights, I knew they required rest, but that they could not rest longer than was absolutely necessary. I directed them to proceed to their camps, provide five days' of rations, take some needed rest, and be ready early next morning for the pursuit."[38]

Later, Grant criticized Rosecrans' decision not to pursue the enemy immediately. Rosecrans *could* have caught Van Dorn, for the Confederates were not moving with notable speed, and they stopped at sunset without even crossing the Tuscumbia, the first natural defensive feature on their retreat westward. Van Dorn had called a halt not to spare his men, but because he had a scheme in mind; a mad scheme, in the view of Price and Maury. "Van Dorn still believed he could take Corinth.... During the night he spoke of his new attack plan to his staff officers. Then he directed General Price to prepare for an attack on Federal-occupied Rienzi the next day. Van Dorn planned to occupy this town and then prepare for another attack upon Corinth from that direction [that is, from the south]." An astonished Price briefed his own staff officers of Van Dorn's plan and then went to see the general, with Maury in tow. The two division leaders talked Van Dorn out of the plan in an impromptu conference that night. Maury practically mocked Van Dorn to his face, calling him by his surname without the title and saying that his reckless love of danger rendered him incapable of reasonably calculating the risks. Van Dorn said blandly in his report that, in the end, it was "deemed advisable" to countermand his order to Price. The army would continue to the Davis Bridge over the Hatchie River, thence to Ripley.[39]

The next morning, Van Dorn learned that the Federals intended to challenge his crossing of the Hatchie. Confederate cavalry under Colonel Wirt Adams had already clashed with them. Choosing from a short list of options, Van Dorn decided to engage "the enemy until I could get my train and reserve artillery on the Boneyard road to the crossing at Crum's Mill," six miles up upstream (south).[40]

The Federals were Major General Stephen A. Hurlbut's 4th Division of the Army of the Tennessee, commanded on this occasion by Major General Edward O.C. Ord. Union and Confederate cavalry clashed as the day was ending on the 4th, three miles from the Hatchie River. On the morning of October 5, they tangled again. Federal artillery was brought forward and a few rounds served to drive the enemy horsemen back to Davis Bridge. More soldiers came up and pitched in on both sides.

It was the start of a fight in which the contenders had what one might call asymmetrical goals. The Federals felt they must win and the Confederates knew they did not have to. For them, it was only a holding action. After six hours of fighting, they learned that Crum's Bridge, six miles south, was ready and could be crossed. The Rebels fighting Hurlbut and Ord fell back. General Price was on hand to conduct the traffic over Crum's Bridge. More than forty years later, veteran J.R. Perkins still remembered Price's role in the aftermath of Corinth. He said, "Price conducted the crucial part of that retreat"; and that his "subjective soldier instincts" were never better displayed. The sad parade continued over the Hatchie until 1:00 a.m., October 6, and then, as if to symbolize the mood of the army, it began to rain. The retreat continued past dawn and through the day. Cozzens says, "Lovell's division had become the glue holding the army together. At each report of the enemy's approach, Lovell faced his command to the rear and made ready to do battle." Lieutenant Colonel Frank A. Montgomery of the 1st Mississippi Cavalry said that Armstrong's cavalry brigade helped cover the retreat from the Hatchie River. He said, "The enemy made a vigorous pursuit almost to Ripley, and my regiment was kept continually in the rear without wagons or rations … a dozen times in a day I was ordered to halt and hold the position assigned me till further orders, but always as the enemy advanced, and just as the skirmishing became brisk, I would receive an order to retire to another position, a little in rear." Finally, the enemy ended their pursuit and the weary horsemen were "permitted to go to our wagons," to rest and eat. The infantry had been at Ripley since early morning, half-starved and many of them wounded. The women of the town cooked to feed them. Van Dorn and his staff returned to the home of a family named Cole and made it their headquarters, as it had been during their first visit a few days before. The family was invited to leave. They willingly complied; it was their impression that Van Dorn was going to make a stand at Ripley. Mrs. Cole said, "Now began a scene of terror and confusion indescribable." She packed a wagon and a buggy and left town with her children and eight of her slaves.[41]

Van Dorn did not make his stand at Ripley. The Confederates paused only briefly before continuing toward Holly Springs. The Yankees came in the next day, and it was there that Grant ordered Rosecrans to call off the pursuit. Rosecrans argued against the halt, pleading that the weather was perfect, the roads firm, and the fall crops ripe for the sustenance of his men. There was every reason to continue after the Rebels, but Grant said no Three times he refused Rosecrans permission to continue the pursuit. Finally, General Halleck became involved. When he found merit in Rosecrans's point of view, Grant became petulant and even dishonest, "inventing new reasons to call off the pursuit." He conjured up the image of phantom hordes of reserves on their way to join Van Dorn. He insisted that allowing Rosecrans' exhausted troops to continue would expose Corinth to danger because the Mobile & Ohio Railroad was "open to the enemy to near Rienzi," and complained that, by the many reinforcements he had sent Rosecrans, he had exposed the M&O in the vicinity of Jackson to raids by guerrillas. In the end, Halleck would not *order* Grant to unleash Rosecrans. The Confederates completed their retreat in safety, and the Federals remained in Ripley, a disaster for the residents.

Mrs. Cole returned to Ripley three days after she left. Finding the Federals in possession of her town, she exclaimed, "God help us; all is lost." The bluecoats demanded that she cook for them "with frightful oaths." The town was still filled with wounded Southerners. Private citizens helped relieve the crowding in the hospital; the Coles took in three of the invalids. Mrs. Cole and her sister tended them and cooked for them, "but the Yankee ruffians would often snatch it from the stove before it was done."[42]

The occupiers delighted in vandalism and theft. They "broke open every store in town, of course, ruining and destroying what they did not take off," Mrs. Cole told her cousin. "The square is strewn with goods; even the fence around the courthouse was festooned with muslins and tarlatans. They robbed the meat houses and pantries, leaving some families without a mouthful to eat. They took all the corn and fodder, took every horse worth the taking, shot down our cows and hogs wherever they found them, leaving them to rot and fill the atmosphere, already polluted with their awful breath." They insulted the people by their indecent language, gutted abandoned houses, and, Mrs. Cole suggested, committed some rapes. The last night of the Yankee occupation, the soldiers of that "uncivilized old Hessian" Rosecrans burglarized the Cole home. The family had anticipated it, and the thieves "found but little to reward their pains.... Fifty dollars would cover our losses that night," Mrs. Cole said. However, their overall property losses they estimated at $4000. When the Federals left Ripley the next day, they carried away from three to four hundred blacks.[43]

The Southerners had failed to win back Corinth, their vital railroad junction, but failure had been the Confederate byword across the map that bloody and calamitous fall. Their gamble had failed on every front. Van Dorn failed the worst; he had never even gotten out of Mississippi, his starting point, but the other prongs of the great invasion had fared no better in the end. Robert E. Lee had fought through the bloodiest single day in American history at Antietam Creek in Maryland. His army had survived but in such a weakened state that it had to retreat into Virginia. The combination of Generals Braxton Bragg and Edmund Kirby Smith in Kentucky had likewise failed to achieve any permanent gains. Both men had fought small actions, but the climax came at Perryville, where Bragg alone had fought General Don Carlos Buell to a bloody draw. Afterward, his army and Kirby Smith's had joined for the long retreat to Tennessee. General Buell was relieved shortly after because he had shown little desire to chase the Confederates as they retired south. Buell's dismissal created a need for a new leader for the Army of the Ohio (soon to be renamed the Army of the Cumberland), and that created an opportunity that became the solution to a considerable problem. The disagreement over the pursuit of Van Dorn had been the final blow to the friendship between Grant and Rosecrans, and there was a question of how well, or even if, they would be able to work together going forward. In the end, the question did not have to be answered. The hero of Corinth, General Rosecrans, was assigned to succeed Buell in Kentucky.

For the time being, however, Rosecrans was still in charge of the Army of the Mississippi. He led them from Ripley back to a Corinth in shambles. Cozzens says that Corinth, the once proud railroad town, was "awash in suffering, its landscape blasted and torn. The forests were littered with broken branches and treetops lopped off by cannonballs. Fields were pounded to dust. The stench of bloated corpses permeated the town. Wounded men by the thousands lay in homes, hotels, schools, and stores." Those same homes, hotels, schools, and stores had broken windows, holes in the walls and roofs, and floors so stained with blood they would never look clean again. And the fields outside of town where the battles of October 3 and 4 were fought were ghastly. Oscar L. Jackson of the 63rd Ohio was describing the aftermath of Iuka, but what he wrote would apply equally to Corinth: "A battle field is a strange, melancholy sight after the conflict is ended. As you walk over it, some strange curiosity impels you to examine the countenances of the fallen and the nature of their wounds. On an eminence perhaps the bodies of friend and foe lie mixed indiscriminately, showing where the struggle was warmest. A little farther on and you find them scattered and as you reach broken or wooded ground, you hunt for them as strawberries in a meadow. Then the different postures of the dead. Some fall dead instantly. Others struggle into the dark region of the hereafter; whilst many, placing themselves in fantastic or grave positions, appear to leave life as if it all was a farce, or in calm meditation." He noticed an oddity among the dead, "the peculiar expression on the faces of those killed by the bayonet. They have a contorted appearance, as if cramped, that enables them to be selected from among a pile of dead who were otherwise slain." In a sign of the changing nature of warfare in the mid-nineteenth century, he added that bayonet wounds "are very rare on any battle field."[44]

If there was a bright spot to be found amidst the ruins at Corinth, it was in the condition of the railroads. North of Corinth, the Federals controlled the Mobile & Ohio all the way to Columbus. There were stockades, entrenchments, and abatis at weak points, and the amount of manpower was impressive. Any minor incidents of vandalism by raiders could be quickly repaired.

Even the Confederates could find something hopeful in the aftermath of their defeat. The recent campaign had barely touched the railroad south of Corinth. The Memphis *Daily Appeal* reported, "The Mobile and Ohio Railroad is not seriously injured. The telegraph is repaired to Corinth." Furthermore, Confederate authorities were determined to lose no more of the M&O. They assured the public that they would defend and hold their railroad from Tupelo to Mobile "against any odds. A considerable force now holds it, and is being reinforced."[45]

Chapter Six

Van Dorn in Mississippi, Forrest in Tennessee

Major General William T. Sherman, whose understanding of the greater picture was exceptional, wrote, "The effect of the battle of Corinth was very great. It was indeed, a decisive blow to the Confederate cause in our quarter, and changed the whole aspect of affairs in West Tennessee." Corinth was important, but there was a greater prize waiting to be won: Vicksburg. The campaigns that followed against that river bastion temporarily pulled the war away from the Mobile & Ohio, but it continued to play an important role as the lifeline of Grant's army from his supply base at Columbus, Kentucky, to his army in the south.[1]

The year 1862 had been professionally satisfying for Grant, discounting a few setbacks and embarrassments. He had won the battles of Fort Donelson and Shiloh and maneuvered the Confederates out of western Kentucky and Tennessee into Mississippi, and forces under his command had kept the Confederates from retaking Corinth. After that, he had risen from district command to command of the Department of the Tennessee. Now it was fall, and Major General Grant hoped to crown his exceptional year by the capture of Vicksburg, the Confederate stronghold that prevented free Federal navigation of the Mississippi. He sent a message to General-in-Chief Halleck on October 25, recommending that "the rail lines be destroyed in all directions leading from Corinth to be followed by a concentration of the Union forces at or near Grand Junction, Tennessee." Halleck apparently did not respond, and Grant decided to proceed on his own initiative. He assembled ten thousand men from the garrisons in Tennessee and northern Mississippi and stepped off on November 2. The same day, Grant wrote Halleck from Jackson, Tennessee, "I have commenced a movement on Grand Junction [Tennessee], with three divisions from Corinth and two from Bolivar. Will leave here to-morrow, and take command in person. If found practicable, I will go to Holly Springs, and may be, Grenada, completing railroad and telegraph as I go." A week later Grant had reached Grand Junction and La Grange. The first steps on his first campaign against Vicksburg were a success, but as his army proceeded south, a rumor spread that the Emancipation Proclamation, set to go into effect on January 1, was to be rescinded. The story had "a most depressing effect" among the soldiers, and one wonders if that contributed to their "carelessness" at Bolivar on November 7. They "built a fire contiguous to a row of houses during the presence of a high wind. Six or eight frame structures were consumed" before the fire was brought under control.[2]

On November 9, Grant sent two infantry divisions and a regiment of cavalry to Holly Springs, which he had "selected for my depot of supplies and munitions of war, all of which at that time came by rail from Columbus, Kentucky." He himself caught the train north to Columbus for a council of war with Sherman, who came up from Memphis by paddle wheeler. By the end of their conference, it was understood that Sherman would move down the east bank of the Mississippi to threaten Vicksburg while Grant continued south toward Jackson before turning west to threaten Vicksburg by an inland route. In his written orders to Sherman, Grant said, "Inform me at the earliest practicable day of the time when you will embark, and such plans as may then be matured." He explained in his memoirs that Sherman's movements and his own "were to be cooperative," and that he hoped to hold the enemy's attention "in my front while Sherman should get in his rear and into Vicksburg."[3]

Grant resumed his movement south about November 27. In front of him was General Earl Van Dorn with 24,000 men. After Corinth, Van Dorn had found himself caught in a professional thicket. He believed he was in command of the military forces in Mississippi, but the War Department in Richmond had ordered Major General John C. Pemberton "to proceed to Jackson, Mississippi, to assume command of the department" on October 1, without informing Van Dorn of the order. He learned on October 12, not from the War Department, but from Pemberton, that he had been relieved. Van Dorn was left with no official assignment. Pemberton soothed his hurt pride only partially when he allowed Van Dorn to remain "as operations officer over the army concentrated in and around Holly Springs."[4]

Ironically, it was Grant who saved the demoted Van Dorn from wallowing in ignominious self-pity. From his post at Holly Springs, Van Dorn had been the eyes of the army and the first line of defense against the Federal advance down the railroad, but until reinforcements arrived harassment was the most he could offer in the way of resistance, and to do that he must evade capture at all costs. On or about November 8, Van Dorn withdrew from Holly Springs. The Federals were close. His horsemen struck a blow against their communications on November 25, when "250 rebel cavalry took the town of Henderson on the Mobile and Ohio Railroad, burning the station house and other property. They also took one company of the 49th Illinois Infantry prisoners." Grant ordered Brigadier General Jeremiah C. Sullivan, commander of the District of Jackson, to pursue the raiders and "place men on the road to repair it at once."[5]

Van Dorn feinted and jabbed, and he reported faithfully to Pemberton. As the Yankees proceeded south, Pemberton fell back across the Yalobusha River and ordered the Memphis & Charleston and the Mobile & Ohio railroads to cooperate in the removal of machinery and military stores from Columbus, Mississippi. It was essential that Van Dorn hold off the Yankees that nipped at their heels. On the afternoon of December 3, Van Dorn's cavalry and some Confederate infantry clashed with Colonel Edward Hatch at Spring Dale. They fought until dark and continued on the morning of December 4, when the Federals pushed the Southerners back to Water Valley and beyond. Colonel Hatch had taken prisoner ninety-two of Van Dorn's men at Spring Dale; in the fighting around Water Valley he bagged another 183, along with some wagons and equipment, which he ordered burned.

Though he was active against the Federal advance, it was not Van Dorn who finally fought them to a stop. It was the infantry of General Mansfield Lovell, who met them at Coffeeville. On December 5, the day after Van Dorn fought Hatch at Water Valley, Colonel Albert L. Lee's bluecoat cavalry brigade (of Colonel T.L. Dickey's division) appeared at Coffeeville. General Lovell moved out of Coffeeville to meet them. He pushed out his skirmishers and sent the main line to follow a hundred yards behind. General Lloyd Tilghman said, "Nothing could stop the onward movement, and our men moved forward without slackening their pace in the least." They pushed the Federals out of successive positions all the way to the intersection of the Water Valley and Panola roads. Three hours of battle saw the bluecoats retreat three miles and all that saved them from a complete rout was nightfall.[6]

The same day that Lovell and Tilghman defeated Lee and Hatch at Coffeeville, General-in-Chief Halleck sent Grant a cautionary wire that read, "Destroy the Mobile road, as you propose … but I think you should not attempt to hold the country south of the Tallahatchie." Grant, who sometimes remembered others' ideas as his own, wrote in his *Memoirs* that he had never contemplated "going further south than the Yallabusha [sic]. Pemberton's force in my front was the main part of the garrison of Vicksburg, as the force with me was the defence of the territory held by us in West Tennessee and Kentucky. I hoped to hold Pemberton in my front while Sherman should get in his rear and into Vicksburg…. It was my intention, and so understood by Sherman and his command, that if the enemy should fall back I would follow him even to the gates of Vicksburg." Therefore, it was not advantageous to drive the Confederates too far south.[7]

That is the way Grant recalled it, and perhaps it was his idea and not Halleck's to halt north of the Yalobusha. In any case, a halt was called, and Grant settled in at Oxford. He had advanced "some sixty miles from his starting point north of the Tennessee line," but there was always the danger of overreach, especially since his supplies "were still being drawn from Columbus, Kentucky, over a single-track railroad." The time had come to take stock of the situation, and prepare for the next phase of his campaign. He repaired his railroad connection to Corinth and "established a depot at Grenada to supply his planned Vicksburg move." At the same time, he ordered Colonel T.L. Dickey, commanding the cavalry division, to rest his men and horses for a strike at the Mobile and Ohio Railroad.[8]

The relaxation of Federal pressure on his front gave Van Dorn an opportunity. On December 7, he had been appointed to the command of Pemberton's I Corps, and he was ready to quiet the critics of his performance at Corinth with a bold strike. Someone, either Pemberton or his senior, General Joseph E. Johnston, proposed a raid to destroy Grant's supply base at Holly Springs. This was the very sort of action at which Van Dorn excelled, and he accepted the assignment eagerly. Within days he had the expedition organized, and on December 15 he sent forth three mounted brigades, 3500 men, from Grenada, Mississippi; he joined them the next morning. Hartje says that Van Dorn's men were "supplied with fifteen days' rations, a bottle of turpentine, a box of matches, and sixty rounds of ammunition."[9]

Grant almost defeated Van Dorn's expedition, inadvertently. On December 13, he had ordered Colonel Dickey to "strike the Mobile road as far south as possible and follow up north, destroying it all you can." Dickey divided his command so as to hit the Mobile & Ohio at both Tupelo and Coonewar Station, south of Tupelo near Colona. He accompanied Colonel Edward Hatch's brigade into Tupelo while Major Datus E. Coon led the Coonewar column. Coon and his men dashed into town in the afternoon, "made a few prisoners, captured some stores, seized the telegraph office before an alarm could be given and then quietly posted themselves to await the arrival of a passenger train about due." When the train appeared, the engineer somehow sensed the danger and tried to escape by putting the train in reverse. Chicago *Times* war correspondent Sylvanus Cadwallader wrote, "No one had taken the precaution to have the track blockaded, or torn up in the rear." Colonel Dickey reported that the soldiers rushed the train, some of them firing "on the full gallop," and one cavalryman, "leaping from his horse, pistol in hand, mounted the side of the tender under way." The one soldier who boarded soon jumped off, "to avoid a leaning post standing close to the track and just ahead of him." His deed was brave, but the train escaped. It was but a minor setback, and Major Coon returned to his primary mission. He spent the rest of the day "destroying the stores, and the railroad each way as far as possible."[10]

That night, Colonel Hatch's men could see to the south the fires of Major Coon's destruction at Coonewar. The next morning, they began their demolition work up and down the track from Tupelo. Colonel Dickey reported, "all the trestle work and bridges from Saltillo to Okolona, a distance of 34 miles, and a large bridge south of Okolona, across branch of the Tombigbee River, were thoroughly destroyed, as well as large quantities of timber laying along the railroad side for repairing purposes." They captured and destroyed "eighteen large boxes of infantry equipments complete ... several boxes of canteens, a quantity of Confederate army clothing, over 100 new wall tents, with flies, etc., complete, some commissary stores (embracing several barrels of sugar), small-arms, and ammunition." They spent the night of December 17 in Harrisburg, "a deserted town about 2 miles northwest of Tupelo," and struck the next morning for their rendezvous with Major Coon at Pontotoc.[11]

About noon on the 19th, Colonel Dickey received word that a large force of Confederate cavalry had been seen in Pontotoc. He believed they had been dispatched to capture him, and he quickly ordered his men to the north "with a view of passing some 4 miles north of Pontotoc." They skirmished with the Rebel "flankers or stragglers" and discovered that the main column was moving north on the Ripley Road; by continuing on his route, Dickey would run right into them. He later said, "It was deemed imprudent to encounter an enemy so superior in numbers and mounted on fresh horses." He changed direction and moved directly toward Pontotoc, where he saw the tail of the enemy column leaving. The Confederates spotted them, but ignored them and continued north toward Holly Springs. Dickey had had a close brush with Van Dorn's raiding party. He ordered his swiftest couriers to ride ahead to Oxford "to advise the general commanding that this [Rebel] force was moving north." The slower main column would follow as soon as possible. Cadwallader said, "Guides were seized, all extra wagons and baggage burned, and a forced march made towards Oxford." Expecting even now to be pursued, Dickey ordered every bridge along their line of march be destroyed.[12]

The next day, at the Yocknapatawpha River, Dickey discovered that the "couriers by a fatal misapprehension of my orders had not left the column." He dispatched other couriers, but they got lost on the way and actually reached Oxford after Dickey did, on the evening of the 19th. He went immediately to Grant's office to make his report. When he heard about Dickey's near encounter at Pontotoc, the general understood in an instant what was occurring. He did not even listen to the end of Dickey's report before he rushed out to the military telegraph office and began sending "dispatch after dispatch" to his post commanders to prepare to repel a large force of Confederate raiders. One of the wires went to Colonel Robert C. Murphy, who was in charge of the great supply depot at Holly Springs. Murphy was the same officer who had abandoned the vast quantities of government stores at Iuka when General Sterling Price approached the previous September. He soon showed that he had learned nothing in the interim. With twelve hours' warning that he might be attacked, Colonel Murphy did not even send out patrols. Van Dorn's Confederates reached the outskirts of Holly Springs undetected, on the evening of December 19.[13]

They dashed in on the morning of December 20 "with full throated rebel yells." They began by burning the Federal tent village. They continued to the warehouses down by the Mississippi Central Railroad, and lucked onto "enough cars to make three normal-sized trains." The raiders "crammed their saddlebags with all they could carry and torched the rest. They burned buildings and tore up railroad track, and they destroyed two locomotives and sixty rail cars." Uptown, they burned the courthouse and the other government buildings. They burned the U.S. hospital. They set fire to the powder magazine, which went up with an explosion that knocked over some surrounding buildings and was felt all over town. Before disabling the telegraph service, Van Dorn sent a short wire to Pemberton, announcing that he had "surprised the enemy at this place at daylight this morning, burned up all the quartermaster stores, cotton, etc.—an immense amount; burned up many trains, took a great many arms and about 1500 prisoners. I presume the value of stores would amount to $1,500,000." It was the nearest to a report that Van Dorn would produce "about one of the most significant raids of the war."[14]

By 8:00 a.m., Van Dorn had accomplished all he had intended. The hungry, ragged Rebels took everything they wanted—boots and pistols were mentioned as popular items—and the contrabands that had followed the Federals into Holly Springs on an earlier day "began to loot and pillage as never before." The Confederates rode out of town about 4:00 and began a winding return to Grenada. They arrived December 28, completing a circuit that carried them five hundred miles in fourteen days. James W. Rabb says, "Van Dorn's army, with limited striking force and little bloodshed, accomplished more to stop Grant's Mississippi adventure in the last two weeks of the year than the combined Confederate army had done in the previous three months."[15]

After the destruction of Holly Springs, Halleck ordered Grant, "Concentrate and hold the more important points." Grant had already decided to move his headquarters back to the ruined town and to begin drawing in his troops. To feed them, he said, he dispatched "all the wagons we had, under proper escort to collect and bring in all supplies of forage and food from a region of fifteen miles east and west of the road from our front back to Grand Junction, leaving two months' supplies for the families of those whose stores were taken." Months earlier, it had been reported in the Northern papers that there was starvation in Mississippi. Grant found the situation to be otherwise. He wrote, "I was amazed at the quantity of supplies the country afforded. It showed that we could have subsisted off the country for two months." When the locals came to complain, Grant remembered telling them, "we had endeavored to feed ourselves from our own northern resources while visiting them; but their friends in gray had been uncivil enough to destroy what we had brought along, and it could not be expected that men, with arms in their hands, would starve in the midst of plenty. I advised them to emigrate east or west, fifteen miles and assist in eating up what we left."[16]

The newspapers painted a harsher picture than Grant's benign portrayal of his men's collection of supplies. The Memphis *Daily Appeal* characterized it as a "reign of terror" and said that the "ruthless and more than savage soldiers were turned loosed upon the helpless citizens. They bursted open the doors, entered private rooms, threatened to kill and murder, abusing and insulting in the most vulgar manner defenseless females, broke locks, pillaging and destroying everything before them, robbing men of watches and money, and stealing from the most useless to the most valuable articles, applying the torch at midnight, burning homes and turning women and children out at midnight upon the severities of mid-winter." Because Grant had ordered his men to live off the land, "they were duly licensed to commit any act, except taking life; thus grey hairs were dishonored and innocence outraged with impunity."[17]

It was little wonder, then, that the people thrilled to the exploits of their hero Nathan Bedford Forrest, who was even then raiding along Grant's M&O supply line in Tennessee. Van Dorn had dealt the Federals in Mississippi a serious blow; Forrest would bring their adventure to an end by a combination of unmatched boldness and dazzling innovation. In his article titled "A Year with Forrest," W.H. Whitsitt wrote, "The northern general still proceeded on the sleepy idea that it was the main function of cavalry to serve as the eyes and ears for infantry. Forrest had gotten beyond that standpoint long before, and no cavalry trained upon the ancient maxims was able to stand against us." General Dabney Maury agreed that Forrest had notable skill and judgment. He called him "the greatest soldier of his time," and said his "natural qualifications as a soldier were phenomenal." A modern observer, James M. McPherson, agrees. He says, "Forrest became one of the South's most innovative and hard-driving commanders. He developed combined mounted and dismounted tactics not mentioned in military textbooks—which he had never read—but ideal for the wooded terrain of western Tennessee and Northern Mississippi." By his genius for tactics and his abundant reserves of energy, Forrest earned his sobriquet "The Wizard of the Saddle."[18]

General Braxton Bragg had released Forrest to return to west Tennessee at Pemberton's request

General Nathan Bedford Forrest.

for reinforcements. The raid did not get off to a promising start. Forrest reached the Tennessee River on December 15. He crossed his men by night, ignoring a persistent rain, using two flatboats that could transport only twenty-five men and horses at a time. Forrest posted sentries well up- and downstream, and the men waiting on the bank for their turn to cross stayed back in the trees in case the Union gunboats appeared. The men had no tents or shelters and they were thoroughly drenched. When the general called a halt en route to Lexington so that his men could dry their clothing and check their arms, they discovered that their percussion caps "had become wet and unserviceable." But luck born of intelligent foresight saved them. Forrest had sent forward for a supply of percussion caps to be ready for his men, and one of his west Tennessee operatives now appeared with fifty thousand caps for shotgun and pistol. Ready to fight once more, Forrest pressed on to Lexington where on December 17 he defeated Colonel Robert G. Ingersoll and, the newspapers said, "made a stampede that Bull Run can in no wise surpass." Brian Wills says, "Most of Ingersoll's men broke and ran for Jackson, leaving the colonel, 147 of his men and a sizable amount of weapons, ammunition, and other supplies in Forrest's hands." These prizes included two field pieces and seventy horses. From Lexington, Forrest struck due west toward Jackson, one of the most important towns on the M&O RR and the headquarters of the military district. The Federals knew now that a major raid was underway, but, as usual, they exaggerated the numbers of the invading force. Ingersoll reported to Grant that "3000 infantry, 800 cavalry, and six pieces" were on the move, and Grant wired David Dixon Porter than the enemy force numbered "from five to ten thousand men." General Jeremiah C. Sullivan at Jackson estimated the number of invaders heading his way at from "ten to twenty thousand." Even with such panic evident among the Union leaders, Forrest knew there was no time to waste; the Yankees would eventually regain their composure, and, as John Allan Wyeth observed, "The work in hand was dangerous and must be done quickly, and the more rapid the execution, the less danger of a concentration of troops in sufficient number to prevent him [Forrest] from recrossing the Tennessee."[19]

The raiders reached Jackson to find the Federals forming for battle. General Sullivan had been calling for reinforcements from posts up and down the Mobile & Ohio to board the trains and hurry to his aid. His regular garrison of five thousand men had grown to at least ten thousand and perhaps fifteen thousand. The raiders could hear trains in the distance, presumably bringing even more men to Sullivan. Forrest could not afford to wait; he advanced into Jackson. Sullivan threw out his skirmishers, but Forrest drove them back toward their works, "a heavy line of infantry epaulements connecting some five or six open-gorge works for fieldpieces." In an hour, the preliminary fighting was concluded and Forrest deployed his men around the works. It was obvious that even the Wizard of the Saddle could not overpower ten thousand or more entrenched Federals, but he remained in place to intimidate the enemy and protect the detachments he sent out to dismantle and burn sections of the M&O north and south of Jackson. Colonel George G. Dibrell went to Carroll Station, north of Jackson, to burn the railroad bridge over Spring Creek; a second and third group under Colonel A.A. Russell and Colonel N.N. Cox rode south to hit the railroad between Jackson and Bolivar. Dibrell later reported that he moved around to the north side of Jackson as ordered and arrived at the M&O, fired into a passing troop train, and charged the stockade, where the Yankee outpost of one hundred infantry was soon captured along with their arms and stores. The raiders burned the stockade, destroyed a "considerable" length of railroad, and rode back to join Forrest. No one recorded the details of Russell's and Cox's strikes against the M&O south of Jackson, but they presumably had similar success, for Jordan and Pryor wrote, "Each detachment tore up sufficient of the railroad to make a substantial obstruction to the approach of trains from their respective directions."[20]

Forrest pulled back from Jackson late on the night of the 19th and moved north toward Trenton. His detachments rejoined him en route, and the quantity of weapons they brought to distribute among the men was testimony to their success. Forrest needed the additional arms; his force was even then being augmented by "sixty newly-raised volunteers from Hickman and Perry Counties of Middle Tennessee," who came to join the raiders on the 19th and 20th. The raiders arrived at Trenton on the afternoon of the 20th. Once again, Forrest detached various bands; he sent Dibrell "to destroy the bridge over the Forked Deer River between Humboldt and Jackson," and Colonel J.W. Starnes to attack Humbolt. Forrest ordered the rest to the main attack. Dividing his men into two columns, he led one and Colonel Jacob B. Biffle was "sent so as to get in the rear of Trenton." The commander at Trenton was Colonel Jacob Fry, and he had been preparing for days to resist Forrest, but he was at a disadvantage. Colonel Sullivan had stripped his garrison for service at Jackson, and Fry was left to cobble together a force of "convalescents, stragglers, fugitives and other soldiers" he snagged from commands passing through from other posts. He urgently asked General Thomas A. Davies at Columbus, Kentucky, to send him reinforcements; he received no reply at all to his first request and a flat denial to the second. Fry was on his own. His sense of isolation grew on the morning of the 20th when the telegraph service went down. Fry's 250 men were too few to man his rifle-pits, so he barricaded the M&O depot with cotton bales and placed sharpshooters on the roofs and upper floors of nearby buildings.[21]

The attack came at three o'clock in the afternoon. The raiders charged in from two directions. Forrest wrote, "I dashed into town and attacked the enemy ... they were fortified at the depot, but were without artillery." Colonel Fry reported that his sharpshooters opened a "deadly fire" on the attackers. The men in the works kept up a steady fire as well, and, said Fry, both of the attacking columns "were repulsed with considerable loss in killed and wounded." Forrest claimed only two killed and three wounded from the supposedly "deadly fire," but it was hot enough that he ordered his men to fall back and dismount. He engaged the sharpshooters, drove them from their snipers' nests, and then he brought up his artillery. They unlimbered at three hundred yards and opened fire. After three rounds, "numerous white flags were displayed from all quarters of the Federal fortalice." Trenton was won.[22]

Fry claimed that, while only one of his men was killed, the Rebels "could have leveled the stockade, depot, and all in thirty minutes, and probably killed and wounded a large portion of our men, while we could have done them no damage, being armed only with old guns, without bayonets, and therefore unable to make a charge." Fry agreed to an unconditional surrender. When the two leaders met, Fry handed Forrest his sword with the comment that it had been in his family for forty years. Forrest took the sword, examined it, and then returned the heirloom to its owner, noticing about the same time a column of smoke rising from behind the depot. In the midst of Fry's surrender, the Federals were burning what had now become the legal spoils of war. Forrest forced the arsonists to put out their own fire before too much damage was done and declared to Fry "his determination of punish in the most summary manner any such perfidy." The misbehavior was not repeated, and Forrest tallied his prizes. It was a bountiful haul at Trenton: four hundred prisoners; one thousand horses and mules; twenty thousand rounds of artillery ammunition; four hundred thousand rounds of small arms ammunition, twenty wheeled conveyances of different types, and tons of stores. Most of the horses they seized proved upon examination to be of no value. The raiders selected the best of them and distributed the rest among the townsfolk. The men kept what they needed of the ammunition, weapons, and supplies and destroyed the rest "for want of transportation." The prisoners were paroled; the Tennesseans among them were allowed to return home and Forrest sent the rest north under Lieutenant Colonel N.D. Collins to Columbus, Kentucky, "there to spread bizarre reports of his strength."[23]

Forrest and his men remained in Trenton overnight. The next morning, Forrest fired the Mobile & Ohio depot, "burning up the remaining supplies, with about 600 bales of cotton, 200 barrels of pork, and a large lot of tobacco in hogsheads, used by the enemy for breastworks." Once the destruction was complete, he led his column, "now well armed, equipped, and supplied, as well as somewhat stronger than when it had entered west Tennessee," in the direction of Union City. As a precaution against surprises, Forrest instructed Colonel Dibrell to remain in Trenton through the next day. Surprisingly, even now, the Federals were still not entirely sure who was leading the raid. A news item with the dateline Cairo said, "The strength of the rebels is not known, nor do we yet know the name of the commander. Cheatham, Morgan, and Forrest are conjectured."[24]

Colonel Dibrell had rejoined Forrest at Trenton after a failed attempt against the garrison at Forked Deer River. The Federal works there stood between two creeks and a swampy bottom that made it impossible for cavalry to come close. Dibrell dismounted his men, but as they began their advance on foot, a train arrived from Jackson with an infantry regiment. Lieutenant John W. Morton was a young artilleryman on his first ride with Forrest, the beginning of a legendary partnership. On this day, he was with Dibrell, and he opened fire on the train with the two Rodman guns that Forrest had taken away from the Yankees at Lexington. The troops disembarked and got into the stockade and the train escaped. The guns could not be rolled forward over the miry ground and through the scrub timber to get within range of the stockade, and dismounted cavalry alone could not force the surrender. About dusk, Colonel Dibrell broke off the attempt at Deer Forked Creek and returned to Forrest.

Colonel Starnes and his detachment had been more successful in their expedition to Humboldt. They had captured the two hundred man garrison after a brief skirmish and torched the stockade, the M&O station, and the nearby trestle. They seized a trove of prizes, including four caissons with horses; five hundred stand of small arms; 300,000 rounds of ammunition; and quantities of quartermaster and commissary stores. Everything was placed in the stockade to burn except for the best of the weapons and ammunition and the caissons.

Seven miles north of Trenton, Forrest captured a garrison of thirty men and burned their stockade, a railroad bridge, and a trestle. Seven more miles and the raiders came upon the garrison at Kenton Station, 250 men of the 122nd Illinois Infantry, who fell back into their works for protection. To bring them out, the Wizard brought forth his six guns and fired a volley. One unison round was enough to force the Federals' surrender. Forrest burned the stockade and trestle, ripped up track and destroyed two railroad engines and some cars. He pushed on to the Obion River bottoms, where he destroyed another long trestle before settling down for the night, a welcome rest after a long day of demolition. Before retiring, Forrest ordered Colonel Starnes to take his men the next morning and destroy the M&O tracks "through the bottoms of the Obion, a distance of some fifteen miles." The main party would continue to Union City. There, on December 21, they captured 106 of the enemy "without firing a gun." They destroyed four miles of trestle and two railroad bridges over the forks of the Obion.[25]

That night, Forrest ordered an unnamed officer and a detail of forty men to proceed north across the Kentucky line and destroy an M&O RR bridge that spanned a bayou near Moscow. The men arrived the next morning, December 22. At the stockade, "a charge was made, with a loud shout, into the very heart of the position, the commander crying aloud for the 'artillery' to be pushed 'forward.' The Federals thereupon fled precipitously out of their works in the direction of Columbus, leaving possession to the Confederates." The Rebels burned the station, the trestlework, and the U.S. blockhouse.[26]

The arrival of a Confederate party less than fifteen miles away threw a terrible fright into the Federals at Columbus. Only a month before, the garrison was complaining of boredom. They were stuck far behind the lines, at Mile One on the M&O, the very starting point of the war in western Kentucky. The front had moved far to the south. Colonel Frederick A. Starring of the 72nd Illinois described his regiment's duty at Columbus as "irksome" to men who were "desirous of being in service." Now, with Forrest's men so near, there was "considerable excitement at Columbus in anticipation of a rebel visit." General Davies, commanding at Columbus, was worried. He had no communications south, and only knew that the Rebels had taken Union City and made a raid on Moscow. He had said on December 22 that he expected his post to be attacked, "but am ready for any force they can bring." By December 24, he was not so confident. He ordered all the commissary stores and other public property—worth an estimated $13,000,000—to be moved onto boats in case he had to abandon Columbus. General-in-Chief Henry W. Halleck was determined that would not happen and had been making moves to prevent it. On December 21, Halleck had wired Major General Samuel R. Curtis at St. Louis, "Re-enforce Columbus as quickly and strongly as you can." To the commanding officer at Cairo, he said, "Send to Columbus all your available forces." Halleck wired General Davies that reinforcements were on the way and directed him to "Do everything in your power to reopen and protect the railroad. Notify General Hurlbut and the commanding officer at Memphis of the condition of affairs."[27]

Davies remained in a state of alarm, but Forrest did not move farther north. He gave his troops a holiday "after their four-day rampage with axes and sledges," and he sat down to write the report of his raid to date. It was there that rumors began to reach Forrest that a force of twelve thousand or more of the enemy had collected at Trenton for the purpose of blocking his return south to Confederate lines. On the day after Christmas, to the relief of Davies, Halleck, and everyone who was worried about the fate of Columbus, Forrest led his men out of Union City, south by east along the Nashville & Northwestern Railroad toward Dresden and McKenzie, where the N&NW joined the M&O. General Davies, sounding brave again now that the Rebels had turned their backs to him, reported to Halleck, "Things are easing up in every way. I shall hold the place against any force." He added, "I understand from deserters that the road [M&O] is not much damaged except bridges and trestle work burned."[28]

Two days later, he changed his evaluation of conditions on the railroad completely. He wrote Halleck, "From the best information from persons from Trenton and other points I find the road is greatly damaged, not so much in the woodwork as in the rails. They built fires upon the rails on one side, which expands the rails and throws the track, ties, and all out of place, and when the iron gets so hot that it can push no farther the rail knuckles and when it cools breaks the rails. I understand miles of the road are thus destroyed." He believed the damage to be "so extensive that it might involve a change of base to Memphis or below." However, he said that he was "now in a position to send a construction train out" and vowed again that, with his present strength of six thousand men, he could defend Columbus "against any force which they can bring."[29]

General Grant subsequently ordered Davies to send his spare troops to Memphis and reduce the Columbus garrison to its pre-raid numbers, about eight hundred men. He said, "One regiment is the greatest abundance to hold the place, and has been during all the late scare." General Halleck sustained Grant's orders over Davies's protests and ordered the Columbus post commander to send his surplus troops to Memphis "as soon as transportation can be furnished." When that would be, no one could tell. Forrest's destruction of "the Mobile and Ohio Railroad from Jackson, Tennessee, to Moscow, Kentucky, was complete," said Wyeth, "With one exception, there was not a bridge left on this line. Not a yard of trestlework was standing, not a culvert was left undestroyed, and the rails over much of this distance had been completely ruined." The thoroughness of the devastation along the M&O reduced Columbus to a cypher, its importance as the northern terminus of the road and the overland source of Federal supplies at an end.[30]

Forrest wrecked as much of the N&NW Railroad as he could as he moved toward McKenzie, but speed was becoming more important. By the time he reached the Obion on December 28, columns were converging on him from Jackson, Trenton, Fort Henry, Fort Heiman, Fort Donelson and Corinth. General Clinton B. Fisk at Columbus wanted to take four thousand men and join the chase, but Davies prevented him from doing so. Fisk wrote General Curtis in St. Louis that Davies "is quite nervous about the post; but I am fully convinced that we could defeat him or skedaddle the entire rebel horde." He took a swipe at his commander when added, "I know I am a young general, but I believe I am old enough to see through a millstone with so large a hole in it."[31]

The Wizard was reinforced as he moved toward the Tennessee by over four hundred men led by Lieutenant Colonel T.A. Napier, but such a modest increase in numbers would not save him if he became snared in a box of rain-swollen rivers, gunboats, and approaching Federals. That was not out of the question; crossing the bottom of the Obion was such a slow process that Forrest was, by his estimation, sixteen miles behind where he should have been on the night of December 30. And all the time the Federals were converging, determined to trap him on the west side of the broad Tennessee.

Safety lay on the east side, and Forrest meant to get there, but he knew he must not be caught crossing when the enemy attacked. The only way was to evade them—increasingly unlikely—or to defeat them beforehand and then cross in safety. The showdown came the next morning, December 31, at Parker's Crossroads, where he found a brigade of Federal infantry under Colonel C.L. Dunham blocking the way to the river; Forrest would have to fight. He came forward behind the skirmishers of Colonels Dibrell and Russell, followed by the artillery. He placed Lieutenant Morton's section of guns in the center of the line and sections under Captain Samuel L. Freeman on each flank. Dibrell reported that the guns "opened on them with splendid effect." The Federals fell back and redeployed, but they still stood between the raiders and the river. Forrest's dismounted horse soldiers advanced. Morton's and Freeman's guns continued to boom, and it was the artillery that forced the Federals back to a new position behind a split rail fence. At a range of only three hundred yards, the Rebel artillery poured salvos of grape and canister into the fence and turned it into deadly splinters. Forrest said that "many were killed by rails that were untouched by balls."[32]

Charging the Confederates seemed preferable to waiting to be impaled behind a rapidly disappearing fence. Three times the Federals charged and three times the Rebels drove them back. Forrest saw a chance to get the "bulge." He sent a regiment around the left and a battalion around the right to attack each enemy flank while the front line pushed forward. It was too much for the Federals. They broke and ran. Forrest wrote, "We drove them through the woods with great slaughter and several white flags were raised in various portions of the woods and the killed and wounded were strewn over the ground." In five hours of fighting, the Rebels had about exhausted their ammunition, but the battle was ending. "Thirty minutes more would have given us the day," Forrest said.[33]

Suddenly, a storm of lead and steel erupted behind the Confederates. They were under attack by another brigade of Yankee infantry under the command of Colonel John W. Fuller, accompanied by General Jeremiah C. Sullivan, the timid Union commander at Jackson. The Confederate commander was astonished. He thought he had placed adequate videttes to prevent just such a surprise. Yet, it was true, he was under attack from the rear by a wholly undetected force. Wyeth said, "In all probability, there was not in the history of the war a surprise more complete than that which was suffered by Forrest at the Battle of Parker's Crossroads." The sudden fire from Sullivan's men "caused a stampede of horses belonging to my dismounted men," Forrest said. "They also killed and crippled many of the horses attached to our caissons and reserved guns." About three hundred of Forrest's men, primarily members of the cannon crews, horse holders, and others in what might be called support roles, became prisoners of the attackers within moments of the Federal onslaught.[34]

Enemy in front, enemy in the rear—it was at this moment that Forrest is said to have "responded to an excited staff officer's request for instructions: 'Charge them both ways!'" Forrest did not quote himself as making so folksy a remark, appropriate as it might have been, but he did turn to fight in both directions and "withdrew sideways before his opponents recovered from the shock." Forrest merely said, "Finding my command now exposed to fire from both front and rear I was compelled to withdraw, which I did in good order, leaving behind our dead and wounded.

We were able to bring off six pieces of artillery and two caissons, the balance, with the three guns we captured, we were compelled to leave, as most of the horses were killed or crippled and the drivers in the same condition." Once free of the Yankees, Forrest's men traveled twelve miles to Lexington, where they stopped to tend the wounded and to feed the men and horses. It was New Year's Eve, but the transition from 1862 to 1863 went unnoticed as the men resumed their march and kept moving through the wee hours toward the Tennessee River and safety.[35]

General Sullivan had the satisfaction of sending Grant a somewhat exaggerated dispatch that said, "Forrest's army is completely broken up. They are scattered over the country without communication. We need a good cavalry regiment to go through the country and pick them up." Grant replied, "You have done a fine job," and he reminded Sullivan, "I sent a fine regiment of cavalry to you. They left here [Oxford] on the 31st."[36]

Forrest wrote, "Considering my want of ammunition for small-arms and artillery and the worn-down condition of our men and horses, I determined at once to recross the Tennessee River and fit up for a return." He said if he had won the battle at Parker's Crossroads he would have lingered long enough to strike Bethel Station on the Mobile & Ohio, "but after the fight, and knowing we were followed by Federals in heavy force.... I deemed it advisable to cross the Tennessee." Major Jeffrey Forrest, the general's brother, pushed on ahead to the river and sent back a rider with the news that his detail had encountered a heavy force of the enemy at Clifton. A few miles farther and General Forrest met 1200 cavalry under Lieutenant Colonel W.K.M. Breckinridge blocking his way. The Federals were still behind Forrest; he could not retreat. He turned to Colonel Dibrell and ordered him to charge Breckinridge's cavalry, which he did, while Colonels Starnes and Biffle swung around to hit them on the flanks. The bluecoats scattered, and the gray column continued unmolested toward the river.[37]

They had paroled all their prisoners, but they still had their artillery and the train. They arrived at the river mid-day on January 2 and began crossing. The horses swam, the wagons and artillery crossed on a flatboat that, because of the strong current, had to be poled a half-mile upstream in order to hit the opposite bank at the right place. Jordan and Pryor say, "It was a spectacle full of life and movement, quite as many as 1000 animals were at one time in the river, which was about six hundred yards broad with favorable banks," while the slow "ferriage" of the wheeled vehicles— five artillery pieces, six cannon, sixty wagons, and four ambulances— fought the current on the frail raft. The crossing took from eight to ten hours, depending on the account one reads. All agree that it finished after nightfall.[38]

Forrest had a difficult time getting over the defeat he had suffered at Parker's Crossroads. He returned to it repeatedly in his post-action report. Near the conclusion he complained about the four companies he had sent out to watch for the enemy and said, "Had they done their duty by advising me of the approach of the enemy I could have terminated the fight by making it short and decisive, and without such advise I was whipping them badly with my artillery, and unless absolutely necessary was not pressing them with my cavalry. I had them entirely surrounded and was driving them before me, and was taking it leisurely and trying as much as possible to save my men." There, he abruptly ended his recapitulation, and one can almost imagine him throwing down his pen in disgust.[39]

Although he had been embarrassed at the end and had suffered a regrettable number of casualties killed, wounded, and captured, Forrest's raid was a success. He wrote, "We have worked, rode, and fought hard, and I hope accomplished to a considerable extent, if not entirely, the object of our campaign, as we drew from Corinth, Grand Junction, and La Grange about 20,000 Federals." He had armed his men with modern long arms taken from the enemy and had remounted them on captured horses. He had occupied the attention of dozens of regiments and thousands of soldiers in their posts. Most importantly, he had crippled the Mobile & Ohio Railroad, the Federals' life line from Columbus.[40]

Forrest's West Tennessee Raid, along with Van Dorn's destruction of Holly Springs, closed the book on Grant's first Vicksburg Campaign. Bruce Catton says, "Grant's army, deep in Confederate territory, abruptly found itself with no supplies and no supply line, in an area where no living white man would give any assistance to a Yankee army if he could help it. Taken together, Forrest and Van Dorn had completely canceled Grant's campaign plans." The general called it quits and moved his base to Memphis for the winter.[41]

The year 1862 had seen both setbacks and gains for the Federal and Confederate armies. The same was true of the Mobile & Ohio Railroad. By year's end, the railroad had lost the northern half of its original length, from Columbus to Okolona. The ruin left by Forrest in his raid did not count against the corporation, for it was behind the lines, in that section controlled by and used exclusively for the benefit of the Federals, but the destruction of the M&O tracks, trestles, bridges, engines, railcars, warehouses, water tanks, and depots at Tupelo and Coonewar Station by Colonel Hatch and Major Coon was a costly blow to the M&O and to the Southern war effort. Scarce materials and a shortage of manpower made repairing the present damages difficult, and future damages were a certainty. The enemy's army was still poised on the border and his navy still blockaded the coast.

CHAPTER SEVEN

Mobile, 1863

A City and Its Lifelines

Mobile was the headquarters of the M&O Railroad. At the fifteenth annual stockholders' meeting there in April 1863, President Milton Brown reported that the company had earned a profit of $1,379,906 in 1862. There were outstanding debts to the various states and to foreign investors; there was also a legal question about what was owed to investors in the United States. Brown said, "The debts owing to parties in the United States have been attached by the Confederate authorities under the confiscation laws, but as they are due on bills payable, they may have passed into other hands, in due course of trade, and therefore, no judgments can be rendered on them."[1]

The company's assets on hand amounted to over $2,308,000, a total that was deceptively impressive. The company had reserves of money because it could not *spend* its money. There were the unpayable debts mentioned above, the blockade made it impossible to buy replacement rails and rolling stock, and the holders of income bonds refused to present them in return for money, "the bonds being above par." President Brown said, "Had our bills payable and Bonds been presented for payment, and the blockade had been removed so as to allow the purchase of rails and other materials for the repair of the Road, a large portion of this fund would have been absorbed."[2]

Brown made special mention of two other corporate assets. The Mobile & Ohio had 2,055 bales of cotton worth almost $157,000. The cotton was slated to be sent across the Atlantic to the railroad's English creditors "as soon as the blockade will permit." In addition, the M&O had purchased sixty slaves for $98,500 and expected "to increase the number to one hundred, if they can be had at reasonable prices, and of good quality." The president talked about the importance of the lands held by the railroad and the necessity of keeping the line in the best possible state of repair. He concluded by recommending that the board of directors declare a stock dividend of six percent, payable after June 15, 1863.[3]

In his report, Chief Engineer L.J. Fleming alluded more to the military situation. He said the war increased the demand for maintenance and forced the construction crews to use up a rapidly dwindling supply of stockpiled materials. He added that replacement materials had sky-rocketed in price. He said, "In addition to this, the military authorities assumed the supervision of the Road, and trains were forced to run out of time, while the cars were forced upon other Roads, and mutilated and destroyed while thus diverted from the control of the Company's officers." He protested the policy of "interchanging cars," saying that it had ruined 141 M&O rail cars, and adding, if the policy continued, it would "ruin every Road in the Confederate States."[4]

As an engineer, Fleming understood the problem of interchanging cars in a way that was not obvious to the ordinary stockholder. He explained, "Each Road has had its cars constructed from peculiar patterns, and is prepared with brass and castings to keep them in good running order; but when sent upon another Road, that road has not the necessary parts to repair them, so that when out of order, they are placed on the side tracks [where] they are rendered useless, and are frequently broken up and destroyed." He said that the rail cars lost in 1861 and 1862 by this misguided policy "cannot be replaced until the close of the war."[5]

Fleming prepared a chart showing the depreciation of the existing rails, buildings, locomotives and rolling stock of the railroad, the number of cars and locomotives lost, and the number of rails removed from the track for use elsewhere from "that portion of the Road in our possession, extending from Mobile to Okolona." The total from losses and depreciation came to nearly $1,300,000, which should be included in expenses. He recommended that "a special fund be appropriated out of the year's earnings and set apart for the renewal." He did not attempt to tabulate the losses and depreciation for the M&O above Okolona. That portion was in Federal hands and the available information was "too meagre to authorize the making any estimate of the amount required to repair them."[6]

Fleming called the stockholders' particular attention to the importance of maintaining a high quality of rails because poor rails meant broken axles, "now justly regarded as the most terrible form of accidents." This led him to address, finally, the matter of accidents, which had become more frequent. There had been multiple accidents along the M&O RR in recent months. One of them occurred during the second week of August last near Citronelle. A train ran into the rear end of the one ahead, "cutting in two a car filled with soldiers, a number of whom were killed and wounded." Fleming said, "Before this war, it had always been with great pride that I informed the Board that no passenger had ever lost his life on this Road, and but for the interference in its management, the Government and the public would have been better served, the machinery would have been in better condition, and the same record of personal safety would again be written."[7]

The blockade was obviously having a depressing effect on the maintenance of the railroad, but President Brown and Chief Engineer Fleming seemed to have more of a grievance against their own government and its military than against its avowed enemies in blue. In January 1863, Brown filed a complaint with Major General Simon Bolivar Buckner, commanding the District of the Gulf. The previous month, the Kentuckian had been detached from duty with Bragg's army in eastern Tennessee and ordered to Mobile to succeed General John Forney, who was ill. Buckner faced manifold problems. His biographer Arndt Stickles says Buckner was expected to guard the harbor and the city, make contracts for supplies, and "determine the solution of problems concerning export trade." These last two touched upon President Brown's complaint to General Buckner.[8]

About three weeks earlier, on December 12 of the previous year, General Pemberton had issued a directive which he hoped would end the speculation in corn. Corn was rightly regarded in the South as the "basis for food." The Memphis *Daily Appeal* told its readers, "Make food enough and we can fight the Yankees forever. Fail to make it, and not only your other crops will do you no good, but you will lose your lands, your negroes, and your country's independence." The harvest was abundant; it was transporting it to those who needed it that proved difficult. Speculation was an inevitable but unfortunate reality of the war-time economy. Speculators' freight competed for the limited space on the rail cars, space that was needed for supplies intended for the subsistence of the troops, and Pemberton intended to stop it. He instructed Brown that "no more corn for private parties be transported over your road within this department."[9]

Brown said to Buckner that, rather than put an end to speculation, Pemberton's order had actually increased the problem; those in Mobile who held quantities of corn had immediately raised their prices, "thereby increasing the distress of the country." The people, said Brown, had petitioned Pemberton to rescind or at least modify his order, and the general, responding to their pleas, attempted to soften its effects. On January 6, he sent to the head office of the M&O a revised order that said, "Corn for the use of families may be transported when it is satisfactorily shown it is not for speculation." The railroad issued a notice above the name of L.J. Fleming that corn could be transported in accordance with the January 6 order, "upon affidavit filed in my office stating that it is exclusively for family and not for speculation." Pemberton was not satisfied. He informed Fleming that no one other than the quartermaster was authorized to "judge whether the produce is for speculation or not."[10]

At this point President Brown put his foot down. He wrote a heated note to Pemberton that said, "By your order to our superintendent you seem to put private shipments of corn under the control of quartermasters. Please answer if this is your design. I suppose there is some mistake about the matter. There are four or five quartermasters on the road and the confusion will be endless. We will respect quartermasters' orders in regard to Government freight and in all cases give preference to such freight, but their assuming control over private shipments is a different matter." Brown received no reply to his letter. He made Buckner aware of the controversy. Brown said to the general, "This order putting private shipments under the control of quartermasters is plainly without authority of law and opens a door to favoritism and abuse without limit." He asked Buckner to present the facts to General Joseph E. Johnston. Johnston was head of the Department of the West and Pemberton's superior.[11]

General Buckner wrote to Johnston at his Chattanooga headquarters on January 12, 1863. He echoed President Brown's observation that General Pemberton's order was "liable to great abuse," adding, "The rule I have adopted with reference to railroads is to require that all Government freight should have precedence of all others, if necessary, to the temporary exclusion of other freights, but beyond that I regard an interference of the military authorities with the concerns of individuals and corporations as illegal and impolitic." Buckner respectfully suggested that Johnston "endorse and continue this policy."[12]

When Johnston acted on the question nearly a week later, he simply referred it back to Pemberton, who sustained his own order, saying, "I do not think it advisable to change the spirit of my orders as to transportation." Quartermasters would remain the judge of whether or not affidavits presented to them were satisfactory to permit the transportation of corn on the M&O Railroad.[13]

On February 7, Johnston wrote to Buckner, "Is distress or inconvenience in Mobile produced by any order of Gen. Pemberton as to transportation of corn by railroad? Cannot the rivers supply the city with corn?" He sent Mobile Mayor R.H. Slough and Mississippi Governor J. Gill Shorter almost identical wires saying, "I cannot, at this distance, interfere with Gen. Pemberton's mode of supplying his troops" and recommending as he had to Buckner, that Alabama could feed Mobile via the Alabama River.[14]

While Johnston dithered, the distress of the citizens continued. Minds at the highest level were wrestling with legal and ethical questions having to do with the proper relationship between the government and private interests and about how to fairly meet the demands and needs of each in a time of war. Secretary of War James A. Seddon wrote to General Johnston, "The complaints of the conduct of the quartermasters in the department of Lieutenant-General Pemberton have been incessant. Imputations upon their integrity have come again and again to the [War] Department." He said that the order "appropriates the control over the railroad system of the State, and creates an embargo upon the domestic trade of an entire people. These are the highest powers of sovereignty, and are not to be justified unless upon an urgent and present necessity." However, he also understood the difficulties confronting Pemberton, who was under orders to defend Vicksburg at all costs with men whose fitness to fight was increasingly difficult to maintain. Seddon said, "The reasons assigned by General Pemberton are ... recognized as very cogent, and their sufficiency must be judged by you."[15]

At the same time, Major J.M. McMahon, quartermaster at Meridian, defended Pemberton's policy unequivocally and made clear his view that private interests must be made subservient to the military. He wrote, "From the first promulgation of these orders, there has been on the part of the management of the Mobile and Ohio road, a spirit of discontent and ungracious obedience amounting almost to resistance. Parties to whom I have given permits to transport corn down the road for domestic consumption, have been told by the superintendent of the road that such permits were worthless; that the management of the road was vested in the owners and directors of it, not in General Pemberton." Major McMahon believed that the "barrier to extortion" must be sustained.[16]

Major Livingston Mims, Chief Quartermaster of the Department of Mississippi and East Louisiana, endorsed McMahon's letter, saying it "properly represents the spirit of annoyance and opposition that has characterized the Mobile and Ohio Railroad as far as compliance with the later orders of the lieutenant-general commanding, concerning the shipment of corn, is concerned." He urged that Major McMahon be given a special order to inspect, and, if necessary, to prevent shipments. It was "positively required."[17]

The controversy continued into March. The railroad and the hungry people had an ally in the local press. The Mobile *Register* said, "Efforts are being made by the Mobile and Ohio railroad to stay the famine effects of Gen. Pemberton's order prohibiting the shipment of flour and meal southward, but as the railroad agents had no bayonets the evil continues unabated." Bergeron says that the shortage of grain became critical as March turned into April. Buckner did what he could to relieve the people's suffering, including "authorizing his chief of subsistence to impress cattle and other stores held by speculators," and relaxing "restrictions on fishing around Mobile Bay." He also "received permission from the War Department to sell excess military supplies at cost to the needy." The situation was growing tense. Signs reading "Bread or Peace" began to appear around the city. A populist insurgency was percolating below the surface.

Seventy-four wealthy gentlemen of Mobile felt such concern that they formed the Mobile Supply Association. They pooled their money to buy supplies for the relief of the city, and when they raised their voices about the crisis, the military and political authorities began to listen. "The association's secretary, T.A. Hamilton, appealed to Johnston to permit the purchase of corn in Mississippi and its shipment on the Mobile and Ohio Railroad." Johnston agreed, and procurement agents were dispatched across the state. Secretary of War Seddon "approved a plan put forth by Colonel Lucius B. Northrop, commissary general and head of the Subsistence Department, which called for the creation of chief commissaries in each state to supervise the collection, storage, and distribution of supplies." It was this reform, as well as the efforts of the Mobile Supply Association, that finally eased, for a time, Mobile's "supply difficulties." Fleming and Brown of the M&O also seem to have been mollified by the change.[18]

As Fleming had pointed out in his annual report to the M&O stockholders and as the above controversy showed, the relationship between the military and corporations was complicated and often tense. It was intensified by the situation of a new nation at war, as each entity tried to protect its own interests and serve its own needs and, at the same time, contribute to the ultimate victory. It was a fundamental question, touching upon Americans' prickly sense of individuality in a situation where a collective effort is necessary. The passing of the crisis in Mobile was not the result of the universal answer to an eternal question. It simply represented a momentary solution to a specific problem. At least the people had food.

As alarming as the specter of starvation was, Mobile was spared the worst horrors of the war in the spring and summer of 1863 simple by virtue of its location. Flag Officer David G. Farragut had hoped all through 1862 to attack Mobile, but the Secretary of the Navy, Gideon Welles, would only authorize the continuing blockade. The blockading fleet lay about seven miles outside the mouth of the bay. It was not fool proof. An incident embarrassing to the Federals (but exciting to the Confederates) had occurred in September 1862, when the C.S.S. *Florida* ran the blockade to enter the harbor. Though she had been at sea so long that her guns would not fire and her crew was reduced by yellow fever, the *Florida* made a daytime run, flying English colors as a *ruse de guerre* to fool the blockading fleet for as long as possible. She threaded the needle under fire and came through to the cheers of the men at Fort Morgan and a twenty-one gun salute. Lieutenant John N. Maffitt said, "When we anchored under the guns of Fort Morgan, shortly after sundown, the *Florida* was a perfect wreck."[19]

The *Florida* proceeded up the bay to Mobile the next day. Because of the yellow fever aboard, she was quarantined, but with adequate medical attention the crew recovered, and "the yellow flag of quarantine finally came down on September 30." Repairs began four days later, but, plagued by the same shortages of material as the railroad faced, the work progressed by fits and starts. "Slow, slow, slow," Lieutenant Maffitt wrote, "This fitting out in an open bay, where so much is to be done, is bad business." Recruiting was also a frustrating process. "Crew coming on in driblets," Maffitt wrote on October 12. It was January 11 before the *Florida* was ready. That day, Lieutenant Maffitt moved down the bay to Fort Morgan, where he looked out to see what he faced in the way of blockaders. He saw that the Federal navy had increased the number of ships outside the bay from four to thirteen, including one vessel, the *Cuyler*, which Maffit knew could outrun him under most circumstances. On the night of January 15–16, a driving rain began, limiting visibility. The moment had come. At 2:00 a.m., Maffitt raised steam, lifted the anchor, and the *Florida* zipped past Fort Morgan. She was soon spotted by the blockaders. She sped away, a pack of sea hounds in her wake. As Maffitt expected, only the *Cuyler* proved to be a problem. The *Cuyler* stayed with the *Florida* all morning, long after the others had fallen behind, but the heavy seas gave her trouble and the wind carried away one of her yard-arms, and at dusk the *Cuyler* vanished from sight.[20]

The incident of the *Florida* became a Southern legend, but it was not quite unique. Blockade runners constantly made their way into and out of the bay. Mrs. Ella Palmer worked in the hospital at Fort Morgan. She said, "Almost every dark night there would be great cannonading at sea, for those were the nights the blockade runners selected to run the blockade. Many vessels were destroyed or captured; but a greater number were of lighter draught and could run over the bar into Swash Channel, which was next to shore, [and] got through." The hospital at Fort Morgan was ready in case the Federal fleet came in. Mrs. Palmer said, "In this hospital everything was packed every day and everything was arranged so that the people at the hospital could go at a moment's notice into the fort, which was half a mile away."[21]

But the Federal fleet was not coming. General Benjamin Butler in New Orleans would not contribute any manpower for a campaign against Mobile, and Farragut had small chance of victory without him. In December 1862, Major General Nathaniel P. Banks succeeded Butler as commander of the Department of the Gulf. He had more interest in Mobile than his predecessor, but the War Department expected him to focus his efforts on opening the Mississippi. The Navy Department ordered Farragut to cooperate. Vicksburg and Port Hudson would be the objectives of the summer of 1863.

Needing to prepare for whatever the Federals might be planning, General Buckner had done a masterful job of maintaining and strengthening Mobile's defenses. A report from that time said that the city was "strongly fortified, and General Buckner in command with 20,000 troops."

The informant continued, "Mobile is protected on the north side by a triple line of works, a distance of 3 miles from the city. The harbor is driven full of piles, leaving a winding channel commanded by heavy guns." The report added, "The Mobile and Ohio Railroad is run no farther north than Okolona, where there are 2000 cavalry."[22]

It was Vicksburg, however, that remained the major concern of the Confederates, and the situation there soon became worse. On April 16, Rear Admiral David Dixon Porter's flotilla of gunboats and transports ran past the guns of Vicksburg and hardly sustained any damage at all. Grant said, "My mind was much relieved when I learned that no one on the transports had been killed and but few, if any, wounded." He began looking for a place below to land his soldiers.[23]

It was one of the vagaries of war that the existential threat posed by General Grant on the banks of the Mississippi gave Mobile and the M&O Railroad a respite. From May 1, when Bowen fought Grant's troops at Port Gibson, until July 4, when the siege of Vicksburg ended, the attention of the armies was mainly focused on western Mississippi, not eastern, and the city of Mobile was barely on the mind of anyone in the high command.

It was very much on the minds of the Mobile city leaders, though. On May 12, Mr. Peter Hamilton, chairman of the Committee of Safety in Mobile, wrote to Governor John G. Shorter, "We are nearly stripped of soldiers, and it ought not to be so. The enemy has large forces in Louisiana and has command of the sea. It is in their power to land a sufficiently large number of men on the Mississippi coast and by a rapid march threaten us in the rear. Why should Mobile be so left? It has certainly done its share in this war, it is of great consequence to the State, and is probably the largest city in the Confederacy." He continued, "By water we are probably safe, but our land works ought to be guarded. The late raid into Mississippi has shown the enemy some of our weakness…. The destruction of a few bridges and a small portion of the Mobile and Ohio Railroad would deprive us of aid from the Army of the Mississippi, and the city might fall."[24]

It seems that the complaints of the Mobile Committee of Safety got the attention of at least some of the Southern leaders. On May 20, Lieutenant Colonel J.L. White, commanding the Selma Arsenal (up the Alabama River from Mobile), stated that he had orders from Richmond to supply 1500 rifles for Mobile. He said that the order was "being filled as rapidly as possible," but White had complaints of his own. He was short of manpower and asked that disabled soldiers be sent to him to help him fill his orders. He pointed out that he could only repair thirty to forty rifles a day because he had too few gunsmiths and mechanics. Furthermore, he could not complete his orders for ammunition because lead had become scarce. With a sufficient supply of lead, he could turn out as many as thirty thousand cartridges a day, and if he could get those disabled soldiers he could produce even more. Richmond had ordered rifles and cartridges be delivered to Mobile, and if they were not coming as fast as the people of the city would have liked, at least they were coming.[25]

As for the committee's fear that the M&O was so poorly defended that Mobile might be left isolated by the destruction of "a few bridges and a small portion" of track, the danger was relieved by some shuffling of troops. In mid–May, a Federal spy reported to Memphis, "the whole line of the Mobile and Ohio Railroad heavily guarded; 4000 troops under Ruggles, at Okolona; no force at Columbia [sic]; Roddey re-enforced at Courtland; part of cavalry at Clifton; Forrest reported daily at Okolona; the Mississippi militia under Gholson, organizing to move to Okolona." Another report noted, "all the bridges on the Mobile and Ohio Railroad strongly guarded."[26]

The number of troops on the M&O Railroad were not merely for the purpose of protecting Mobile; they were also stationed along the line to guard vast quantities of supplies. In May, Major A.D. Banks at Mobile was able to report, "The commissary arrangements in this district look well." The next month, an inventory at locations on the M&O showed that there were 250,444 rations of bacon; 2,500 rations of mutton; 96,300 rations of beef; and 17,100 rations of lard. There were 90,147 rations of flour; 102,276 of meal; over 1,000,000 of corn; 149,000 of peas; and 269,300 rations of rice. There were 20,000 rations of vinegar; 615,170 of salt; 144,133 of sugar; and 69,500 of molasses. There were also 743,975 rations of soap and over 140,000 of candles. Even in one small district of a backwater department in an impoverished nation, the volume of stockpiled goods was phenomenal.[27]

The people might have felt hopeful that their situation would receive more attention after General Joseph E. Johnston arrived during the second week in May. Ordered to move to the area of his department where critical events were unfolding, Johnston finally bestirred himself from Chattanooga and traveled west by train. He installed himself at Jackson. Johnston was popular among the civilians and in the army. He had a sort of genius for preserving the lives of his soldiers and the commissary and quartermaster stores that sustained them. However, he had a blind spot about the importance of defending the strategic locations that others recognized as key to their success. Observers from his time forward recognized it, and one can see in Johnston's own military memoirs, a book with the unwieldly title *Narrative of Military Operations, Directed During the War Between the States, by Joseph E. Johnston, General, C.S.A.*, that he was always falling back. The record is clear: from the Peninsula in 1862 to the gates of Atlanta in 1864, Johnston demonstrated a perturbing urge to surrender territory to the enemy, and he expected his subordinates to do likewise upon his order. Arriving in Mississippi, he urged General Pemberton in the strongest terms to abandon Vicksburg and join him in the open country near Jackson. Pemberton was under positive orders from President Davis to defend Vicksburg to the end, and he was determined to do so. Pemberton hoped that Johnston would come to *his* support, but the Virginian refused to advance westward. He remained in the Jackson area, always pleading the need for more men and drawing reinforcements for his own army from other sectors. The War Department did its best to accommodate him. The railroads stayed busy delivering troops to Johnston. Federal dispatches dated May 18 said, "Scouts report all the cars on the Mobile and Ohio Railroad below Okolona drawn off south to transport troops to Jackson … heavy reinforcements are moving on General Grant from South Carolina, Georgia, and Tennessee…. From 6000 to 10,000 mounted men are concentrating near Okolona."[28]

Then, having received the extra men, Johnston kept them close at hand, dallied and fretted, and repeatedly urged the commanders in the two besieged cities on the Mississippi to abandon their trenches and lead the men out. Neither Pemberton in Vicksburg nor Major General Franklin Gardner in Port Hudson would obey.

On July 1, Johnston reluctantly began to move to General Pemberton's relief. He had advanced as far as the Big Black and was still there when he learned that Vicksburg had fallen on July 4. His mind immediately turned to retreat. He ordered his herds of cattle and his wagons east to the Mobile & Ohio, and he pulled his troops back into the capital city. Sherman quickly moved east from Vicksburg and surrounded Jackson with three corps. Uncle Billy wrote, "On the 10th we pressed close in, and shelled the town from every direction." He isolated the city by cutting its rail lines north and south, and, as he said, "continued to press the siege day and night, using our artillery pretty freely." On the morning of July 17, the besiegers found Jackson evacuated; Johnston had slipped away. Sherman sent a division in pursuit, but after fourteen miles the chase was suspended. He moved into Jackson and set four thousand men to work with sledgehammers, pinch bars, and torches. By the time Sherman led his men back to camp on the Big Black, they had destroyed the rail lines "for 40 miles north of the city, 60 miles south of it, and 10 miles east," along with rolling stock and infrastructure. Sherman wrote Admiral David Dixon Porter, "The good folks of Jackson will not soon again hear the favorite locomotive whistle."[29]

Johnston continued his retreat to Morton, thirty miles east of Jackson. He ordered General James Chalmers to "show a bold front to the enemy, and protect the abundant crop of this year, removing as much of it as you can to the Mobile and Ohio road." He was proud of having preserved his army intact and was content to rest. While the Confederates rested, the Federals did too, unmolested in their Mississippi strongholds, in the interior and on the river, awaiting orders.[30]

The fall of Port Hudson and Jackson affected Mobile directly. The city was flooded with refugees, and food became an issue once again. The Memphis *Daily Appeal* reprinted an article from the Mobile *Tribune* that said, "The subject of provisions is now the principal theme of conversation among our citizens.... We have seen during the last day or two a number of refugees from Mississippi with large numbers of negroes who have not brought enough provisions to feed themselves for two days, and we learn that large numbers are expected daily." Thoughts of the besieged citizens of Vicksburg reduced to eating mule meat and rats haunted them. General Dabney H. Maury, who was Buckner's successor at Mobile, asked General Johnston to rescind Pemberton's still-in-effect restrictions "upon free trade and transportation of subsistence stores between Mississippi and this State." He said, "The population of Mobile is, I believe, steadily increasing by the usual as well as by extraordinary processes, and the scarcity and high prices of subsistence increase in like manner." Johnston replied that he planned to visit Mobile soon, and they would discuss Maury's concerns at that time. In the end, Pemberton's hated decree was lifted, and food slowly began to trickle down the M&O into Mobile. The process was agonizingly slow, however, and the people continued to suffer. The *Daily Appeal* reported, "Some few lots of flour have been received, but so small as to be of no consequence."[31]

The newspaper had hit upon a theme and developed it with enthusiasm. The paper said, "Let our farmers, military men and the people generally, go to work, and gather all the food that is made along the line of the Mobile and Ohio railroad, and have it at once placed in a secure place. Fill up every point that is to be defended, so that we never again have another commander say that he was compelled to surrender because he had 'eaten his last mule.'"[32]

The fear of attack, and worse—surrender—was implied in the *Daily Appeal* article, and it was implicit in the message General Maury sent to Richmond on July 16. He said, "After the fall of Port Hudson, the army of Banks may be available for an early attack on Mobile." He described the harbor as "very defensible, on account of the powerful and well placed batteries, the artificial obstructions to navigation, and the shallowness of the channels approaching the city." On the land side, there was a strong line of nineteen redoubts, which he intended to connect with rifle pits, but the line was at "the very edge of the city proper," and the terrain was "very level and very vulnerable to enemy fire." The number of refugees, prisoners, and other transplanted noncombatants had reached fifteen thousand, Maury estimated; they "should be removed before the attack is made." He told Richmond that he needed stores of every description, and he needed enough reinforcements to increase his garrison to twenty thousand.[33]

Neither the Secretary of War nor General Johnston shared Maury's apprehension of an immediate danger. Inspector General Samuel Cooper refused to send him reinforcements, on the grounds that Johnston had reported that "no present purpose of attack on Mobile seems contemplated." Furthermore, Johnston himself could not send troops to Mobile "without imminent danger of attack." Cooper would not approve his removal of refugees until an attack was certain. And when Maury asked for the return of a brigade he had sent to Bragg on loan, the protector of Mobile was refused even this. Some of the communications from Cooper to Maury fairly dripped with condescension. In one, Cooper wrote, "Report the number and kinds of troops under your command: *we wish to judge* and provide for your needs" [emphasis added].[34]

Maury was, in fact, more prescient than his superiors, for an attack on Mobile was exactly what Grant and Banks had in mind. Banks was particularly eager to make the attack. Back on April 23, he had written to Halleck from his headquarters in Louisiana that if the government would send him twenty thousand men and the "iron clads that were engaged at Charleston" he would not only take Port Hudson but also "take Mobile, hold its forts, and close its harbor against the commerce that now pours into its gates in spite of the blockade." Banks did not get his wish, but now Vicksburg and Port Hudson were won, and Banks pitched his Mobile plan again. This time, he went to Grant. "The capture of Mobile is of importance second only in the history of the war to the opening of the Mississippi," he said. "Mobile is the last stronghold in the West and Southwest. No pains should be spared to effect its reduction." Banks found a receptive listener in Grant, who was thinking along those lines himself; as Ron Chernow points out, Grant hated "to keep his army idle for extended periods." Now was not the time to rest, but to keep going. Grant wrote in his *Memoirs* that "the troops that had done so much should be allowed to do more before the enemy could recover from the blow he had received." Grant wrote to Halleck, promoting a campaign against Mobile, and recommending either Sherman or James B. McPherson as its commander. He acknowledged that Mobile was in Banks's department and believed the expedition should be planned in New Orleans and step off from Lake Pontchartrain. Halleck disapproved.[35]

Nevertheless, Grant and Banks refused to let it go. Banks came upriver to Vicksburg for a conference with Grant on August 1, 1863, and, as

Bruce Catton says, "it seems clear that he and Grant went over the Mobile operation in some detail." Grant reasoned that the Federal occupation of Mobile was not only a desirable goal in itself, but that it would also produce benefits for the Union armies fighting on other fronts. It would force Bragg to divide his army in Tennessee "in order to meet this fire in his rear." Furthermore, the Federals fanning out from their Mobile base could inflict "inestimable damage upon much of the country from which his army and Lee's were yet receiving their supplies." Grant offered to provide "all the troops necessary" for the operation. Halleck said no. General Banks wrote Halleck to point out that works on the land side of Mobile were not yet com-

General Dabney H. Maury.

plete. He felt that Mobile could be taken by an attack on that side "without serious contest." Twenty-five thousand men from Grant's army, plus his own forces at New Orleans could do the job, he said. "The co-operation of the naval force now here is all that is required." He pointed out that the "operation need not last more than thirty days, and can scarcely interfere with any other movements east or west."[36]

Again Halleck refused. He and the War Department were focused on Rosecrans's effort against Bragg around Chattanooga, but there was another reason that Halleck did not make perfectly clear. Bruce Catton explains, "Washington had suddenly lost interest in Mobile and had begun to think about Texas." In a blatant violation of the Monroe Doctrine, the European forces had invaded Mexico in December 1861, launching a war that ended with the occupation of Mexico City in June 1863. The French had plans to install Archduke Maximilian of Austria as their puppet Emperor of Mexico. Lincoln saw clearly that it would be desirable to have a national presence in Texas to prevent the French from undertaking any adventures north of the border and to prevent Maximilian's regime from offering any aid to the Confederacy. The president's secretary John Hay wrote in his diary that Lincoln "is very anxious that Texas should be occupied and firmly held in view of French possibilities. He thinks it just now more important than Mobile.... He wrote in that sense, I believe, to Grant today." Lincoln had, indeed, written Grant, saying, "I see by a dispatch [sic] of yours that you incline quite strongly toward an expedition against Mobile. That would appear tempting to me also were it not that, in view of recent events in Mexico, I am greatly impressed with the importance of re-establishing the national authority in Western Texas as soon as possible. I am not making an order, however; that I leave for the present at least, to the General-in-Chief."[37]

Lincoln had made clear his concern for Texas. Consequently, in the autumn the XIII Corps (formally of Grant's army but transferred to the Department of the Gulf after Vicksburg) was sent to Brownsville. The removal of the XIII Corps from Grant was only one reduction of his force after Vicksburg. The IX Corps was returned to General Ambrose E. Burnside in Kentucky, and five thousand men went to General John Schofield in Missouri. Grant said, "The troops that were left with me around Vicksburg were very busily and unpleasantly employed in making expeditions against guerrilla bands and small detachments of cavalry which infested the interior, and in destroying mills, bridges, and rolling stock on the railroads." Because of Halleck's overweening interest in the Trans-Mississippi, the administration's concerns about the international situation, and the resulting reduction of the number of armed forces in Mississippi, Mobile was once again spared from attack.[38]

But everyone knew the Federals would strike again; the only question was where. North of Mobile, the Confederates were busy gathering supplies and moving them to safety, as General Johnston had ordered. General Chalmers was at Grenada. He reported, "I have about 50 wagons which I can use in the transportation of supplies. And as long as I can maintain my positions and protect this place, it is my intention to make it my depot for supplies, and run a regular wagon train between it and West Point, which will be my depot on the Mobile and Ohio Railroad. By this means I hope to get out a considerable quantity. I will keep the railroad in operation from Panola as far south as can be done with safety to transport supplies."[39]

As usual, competing interests clashed. At the same time that Chalmers wanted to use the railroad to convey his supplies, the Engineer Bureau in Richmond was ordering that iron rails be taken from the M&O for repairs on other lines. Colonel J.F. Gilmer, Chief of the Engineer Bureau, wrote General Johnston, "The condition of the main lines of railroad in the Confederacy is such as to make the collection of railroad iron and rolling stock from some source a vital necessity; for this reason I make an earnest appeal to you for such and support as you can give our efforts to collect these from the roads of Mississippi." Gilmer asked Johnston "to give your engineers authority to collect all necessary labor and materials for repairs of bridges and roads needed for securing the property in question." The practice of robbing one railroad to repair another had become so pervasive that there was in the Engineer Bureau a "Commissioner for the Removal of Railroad Iron"[40]

None of this was to the benefit of the people of Mobile. The M&O was Mobile's "most important supply line," and with various arms of the military and the government wrestling over its use, and with the influx of refugees into the city, the shortage of food became a sore point yet again. It came to a head in September. On the morning of September 4, a group of several hundred poor women gathered on Spring Hill Road. They carried signs that read, "Bread or Blood," a slogan reminiscent of the French revolutionists of 1789. More ominous than the signs, the women had axes, hatchets, hammers, and brooms in their hands. They marched into the city and down Dauphin Street, where they began to break into stores for food and clothing. *Harper's Weekly* reported, "The rioters openly declared that if some means were not rapidly devised to relieve their suffering or to stop the war they would burn the city." General Maury called out the 17th Alabama to restore order, but they refused to take action against the women. Maury next turned to the Mobile Cadets, which the newspapers described as "a fancy military organization." The cadets were no match for the rioters. "The mudsill females routed these young aristocrats, in their first battle," said the news reports.[41]

With the 17th Alabama in near mutiny and the Mobile Cadets in flight from the "Amazonian Phalanx," Mayor R.H. Slough stepped in. He appeared in front of the women, and, by the power of persuasion and promises to see to their needs if they would disband and go home, he restored peace to Dauphin Street. Slough's word was as good as his oratory. That very afternoon he addressed an appeal to the more affluent citizens of Mobile. He asked them to contribute money so that food and clothing could be bought for the needy, and he set up a Special Relief Committee to oversee the effort. The committee alleviated the problem without being able to eliminate it. Finally, even the upper classes began to feel the pinch. Money was in abundance—state bills, cotton certificates, railroad company currency—and people circulated it because they had no choice, but it was almost all worthless. Andrew F. Smith writes, "Six weeks after the Mobile bread riot, a Mississippi newspaper reported that inflation was 'fast reaching a point beyond even starvation prices. We are approaching a state of things that will inevitably culminate in riots and bloodshed among our own people.' The newspaper's prediction was too dire, there was no organized violence in the streets of Mobile, but the short supply of food at ruinous prices meant that an unsatisfied hunger persisted among the people from then on."[42]

This was the situation, then, when President Jefferson Davis visited Mobile on October 24 and 25, 1863. It was actually his second visit that year. Between December 10, 1862, and January 5, 1863, Davis had taken a long train journey across the Western Theater. He had visited the armies in Chattanooga and Vicksburg and had delivered speeches in all the major cities. He had given two brief speeches in Mobile, one on his way west to Vicksburg and another on his way back east.

So much had changed by the time of his second visit ten months later. East Tennessee was held by General Burnside's Army of the Ohio. Vicksburg was gone, Port Hudson was gone, and with them control of the Mississippi River was gone. Shelby Foote writes, "The Confederacy's shrinking fortunes were reflected all too plainly in the fact that this second western journey was necessarily far more roundabout." Davis intended to visit Chattanooga, where Bragg had the Army of the Cumberland under siege, but he could no longer train directly down the Virginia & East Tennessee Railroad; he had to go south through the states of the Eastern seaboard until he reached Columbia, then west to Atlanta before turning north through Marietta and Dalton to Chattanooga. He arrived at the Army of Tennessee headquarters on October 9 and remained there several days. Davis left for Selma on October 17. He toured the cannon foundry, the arsenal, and the various manufactories of Alabama's industrial giant before continuing to Meridian. On October 24, he proceeded down the M&O Railroad to Mobile. As before, he took rooms at the Battle House, but he was not in them much. He was in Mobile to see and to be seen. He toured General Maury's works and the naval yards where he must have seen the ram *Tennessee*, "a dangerous craft" armed with 10-inch Columbiads and heavy Blakely guns and capable of making eight knots. The *Tennessee* had been built in Selma and then floated down to Mobile to be fitted out. Admiral Franklin Buchanan thought she was more of a threat to Yankee shipping than the *Merrimac*, and he should know. During the Battle of Hampton Roads in March 1862, Buchanan had been in charge of the *Merrimac* (renamed the *Virginia*) in her battle with the *Monitor*. Buchanan took the *Tennessee* as his flagship. Her mere presence was intimidating to the Yankees, and she would eventually test her mettle under fire in the Battle of Mobile Bay.[43]

Back at the Battle House, Davis addressed the citizens and refugees of Mobile. He told them that Bragg's victory over Rosecrans at Chickamauga "will practically end the war." He reminded them, too, of the role civilians played in the War for Southern Independence, saying that "those who remain at home, not less than those in arms have their duties to perform." He urged them to "encourage the spirit which can bring success," and he denounced the speculators that had so distressed General Pemberton that he was willing to starve the people in order to rid his department of them. Davis said that "men using the opportunities given by war to make fortunes will be detested by their posterity." A newspaper reported how President Davis's voice carried clearly and without apparent effort from the balcony to the people below and well down the street so that all could hear. But how hollow the content of his message must have seemed to the assembled crowd. They had seen too much of war's reality. One Davis biographer said, "The enthusiasm of former years was conspicuously absent. A sort of apathy seems to have settled down upon the country. At Mobile, Davis was not more successful in arousing the war spirit than he had been elsewhere."[44]

Davis left Mobile on October 25 for his return trip home. He must have known that the Confederacy was failing. He had seen evidence of it across the South. Its soldiers could not keep the enemy from its most important cities and could barely protect its connecting lifelines. Yet, the spirit of the fighting men was still strong. At Montgomery, General Forrest boarded the train. By the time he left the train at Atlanta, he had been promoted to Major General, provided that Congress approved, and had been promised a transfer away from Tennessee and the army of the hated Braxton Bragg to north Mississippi, where he could raise and lead his own command. He would not have to start from scratch. Davis promised Forrest two battalions of his "veteran troopers plus Morton's battery." From this nucleus, Forrest would build a legendary organization.[45]

William Tecumseh Sherman called Forrest and Southern cavalry leaders like him "the most dangerous set of men that this war has turned loose upon the world. They are splendid riders, first rate shots, and utterly reckless." Now, Major General Forrest had been "turned loose" again in Mississippi, and he would soon show the enemy just what a reckless and dangerous man he was.[46]

CHAPTER EIGHT

The Meridian Campaign

In the summer of 1863, a traveler made a trip through northern Mississippi to Jackson, Tennessee. He took the Mobile & Ohio Railroad as far north as the line was still in service and then continued on horseback. He had plenty of time to observe what war had meant to the planters and to the towns along his route, Okolona, Pontotoc, Ripley, Humboldt, and Jackson. What he saw was not good. The towns had been burned, and the planters all along the way had been robbed of their "horses, mules, and negros [sic], and their supplies taken to nearly destitution." He said, "All these places have been occupied. It is needless to say that pleasant and beautiful homesteads are to be found no more in all this region, or that none of the elegancies or comforts of life are left to the people." Even the churches had been "polluted and robbed," as had Masonic Lodge halls.[1]

The traveler said, "Very nearly all these people have taken the oath to support the Union, but they hate the Union with a hatred as rank as the weeds which grow fence high in their fenceless fields." He said, "The taste they have had of the stars and stripes has done its work. The most ultra Union man of the earlier days of the war is a Union man no more." What the people needed, he said, was a "bold and dashing" leader to put into action the "encouraging spirit of resistance." Consolidated and led by such a "judicious and dashing" figure, the small and scattered bands of Confederate cavalry in the region could destroy communications on the railroads and the rivers and drive the Lincolnites in large numbers to cower inside their works.[2]

The leader for whom the anonymous writer wished was on his way. In October 1863, on his way back to Richmond after a rather disheartening tour of the Western Theater, President Davis gave Nathan Bedford Forrest the rank, the independence, and the authority to raise and lead a force of his own in northern Mississippi. The Wizard wasted little time. With typical boldness, he passed through Union lines into Tennessee to pursue his purpose. In December, the new major general came to Jackson, Tennessee, where he "was ever a welcome guest." He told the people there that he "had not come into West Tennessee to make a raid; that he intended to permanently hold West Tennessee if he had to fight a battle three times a day." He set about recruiting new horsemen, collecting supplies, and, to prevent surprises by a fast-moving foe, destroying the Mobile & Ohio Railroad. It was reported that Forrest's Rebels "are burning the remaining trestles and bridges, and taking up the track and burning the ties."[3]

Up until mid–December, Forrest went about his business, but the Yankees knew of his presence in Jackson, and they intended to stop him. Brian Steel Wills writes, "Strong columns of Federals marched toward him from nearly every direction: A.J. Smith's from the north, starting at Columbus, Kentucky; William Sooy Smith's from the east, out of middle Tennessee; Joseph A. Mower's from the southeast, out of Corinth, Mississippi; George Crook's from the east, from his base at Huntsville, Alabama; and Benjamin Grierson's from the southwest, coming from La Grange, Tennessee."[4]

To avoid being trapped by them, Forrest started his men south toward C.S.A. lines on December 23. Now the two hundred head of cattle and the three hundred hogs that he had so painstakingly collected became a burden. Luckily, he had also recruited upwards of three thousand men who, for the time being, became not soldiers but drovers. There was some light skirmishing, but the graycoats reached the Hatchie River on the night of December 24. They spent Christmas Eve and half of Christmas Day crossing themselves, their animals, and fifty wagon loads of supplies. Though they were getting closer to Rebel lines, the Federals persisted. Forrest had to fight his way through to the Wolf River, but "by nightfall on December 27, the men were well on their way to Holly Springs." Two days later, Forrest reported to Lieutenant General Leonidas Polk at his headquarters in Meridian. Polk had succeeded General Johnston as department commander. After his defeat on the seemingly unassailable Missionary Ridge, Braxton Bragg gave up command of the Army of Tennessee, and Johnston was transferred east as his replacement. Forrest expressed to General Polk "his regret at leaving western Tennessee so quickly, remarking that if he could return, he would bring out three thousand more recruits." It was Polk who informed Forrest of his formal promotion to Major General, and before Forrest left to set up his own headquarters in Oxford, he was given the independent command that President Davis had promised. It was called Forrest's Cavalry Department, and it consisted of all the Confederate mounted forces in northern Mississippi and western Tennessee.[5]

At the time of Forrest's visit, Polk was himself a newcomer to Meridian. He had only been there since November, and was "still trying to familiarize himself with the novelties of his position as commander of the department that was about to be renamed the Department of Alabama,

Mississippi, and East Louisiana." His fighting arm was the Army of the Mississippi. His four principal commanders were Major Generals William W. Loring and Samuel G. French, who commanded the two infantry divisions, and Major Generals Stephen D. Lee and Nathan Bedford Forrest, who commanded the two cavalry departments. Polk needed every man, for trouble swirled all around him. "In late January he was warned by General Johnston from Georgia 'that there was every reason to believe the enemy was preparing a raid against the coal and iron fields of central Alabama.'" Simultaneously, intelligence reached Polk's headquarters of other Federal incursions coming from the direction of the Gulf Coast, Vicksburg, and Memphis.[6]

And if those threats were not enough, Polk had a homegrown rebellion on his hands. A Confederate deserter named Newton Knight organized an insurrection among other poor and dissatisfied Mississippians in Jones County. They had decided, in the familiar phrase, that it was a rich man's war and a poor man's fight. They and their supporters in Jones County seceded from Rebeldom, if not legally, then at least in their hearts, and they considered themselves at war with the Confederacy and with the M&O Railroad. Polk called them "lawless banditti," and was forced to divert his attention from greater dangers to deal with them. On February 7, Polk wrote to General Dabney Maury, "I find the officer in charge of the guards at Red Bluff bridge, on the Mobile and Ohio Railroad, has been made uneasy by the messages he has received from those deserters, etc. in Jones County, that they propose to burn the bridges on that road. I advise that Colonel [Henry] Maury proceed without delay on his expedition against them. He will find 500 men ample for this work.... His best place to proceed to is Winchester, on the Mobile and Ohio Railroad, where I have ordered a half a dozen guides to be sent to meet him and report to him." The guides selected came from among Knight's victims, "men whose homes have been burned by them, and whose families have been insulted." The depredations of the "Knight Company" were far more serious than mischievous pranks; they included murder (beginning with that of Major Amos McLemore, who had come to Jones County to arrest deserters), and arson, and now they were about to graduate to bridge burning, which would affect the whole region. Polk wanted them "dealt with in the most summary manner," and reminded Maury that there was no time to lose.[7]

General Dabney H. Maury said that his kinsman Colonel Henry Maury "broke up the cover of these malcontents, put several families into mourning, and scattered the military powers into the neighboring swamps and fastness." He said that the outlaws left the country and relocated in the Delta. However, Victoria E. Bynum, historian of the Free State of Jones, says that General Maury exaggerated his claims of success, and "the self-proclaimed Southern Yankees remained defiant." Conditions in Jones County were described as "deplorable" and one officer complained to Secretary of War Seddon that the deserters' organization was so effective that they could rendezvous in a matter of hours "at any given point prepared to attempt almost anything."[8]

In the meantime, General William Tecumseh Sherman was himself planning a strike against the Mobile & Ohio Railroad and one of its important depots. Having returned to Memphis after the defeat of Bragg at Chattanooga, Sherman decided not to waste the winter waiting for the spring campaign. Instead, he would lead a fast-moving strike force against Meridian, Mississippi. Meridian was not only a rail center, but also a collection point for Confederate supplies and the site of an arsenal. On January 12, 1864, Sherman wrote to both Grant and Halleck, "I think by the 24th I can make up a force of 20,000 men to strike Meridian, and it may be Selma. Infantry will move via Vicksburg, Jackson, and Brandon; cavalry down the Mobile and Ohio Road from La Grange, they meeting about Chunky River. If you think we hazard too much you will have time to notify me by telegraph." Then he went to Vicksburg to begin preparations.[9]

Grant, who had never yet given up his designs on Mobile, wrote Halleck on the 15th, "Sherman has gone down the Mississippi to collect at Vicksburg all the force that can be spared from Mississippi." He repeated Sherman's prediction that he would have twenty thousand men by January 24, and said that he would direct him "to move out to Meridian with his spare force (the cavalry going from Corinth) and destroy the roads east and south of these so effectually that the enemy will not attempt to rebuild them during the rebellion. He will then return unless the opportunity of going into Mobile with the force he has appears perfectly plain." Grant was looking ahead to the spring campaign and the effect Sherman's expedition would have upon it. He said, "The destruction which Sherman will do the roads around Meridian will be of material importance to us in preventing the enemy from drawing supplies from Mississippi and in clearing that section of all large bodies of rebel troops." This was also Sherman's line of persuasion in his subsequent telegrams to General Banks and Admiral David Dixon Porter, but that was not the extent of his goals in making a winter campaign. Sherman wrote in his memoirs, "A chief part of the enterprise was to destroy the rebel cavalry commanded by General Forrest, who was a constant threat to our railway communications in middle Tennessee."[10]

By the time he wrote Grant of his plans, Sherman had already briefed General Stephen A. Hurlbut, commanding the XVI Army Corps, and the cavalry commander, Brigadier General William Sooy Smith. Together they traveled to Vicksburg to explain the plan to General James B. McPherson,

Sherman's XVII Corps commander. Sherman intended Hurlbut and McPherson to travel with two divisions each. General Smith, commander of all the cavalry in the Military Division of the Mississippi, would take only a select seven thousand on the Meridian Campaign. The cavalry's primary mission was to block Forrest and eliminate him, if possible. Sherman took particular care in his instructions to General Smith. He said, "I explained to him personally the nature of Forrest as a man, and of his peculiar force; told him that in his route he was sure to encounter Forrest, who always attacked with a vehemence for which he must be prepared, and that, after

General William T. Sherman.

he had repelled the first attack, he must in turn assume the most determined offensive, overwhelm him and utterly destroy his whole force." He instructed Smith to leave his staging area at Collierville (just east of Memphis) on February 1 and march directly toward Meridian via Okolona. The infantry columns would set out from Vicksburg on February 3. They would all converge on Meridian for a February 10 rendezvous.[11]

Before the infantry set out, Sherman issued Special Field Orders No. 11, which provides a window into Uncle Billy's mind as well as a primer for the nineteenth-century blitzkrieg. Sherman wrote:

> The command designated for the field will be lightly equipped—no tents or luggage save what is carried by the officers, men, and horses. Wagons must be reserved for food and ammunition. Cartridge-boxes must be filled full of fresh ammunition, and a hundred rounds extra carried along in wagons or on pack animals. Ten days' meat and bread and thirty days' of salt, sugar, and coffee will be carried in wagons; beef-cattle driven along, and pack animals, at the rate of one per company, when practicable, in lieu of wagons.
>
> Artillery will be cut down one-half, and that double-teamed, and 200 rounds of ammunition for each gun will suffice, but must be carried in

caissons belonging to each battery. Artillery carriages must not be loaded down with men and packs, nor must imperfect ammunition be carried along, nor shots wasted at imaginary objects. Chiefs of artillery will see that each box is inspected, and the heavy artillery wagons and forges left at the depots.

The expedition is one of celerity, and all things must tend to that. Corps commanders and staff officers will be that our movements are not embarrassed by wheeled vehicles improperly loaded. Not a tent will be carried, from the commander-in-chief down. The sick must be left behind, and the surgeons can find houses and sheds for all hospital services.[12]

As they moved east from Vicksburg, General McPherson was on the south side of the Southern Railroad and Hurlbut was on the north. They marched fast along the same route some of the men had seen the previous summer when Vicksburg was the object. Beyond the Big Black River, they encountered the cavalry of Major General Stephen D. Lee. There was some sharp skirmishing beyond the Big Black River, and it intensified as they came closer to Jackson, but it was not more than the Federals could handle. Sherman wrote, "The 5th [of February] was one continued skirmish for 18 miles, but we did not allow the enemy's cavalry to impede our march but got into Jackson that night." Sherman had burned Jackson twice in 1863, and he showed it no new-found mercy on this, his third visit in eight months. On the evening of February 7, 1864, he sat down and wrote his wife, "I am here again and a new burning has been inflicted on this afflicted town. We had some pretty Skirmishes on our way out and we handled the enemy's cavalry rather roughly. No infantry has yet been encountered…. Weather is beautiful and roads good—all of us in fine condition."[13]

Beyond Jackson, they entered a land of plenty. Buck T. Foster writes in his study of the campaign, "Mississippi corn-cribs and barns, from Jackson to Meridian, now stood full, and the railroad warehouses overflowed with Confederate supplies. Sherman's army marched in the face of the largest Mississippi harvest during the war." Stephen D. Lee's cavalry hung on the enemy's rear and flanks to hinder the advance, but found his efforts useless. Lee wrote, "It was impossible to damage the enemy much, as he marched in perfect order, his trains being divided between the brigades and kept in close order." His cavalry flailed away at the enemy as they continued on their trail of destruction through Brandon to Morton. Loring and French had formed a junction at Morton, but Loring concluded that the odds were too long, and he ordered a withdrawal east toward Meridian on the night of the 8th. Sherman moved into Morton on February 9. There he halted so that McPherson could destroy another length of the Southern Railroad. Hurlbut's column went out in front and kept the lead the rest of the way to Meridian. His persistent opponent, General Lee, had developed a clear picture of what was happening. He wrote to Polk, "The intention of the enemy, I think, is to go to Meridian first. He may then turn toward Mobile (but I doubt it) soon after he reaches Meridian. I think a large column of cavalry is coming down the Mobile and Ohio Railroad, which will unite with Sherman at Meridian." He could not stop them, though. Sherman had left his trains behind with good escorts and was pushing forward faster than ever. Lee detached Brigadier General Samuel W. Ferguson with his brigade and sent him forward to retard the Yankees if he could.[14]

Delay was, indeed, General Polk's game. He had known since late January that Sherman was planning a strike and was soon to move. He had only about twenty thousand men in his whole department and could not hope to outfight Sherman. He warned the War Department, "The whole of my force is very small, inadequate to the emergency." He was convinced by diversions against Mobile by the Flag Officer Farragut and Pascagoula by General Banks that General Maury's destruction was Sherman's goal. Polk went on a flying inspection tour to Mobile, where the garrison troops were discouraged to the point of mutiny. It was reported to him that the garrison at Fort Morgan, one thousand men, had "laid down their arms." Maury had persuaded them to return to their duties, but it showed the iffy morale of the men Mobile counted on to save the city in case of attack. There seemed to be trouble on every hand, but Polk did observe some things in Mobile that gave him hope. Thousands of impressed slaves from Alabama and Mississippi were laboring on the fortifications, which were described as "nearly completed from the old lighthouse to the terminus of the Mobile and Ohio Railroad, near the city, inside the swamps, and Three Mile Creek." Polk would fill the works and stiffen the spine of Maury's fighting force by ordering additional troops to Mobile.[15]

Polk learned upon his return to Mississippi that Sherman was about to march. Knowing that the blue column would proceed east before turning south toward Mobile, he decided to withdraw to Alabama and make his headquarters at Demopolis. He would try to remove every valuable item from Meridian, and, while the relocation of men and materiel was going on, try to defeat Sherman by following President Davis's recommendation "to delay the enemy so much that he will consume his supplies, and press him so closely that he cannot forage to replenish them." Like Polk, Davis believed that Mobile was Sherman's destination. However, he warned the Bishop, "Beware lest his movement in that direction be a feint and his real purpose to be more eastward." Polk remained convinced that Mobile was the objective, and on February 9, the day the Federals entered Morton, he ordered French to prepare to move next morning down the M&O Railroad to Mobile and to report there to General Maury. The order was rescinded two days later. Suddenly alarmed for his own safety by Sherman's moves, Polk decided to retain French in the Meridian area, well behind the front. French was out of the fighting.[16]

Meanwhile, as Loring's meager infantry and Lee's cavalry tried to delay Sherman, Polk was trying to arrange the removal of as many supplies as possible. His private sector counterpart in the effort was L.J. Fleming of the M&O, who was soon able to report to Polk, "By very hard work, we saved all stores at Meridian; all at Enterprise, including all Government cotton in shipping order, except the corn in the shuck." He had overseen the removal of all the rail cars "except eight or ten," and called the whole removal operation, "entirely successful." Polk wrote to General Loring, who was in command of the infantry resistance to Sherman on the western front, trying to explain the big picture. "It has not been my intention to bring on an engagement with the enemy, the disparity of forces being too great to justify it. It has been of great importance to remove all the public stores here and at other points along the Mobile and Ohio Railroad beyond the enemy's reach, for which we wanted all the time we could get.... I have thrown everything beyond the Tombigbee, and my line of retreat will be toward Demopolis." He gave Loring the latitude to decide for himself when to move his division back, but asked to be advised when that time came so that he could get French's division out of the way. Until then, "I send a lot of axes to you to be used by a working party, which you will please detail, to obstruct the roads after the cavalry have passed.... All bridges should be burned." Polk also ordered Lee to push his cavalry forward, get ahead of Sherman, but Lee reported on February 13 that he had not been able to do it. He also complained to General Polk that day of a certain lack of clarity in his orders, saying, "I am at a loss as to my moves, not knowing what your intention [is] as to offering battle, etc."[17]

When the head of the Federal column reached Oktibbeha Creek, they found the bridge burning. Sherman said, "A large cotton gin, however, close by gave us good material, and a couple of hours sufficed for a new bridge." Beyond the Oktibbeha, Colonel Edward F. Winslow, commanding the four regiments of cavalry accompanying the infantry, brushed aside some light opposition and scattered them, leaving the way to Meridian open. The horsemen hurried forward and entered Meridian in mid-afternoon, Sunday, February 14, the first Federals to see the great prize. Hurlbut's infantry marched in that night.[18]

Like Corinth, Meridian owed its existence to the Mobile & Ohio Railroad, which reached the area in 1855, and it owed its prominence to the intersection of the M&O with the Southern Railroad, which arrived in June 1861. Peter J. Lamb says, "With the arrival of the second railroad, the fledgling village of Meridian could now begin to promote its importance as the gateway to the North and the East." The intersection of the two railroads, and the completion of the line from there to Selma in December 1862, made Meridian only slightly less important than Corinth, where the M&O crossed the M&C. Corinth, of course, was in Federal hands, and by the winter of 1863–64, Meridian was the "only major rail crossing left in the state" for Confederate use.[19]

Meridian was a town of several hundred residents; sources vary widely in the count, with estimates ranging from four hundred to 1500. It had about one hundred civilian homes, several railroad hotels, a handful of stores, and two Protestant churches. Meridian had a cobbler, doctor, stone cutter, and the usual different types of millers, and a somewhat depleted workforce, for eighty of its young men formed a company called the Meridian Invincibles and went off to fight Yankees in 1861. The government buildings of Meridian were what interested Sherman; the military hospital and stockade, barracks, store houses, machine shops, an arsenal, and "headquarters for chiefs of ordnance and quartermaster." It was all so raw and new that one Federal soldier commented that it looked as if the town was only a few months old.[20]

For all of this, Meridian felt strangely quiet when the Federals moved in. That very morning the Confederates had completed their withdrawal. Polk had evacuated a handful of troops and successfully removed $12,000,000 in military goods and rolling stock, so that Sherman "found the warehouses yawning empty and the tracks deserted in all four directions." Some residents remained in town, while others had deserted Meridian, abandoning their homes to Yankee vandalism. The looting began immediately. A lady of the town told the Nashville *Daily Union* that "the mob ran around, going into houses, breaking open doors, trunks, locks, etc., tearing up and destroying everything they could. Caught all the chickens in the place in half an hour." She sent a request for protection for her home, and General Hurlbut supplied one, but before the guard arrived five soldiers entered her home and demanded the keys to her trunks and wardrobes. She told them she hoped they would not take her clothes, and "They said no; they only wanted all arms and gold and silver I had. I told them they might have all of both they could find, but I had none." They did take some flour and blankets which they were made to return after the guards appeared and took charge.[21]

McPherson's column came in on the morning of February 15, but there was still no word from Sherman's cavalry chief, General Smith. Uncle Billy was angry at Smith for not arriving with his cavalry in time to prevent Polk's clean escape and for leaving him short of a full complement of horsemen, but at least the infantry was all up. Sherman gave his men a day of rest, and on Tuesday they "began a systematic and thorough destruction of the railroads centering at Meridian." While one half of a corps worked at the demolition, the other half stood guard. General Lee was still on their perimeter. He said, "Attempts were made to stop their work, but their heavy force made it of no avail." Meanwhile, Polk remained at Demopolis with his ten thousand effectives, dreaming of receiving reinforcements from General Johnston in Georgia. With them, he would "chase Sherman back to Vicksburg and headlong into the Mississippi," but no reinforcements were coming from Georgia; General George H. Thomas was holding them in place at Dalton. So the Federals went about their work without interruption. They learned that, while the Fighting Bishop may have succeeded removing everything of value from Meridian itself, the surrounding region had not been cleaned out. In sheds and warehouses up and down the railroads they found and destroyed "thousands of bales of cotton, hundreds of weapons, thousands of bushels of corn, and yards of lumber."[22]

Two of the outlying towns that suffered the most were Enterprise and Quitman. Enterprise was on the M&O about six miles south of Meridian and Quitman was about the same distance south of Enterprise. One of McPherson's men who helped burn the first town wrote, "Enterprise, all and singular with its improvements, public and private, its parole camp, and its conscript camp, with its associations, historic, poetic, and secesh has been—according to compliance—wiped out." Foster quotes a citizen who called the Yankees "low-down pilfering rascals," and said, "No place escaped them." Quitman was another scene of desolation. There, the Yankees destroyed "two flour mills, a fine sawmill, railroad depot, and other storage buildings, with several thousand feet of lumber." Towns up and down the line from Meridian suffered a similar fate as Enterprise and Quitman, and between each station the connecting railroad was wrecked. Captain Andrew Hickenlooper, chief engineer of the XVII Corps, said that destroying the railroad "was effected by taking up the rails and piling the ties together 5 or 6 feet wide and 4 feet high, balancing the rails on their sides with weights on each end and setting fire to the piles. The rails would invariably bend from 30 to 40 degrees. We found this to be the most effective manner of destroying the road."[23]

The men worked for five days with every implement of destruction plus fire to create a circle of desolation sixty miles in diameter with the ruined town of Meridian at its center. The whole time, Sherman expected "every hour to hear of General Smith, but could get no tidings of him whatever." Foster says, "With the continued absence of William Sooy Smith's cavalry, the Union army was forced to delay its departure, consuming all the resources around Meridian." And Meridian itself was not spared. When the temperatures dropped below freezing on the night of February 16, the men warmed themselves by burning not only the public buildings but also many of Meridian's homes. Most of the houses so torched were abandoned, but in a few cases troopers set fire to an "occupied residence." It may have been this night that a well-remembered incident took place in which a soldier set fire to a dwelling with people inside and was arrested for it. When asked why he had done it, he explained that the woman of the house had spat in his face when he was a prisoner of war during the Vicksburg campaign. That was justification enough in the eyes of his officers, and the man was released without further comment.[24]

Waiting beyond their expected time of departure was creating a dangerous spirit in the men. Where was Smith? Without him Sherman was delaying, struggling to decide "whether to continue into Alabama without the cavalryman or to return to Vicksburg." Finally, he decided to turn west, back to his starting place. The Federal column set out on the morning of February 20. Meridian's public buildings, hotels, the hospital, the offices of the *Daily Clarion*, most of the homes; all that lay behind was a "smoldering rubble." Sherman ordered Colonel Winslow to take his cavalry brigade north along the Mobile & Ohio to search for Smith. When they found him, they had orders "to instruct him to meet Sherman at Canton, twenty-five miles north of Jackson."[25]

Winslow could never make contact with Smith. Where *was* he? He was at West Point, about 125 miles up the M&O Railroad from Meridian. He had arrived there in mid-afternoon of February 20, after a "short, sharp fight" with Forrest's cavalry, and the next morning he turned his column back toward Memphis.[26]

Smith's part of the Meridian Campaign had been a tale of woe from the beginning. His orders instructed him to leave Memphis on February 1 and to arrive at Meridian on the 10th, but he missed the deadline. He was awaiting Colonel George E. Waring's brigade from Columbus, Kentucky. Smith wrote to Sherman on February 2 to inform him of the delay and the reason for it, saying that to leave beforehand would reduce his expeditionary force to five thousand men when "in our conversations 7,000 was always hypothecated." He promised, "I have my whole command in readiness to move at a moment's notice." Waring finally arrived on February 8. He was late because of bad winter roads, downed bridges, and flooded streams so dangerous to cross that some men and horses had drowned. Waring's horses were so worn down that Smith decided they must rest. As a consequence, Smith did not commence his expedition until the 11th, the day after he was supposed to have been in Meridian.[27]

Smith's orders were to proceed from Collierville southeast to Okolona, then to turn south on the M&O, destroying everything in his path, every bridge, trestle, culvert, and stretch of track that time allowed for him to make the rendezvous at Meridian. He was instructed, as much as possible, to spare homes, "something too sacred to be disturbed by soldiers," but he was definitely to destroy "mills, barns, sheds, stables, and suchlike" and to "take liberally" of the provender, forage, and horseflesh that would enable him to complete his mission. Sherman had told him, "This will call for great energy of action on your part, but I believe you are equal to it, and you have the best and most experienced troops in the service, and they will do anything that is possible."[28]

And, indeed, they might have. The fault was not in the soldiers but in their commander. Advancing cautiously, Smith crossed the Coldwater and the Tallahatachie unopposed, continued to Pontotoc where he pushed General Samuel J. Gholson's "'rabble of State troops' out of the way," and turned toward Okolona. They rode in on February 18. This was where Smith's main mission was to begin, the destruction of "public property and supplies and the Mobile and Ohio Railroad" all the way to Meridian.[29]

Smith wrote, "From Okolona to West Point we found Government corn in immense quantities all along the road, and this we burned until there was a line of fire from place to place." There was no way to distinguish Confederate grain from that of private citizens, so Smith burned it all, the contents of every crib along the M&O tracks, an amount he estimated as "from 1,000,000 to 2,000,000 of bushels." As the main column burned corn and cotton and tore up railroad by the mile, Foote says, "Stragglers went off on their own missions to burn and plunder and slaves 'driven wild with the infection' rose up to multiply the destruction many times over," payback for lifetimes of unrequited toil. It was undoubtedly some of these "wild" slaves, along with whole families of contrabands just seeking to be free, who began to appear with their bindles along the railroad. They would eventually number 1500, and they became another cause of Smith's slow progress.[30]

On February 20, about a mile north of West Point, Smith found a brigade of Forrest's cavalry waiting for him. Forrest had been shadowing Smith all along, not daring to attack a force that was more than double the size of his own. He and his men had seen the destruction wrought by Smith's men and one said, "Up to that date, nothing like this had been seen in our part of the country, and our soldiers were aroused." They did not give in to their passions, though. They watched and waited until they could fight on ground of their own choosing. It was here. The Confederate brigade, under Colonel Jeffrey Forrest, the general's brother, "fell back toward West Point, skirmishing with them, but avoiding an engagement." General Forrest led two brigades and two artillery batteries to his brother's assistance, but finding Smith's full force in front of him, and expecting General Lee to come soon and join him, Forrest decided to wait before launching a full attack. He fell back across Sakatonchee Creek and stopped near Ellis Bridge. Smith proceeded toward another bridge eight miles upstream. Forrest rode toward the Federal position, "clearly designated by the smoke of the burning mill," with five companies of Kentuckians from William W. Faulkner's regiment. They captured a small squad of the 4th U.S. Cavalry, destroyed the bridge, and fell back to Ellis Bridge. He said, "This bridge I determined, if possible, to defend and preserve, because it was necessary in the event we could drive the enemy back to use it in advancing on them; and had I allowed the enemy to cross it and then succeeded in driving them back they would have burned it behind them, rendering pursuit impossible."[31]

That night, Brigadier General Benjamin Grierson, who was riding with the Second Brigade, found a way around Forrest by means of a crossing a few miles below Ellis Bridge. However, when Grierson returned to headquarters, he learned that Smith had decided "to go no further south." Smith had shown signs of wavering ever since Okolona, when he "became alarmed by reports that the rebels were concentrating at West Point." Grierson studied the maps with him at Okolona and "inspirited him with my own ideas as far as possible." This time, Grierson could not dissuade him from the urge to fall back. Smith said the enemy was "in strong position under good cover, and beyond obstacles which could only be passed by defiles." In addition, the Confederates were protected by creeks on the west and south and the Tombigbee River on the east. Forrest had laid a deadly trap, and Smith wisely decided not to step inside. Besides the tactical difficulties of the terrain in his front, Smith had little faith in the men he commanded. He judged that he had only one reliable brigade and that "any reverse to my command, situated as it was, would have been fatal." Added to all of this, he believed that Sherman had finished his work at Meridian and was on his way back to Vicksburg. He said, "I therefore determined to move back and draw the enemy after me, that I might select my own positions and fight with the advantages in our favor."[32]

The next morning, February 21, the Federals made a bold showing at Ellis Bridge to cover the withdrawal of the main column. Colonel Forrest's brigade was dug in on the north bank of the creek, behind a barricade of logs and fence rails. Colonel Robert McCulloch's brigade was on the south bank in support. The Federals made their attack at eight o'clock. The fighting went on for two hours before the Northerners disengaged. Forrest was delighted to see the enemy retiring. U.S. Grant said, "For the particular kind of warfare which Forrest had carried on, neither army could present a more effective officer than he was." And the particular kind of warfare that suited Forrest best was slashing at an enemy in motion, pressing them, keeping "the skeer on." He was excellent at putting them in motion when they showed a reluctance to go, but Smith had put himself in motion and now Forrest struck. Waring said in his article for *Battles and Leaders* that Forrest fell in behind the retreating blue column "and drove our seven thousand men without difficulty." Forrest later said that he followed cautiously at first, having with him only a handful of men and a section of Morton's battery, but when it became clear that the enemy was in full retreat, he "dashed on after them, sending back orders to General Chalmers to send forward to me, as rapidly as possible, 2000 of his best mounted men" and to bring a battery of mountain howitzers. He hit the Federal rear guard and was fighting when the requested support came up. He charged into them again and again, denying them the chance to make a stand, and when McCulloch's brigade arrived, "we continued to charge and drive them on, killing and wounding 15 or 20 of them and capturing a number of prisoners." The fighting was vigorous. Forrest's men were recently recruited, untested under fire, but he was watching them. When one of them lost his nerve and tried to run away, the general grabbed him, threw him down, grabbed up a switch, and disciplined him in the old woodshed way before sending him back into the fight, blistered high and low by the switching and Forrest's swearing. Between West Point and Okolona it became so dark that Forrest's men fired into one another, each group mistaking the other for the enemy, and Forrest called a halt to the pursuit. The men bivouacked and made good use of the "generous portion of forage and supplies" the Yankees had abandoned in their flight.[33]

The Federals kept moving until well past midnight. They finally stopped near Okolona. But they did not rest. They spent the early morning hours erecting barricades. Early the next morning, while the rest of his men still slept in their bedrolls, Forrest got his escort up and rode out. They discovered the Federal position about a mile away across an open plain, perfect for cavalry. They could also hear sputtering gunfire; Colonel Clark R. Barteau's 2nd Tennessee Cavalry had come up and were already skirmishing with the Federals. Forrest left his escort on the skirmish line and rode around to coordinate with Barteau, and then they attacked simultaneously front and flank.

At first, the Federals showed a fair amount of fight. They fired a volley at their attackers, and then they charged. Forrest remembered that they came at him "with yells, but were handsomely repulsed in the open field and forced to retreat, which they did rapidly and in confusion." Waring agreed that the men around him fell back "in disgraceful flight and confusion, abandoning five of its battery without firing a shot." He continued that, while their behavior was inexcusable, it was understandable, considering the "hurried retreat of the day before" which caused the men to imagine themselves "in the coils of an overwhelming enemy." The command "had lost all confidence in the commanding general, and its discipline dissolved."[34]

Richard R. Hancock of the 2nd Tennessee Cavalry recalled the moments after the Yankees broke. He said, "We dashed into the town by two different streets, and struck the enemy in his very face, just as he was preparing to execute the same movement on us. He seemed astonished and confounded, and his partially executed movements were turned into confusion and disorder."[35]

Forrest, with his escort and the 2nd Tennessee Cavalry, pursued the enemy down the Pontotoc Road. Hancock said, "For the next four miles Forrest's best mounted men were constantly up and in conflict with the worst mounted [Union] fugitives." They fought through a "rolling sequence of temporary defensive lines." Forrest's two brigades had come up by now, but the Confederate column became so intermingled that the general had to call a halt so that the men could re-organize into their proper regiments before continuing the pursuit. The Yankees opened a bit of a lead during the halt, and entered a "broken and hilly country," and there Forrest found them, in place upon a ridge. Smith's men had stopped, placed their guns, and formed a battle line on an open slope. General Forrest ordered McCulloch's brigade to attack. They moved up the left side of the road, and as they passed by Jeffrey Forrest's on the left, they "jeered them unmercifully." The front of McCulloch's column had just come abreast of the other when Colonel Forrest's bugler sounded the charge, and the two columns raced forward together. The Federal guns were firing, and the 4th Missouri Cavalry of Waring's brigade dashed forward to meet the Confederates, who charged into what Captain Henry A. Tyler of the 12th Kentucky Cavalry called "the most terrific volley I ever faced." In this charge, Jeffrey Forrest was shot through the neck and tumbled from his horse, mortally wounded. The general was nearby when his brother fell. He dismounted and held Colonel Forrest's head as the young man died. Jeffrey Forrest's death unleashed a terrible rage in the general, who returned to the fight seeking vengeance. One of his staff officers thought he was "mad with grief." In this savage state of mind, he ordered a charge.[36]

The Federals gave way and fell back half a mile "where the ground offered another favorable position, with abundance of rails available for another temporary breastwork." McCullock charged and dislodged them. They fell back to a farm within two miles of Pontotoc, where they turned for one final stand, counting on their "preparations, numbers, and advantageous position" to give them a late day victory. Forrest was determined to deny it to them. His men were exhausted by the day's fighting, much of it done on foot, and they were nearly out of ammunition, but to surrender the advantage now would invite a disastrous counterattack by the Federals with their superior numbers. The general ordered the charge. Forrest said, "As we moved up, the whole forced charged down at a gallop, and I am proud to say that my men did not disappoint me." The Yankees charged back in what Forrest called "the grandest cavalry charge I ever witnessed." The Rebels repulsed them with a "scorching volley," but the Federals would not quit; a second, third, and fourth charge followed the unsuccessful first. The fourth was the most successful. The enemy broke the Rebel line in once place and the fighting was with revolvers, blades, and fists. McCulloch had been wounded in the hand in some of the earlier fighting and his brigade had fallen behind, but now it appeared, just as it was needed to strengthen the Rebel defense. Simultaneously, Barteau swung around, hit the Yankees in the flank, and silenced a Union battery that was punishing the Rebels with grapeshot, and the Federals fled.[37]

They left the scene "in dismay and confusion, and losing another piece of artillery, and leaving it strewn with dead and wounded men and horses." William Sooy Smith's will to fight was broken. He led his men away as quickly as they could move, burning every bridge behind him to keep off Gholson's state militia. Waring said their retreat "was a weary, disheartened, almost panic-stricken flight, in the greatest confusion, through a most difficult country." His own brigade lost "all of its heart and spirit and over 1500 fine cavalry horses." The Federals arrived safely in Memphis on February 26, but they did not feel proud. Waring said, "The expedition filled every man connected with it with burning shame. It gave Forrest the most glorious achievement of his career."[38]

Sherman's forces had left Meridian by different routes. Lee's horse soldiers could only harass them, not stop them, and they all converged on Canton on February 26. Sherman left General Hurlbut in charge and went ahead to Vicksburg with the cavalry of Colonel Winslow, who had rejoined the main column after a fruitless side mission to discover William Sooy Smith's whereabouts. The veteran re-enlistees, who were due to begin their furloughs, went ahead as well. Those who remained behind picked up their tools and fell to the now-familiar work of destroying the railroad while they waited for Smith. He and his cavalry never appeared. McPherson's column left Canton on March 1, lightly harassed by the enemy's cavalry. Hurlbut remained in Canton until March 3, when he began the four-day march to Vicksburg.

In the North, the immediate reaction to the Meridian Campaign was mixed. Calling it "Sherman's mystic march," *Harper's Weekly* felt let down that the expedition had proven to be little more than a "mere raid, a reconnoissance in force, a diversion," when the prognostications had been for "the capture of Mobile or the turning of Johnston's flank." The paper said, "It was a very fine array of hopes, surmises, theories, possibilities, probabilities. Meanwhile, the solitary fact was that he moved with an uncertain number of men, and with the lightest artillery." *Harper's* chided the national press for its overblown predictions of what Sherman would accomplish and admitted, "Very much of our ill-humor is surely revenge upon our own mistake."[39]

The Nashville *Daily Union* was among those that had no such "ill humor." It said the expedition "has not only cut off the rebel supplies ... but it has also rendered an attack on any point on the Mississippi untenable." The campaign had kept the bumper harvest of '63 from reaching the Rebels in Georgia or Mobile, and, furthermore, "the diversion created by Sherman prevented Johnston from attempting to take any advantage of our weakness; and if nothing but this had been accomplished, the expedition would not only have been fully justified, but absolutely demanded." The New York *Times* called the expedition "one of the most rapid and brilliant in military annals."[40]

Like the Northerners who commented on Sherman's campaign, Southerners also had a mixed reaction. Jefferson Davis condemned the "universal destruction" that was "worse than the vandal hordes" might have committed. General Stephen D. Lee also evoked images of ancient barbarity when he said, "There never was an army in a civilized country that laid waste and destroyed public and private property as did Sherman's army." He calculated the cost to the South at $50,000,000 and believed that seventy-five percent of that was from the unprecedented destruction of private rather than public property. General Polk, on the other hand, said that Sherman's expedition "certainly has not been a successful one." He said in his congratulatory message to his men, "Never did a grand campaign inaugurated with such pretensions, terminate more ingloriously." He claimed, "The vigorous action of my cavalry under General Lee kept him so closed up that he could not spread out and forage.... He was deprived entirely of the rolling stock of all the roads between the Pearl and the Tombigbee Rivers, as well as of the use of all the valuable stores which had been accumulated at depots on those roads, and, finally [because of Forrest], of the services of his cavalry column. This last deprivation was fatal to the further prosecution of his campaign ... he seems to have given it up and gone back toward the Mississippi." Polk went on to call Forrest's defeat of William Sooy Smith "a brilliant affair" that prevented Sherman and Smith from forming a juncture. "That success destroyed his campaign," Polk said.[41]

Modern evaluations of the campaign have varied as much as those of the time. Some consider it to have been an innovative and well-conducted exercise in a new kind of warfare, the model for the Atlanta Campaign and the March to the Sea of later that year. Buck Foster, historian of the Meridian Campaign, does not give much credit to Sherman, however. He says, "Sherman's expedition was largely successful because of the continued incompetency of Polk." Jim Woodrick says that the damage to the railroad was "significant," but points out that "much of it was repaired in a matter of weeks." Admittedly, the repairs did use up "valuable resources that were in short supply and that would be needed elsewhere in the Confederacy in the coming year," but Woodrick suggests that the material damage, though carried out on a scale that "had not been seen prior to the Meridian campaign," was ultimately less important than the "psychological damage of the expedition on the citizens of Mississippi, who bore the brunt of Sherman's policy of engaging in 'total war.'" Sherman destroyed "not just military targets, but also the will of the people to continue supporting the Confederate war effort." He concludes, "the psychological effect of the raid cannot be over-estimated."[42]

Sherman, of course, insisted then and forevermore that his part of the expedition (but not Smith's) was an unqualified success. He reported, "For five days 10,000 men worked hard and with a will in that work of destruction with axes, crowbars, sledges, clawbars, and with fire, and I have no hesitation in pronouncing the work well done. Meridian, with its depots, store-houses, arsenal, hospital, offices, hotels, and cantonments no longer exists." He wrote to General Halleck, "Our loss was trifling, and we broke absolutely and effectually a full hundred miles of railroad at and around Meridian. No cars can pass through that place this campaign. We lived off the country and made a swath of desolation 50 miles broad across the State of Mississippi, which the present generation will not forget. We bring in some 500 prisoners, a good many refugee families, and about 10 miles of negroes." He added that he could now "reduce the garrisons of Memphis, Vicksburg, and Natchez to mere guards, and, in fact, it will set free 15,000 men for other duty." He was thinking ahead to the Atlanta Campaign.[43]

Sherman was bitter that General Smith did not complete his part of the programme. He called Smith's after-action report "unsatisfactory" and said, "The delay in his start to the 11th of February, when his orders contemplated his being at Meridian on the 10th, and when he knew I was marching from Vicksburg, is unpardonable, and the mode and manner of his return to Memphis was not what I expected from an intended bold cavalry movement." He made the disingenuous statement that Smith "had nothing to deal with except Forrest and the militia." Many commanders, including Sherman, had found and would find in the months to come that Forrest and the militia were more than enough to deal with.[44]

Smith's part of the campaign was conducted with a marked lack of determination and drive on the part of the commander, but it was not a complete failure, as Sherman pretended. Smith destroyed thirty miles of the Mobile & Ohio, and burned from one million to two million bushels of corn and two thousand bales of cotton; he carried away three thousand horses and mules and 1,500 contrabands, burned a tannery with two thousand hides, and took away from the enemy tons of forage and provisions for seven thousand men. He also kept Forrest off of Sherman, for which Uncle Billy should have been grateful.

When these figures are added to the totals from Sherman's two corps, it becomes evident just how disastrous was February 1864 was for Mississippi. Sherman's totals: 115 miles of railroad destroyed; sixty-one bridges and culverts destroyed; 6,075 feet of trestle work burned, twenty locomotives destroyed; twenty-eight rail cars destroyed, and three sawmills burned. Sherman did not give an exact tally of horses, mules, and refugees both black and white that his men carried away, but it must have been in the hundreds.

How much of the destruction of railroads was on the Mobile & Ohio is hard to determine exactly. The calculations found in the *Official Records* and the press of the day vary greatly. Some say it was about thirty miles while others say it was over fifty, but these invariably overlook the thirty miles wrecked by Smith's cavalry. Added to this *may be* an unknown number of miles (and bridges and trestles burned) by Newton Knight's men, who were said to be cooperating with Sherman by destroying railroad independent of the Federals. General Stephen D. Lee estimated that about twenty-four miles of the M&O were destroyed. Chief Engineer L.J. Fleming said that the enemy operated along eighty miles of the Mobile & Ohio, and tore up thirty miles of the main stem and sidings, but he was speaking only about Sherman; he barely acknowledged the damage Smith did, which would raise the total closer to sixty miles of rails and crossties actually uprooted and burned. Polk reported, "Sixteen miles of track torn up, iron badly burned, and most of the cross-ties burned on 47 miles of road from a point 5 miles below Quitman to Lauderdale Springs and track torn up in spots. The worst destroyed track is between Enterprise and Marion Station." He added that Sherman's raiders also destroyed sixty miles of "telegraphic communications."[45]

But there is another way to think of it. While the enemy demolished a certain number of miles of railroad, they destroyed the *effectiveness* of many times more by ruining bridges, culverts, and trestles, which rendered the tracks useless for long stretches. When the amount of damage is viewed in terms of railroad effectiveness, it would not be unreasonable to estimate the total at close to a hundred miles, and considering the reduced length of the railroad still under the control of the M&O RR corporation, that was a very large percentage indeed.

Sherman's operations along the Mobile & Ohio in February 1864 were so extraordinary an event that the chief operating officers of the railroad broke with precedent and included a discussion of it in their report to the stockholders at the convention on April 19, 1864. That report was a review of the profits and expenditures for 1863, but Sherman's expedition was included, even though an accounting of the damage done "does not legitimately belong to the present year."[46]

It was a peculiar stockholders' meeting, anyway. Because he was grieving the recent death of his son, President Milton Brown did not submit a report. Then, Sherman's raid had so disrupted normal operations that Chief Engineer Fleming could not get his figures together and complete his report until the morning of the convention. Fleming had been heroic during the evacuation of military supplies and railroad equipment at Meridian. Major George Whitfield reported on March 19 to Colonel F.W. Sims of the Railroad Bureau in Richmond, "Mr. Fleming, Superintendent of this road, has been on the work all the while & has driven things on night & day. He is the best R.R. worker in this or any other country." Though he was hard up against his deadline, Fleming produced ten pages of text and tables to submit to the directors and stockholders. Fleming told them that the company earned a profit of $457,213 in the past year, less than half the profits of 1862. He explained several reasons for the low figure, including an increase in maintenance and repair costs, and "the removal of the large army which occupied Corinth and Tupelo during eight months of the year 1862, the shorter length of the road operated [and] the restrictions place upon the transportation of individual freight by the military authorities." He was referring to Pemberton and his controversial order. Fleming complained, too, about the costly effects of the tax bill recently passed by the Congress in Richmond. He said it did the M&O (and other lines) "great injustice in taxing the whole capital stock and earnings, while one half of the Road is in the hands of the enemy, and entirely unproductive and subject to destruction alike by friend and foe. Other interests are allowed to offset this damage," he said, "and common justice requires that Railroads should be placed upon the same just basis."[47]

Fleming complained about another baneful practice of their fellow Southerners against the railroad. He said that "in every evacuation and retreat from Columbus, Ky., down to the recent raids, bridges, trestlework, and cars which under no circumstances could have been used by the enemy, have been destroyed by our own forces." An order issued by General Stephen D. Lee during Sherman's recent campaign illuminated this issue. Lee had ordered his men to destroy all the M&O cars between "Marion Station and Okolona." It resulted in the destruction of twenty-eight cars. Such promiscuous destruction of M&O property, Fleming warned, "will soon result in stopping the road." He asked the board of directors to protest in the halls of government the ruinous, "universal" custom.[48]

Regarding those repairs to the railroad made necessary by Sherman's expedition, Fleming did not calculate exact dollar figures, but he did say that "notwithstanding rainy weather and freshets this work has been repaired in the short space of 48 days and the regular business of the road resumed." He credited Major George Whitfield for his direction of the reconstruction effort and the black workers for their "commendable energy." He included an interesting digression about the problem of restoring twisted rails to a state of usefulness. The Mobile & Ohio used T-rails. Fleming said that they were so "heavy and strong," that all previous methods used for straightening them proved ineffective, and "we were forced to resort to heat and negro power." He said, "It is almost impossible to make them perfectly straight, but they have been laid again, and make a safe track, but at a lower rate of speed than the former schedule."[49]

And so 1864 began. A devastating raid at the beginning of the year, declining profits, increasing expenses, half its length in enemy hands, its number of engines and rolling stock reduced, and the necessity of slower speeds for those that remained—what else could the year of 1864 possibly bring?

CHAPTER NINE

Fort Powell, Paducah, and Brice's Crossroads

At the time of the Meridian Campaign, Major General Maury had an aggregate of 8415 men present for duty in the Department of the Gulf, a number that increased to 12,512 when those absent were included in the count. In Mobile proper, he had 1851 men present, and in the defenses on Mobile Bay, 2106. Five thousand impressed blacks labored on the fortifications, but they had now become something of a burden. The defenses were nearly done and there was not enough work for all, yet the slaves remained in the city, consuming precious rations at an alarming rate. "The negro laborers have eaten up a great deal of my supply of meat," Maury said.[1]

The refugee population in Mobile continued to be a concern. During his hurried visit to the city in January, General Polk had apparently raised the issue to Maury. A week later the Mobile commander wrote to the Bishop, "I have to state that the removal of the non-combatants of Mobile is entirely beyond our control. I have been endeavoring ever since Vicksburg fell to get the people to go away from Mobile, but the population has continued steadily to increase by natural and other processes." He expected they would still be in the city "when the enemy actually commences operations."[2]

Maury said that Mobile "has been threatened several times" during his tenure as commander of the department. There was no way of knowing if the next time would see the threat become a reality; if it was the time, he was going to need more rations and ordnance. "In anticipation of a siege," he said, "I ought to have six months' supply of meat for 15,000 men, and 800 rounds of projectiles for near 300 guns." He felt that the foodstuffs were less of a worry than the lack of artillery shells. He had meat and bread on hand, and more was available. He said, "There is plenty of meat now being cured in Alabama, and some beef cattle that are awaiting my call." But, as for the ammunition, he despaired. Demands elsewhere had diverted the ammunition that might otherwise have come to Mobile, and his local supplier was unreliable. He said, "Selma arsenal is charged with filling my orders, but they work slowly there." Richmond had promised him more heavy guns, along with two hundred rounds each, but "if they cannot send plenty of ammunition they had as well not send any more big guns," he said.[3]

Fears of an imminent attack increased on January 20, when Rear Admiral David G. Farragut came "over the bar" in the gunboat *Octorara* accompanied by the *Itasca*. The two vessels approached as close as three miles to Forts Morgan and Gaines. The men inside the forts could see them clearly, could pick out every detail of the men and guns on deck, but they gave Farragut no difficulty during his reconnaissance, and no Confederate boats went out to challenge him. He sailed back out of the bay as peacefully as he had come in, but the defenders of Mobile apprehended that Farragut's brief expedition was a preliminary to what was coming. Expectations of a Federal move on the city grew. The inland side, too, appeared to be under threat. The New York *Times* ran an item from an eyewitness who was in Meridian at the same time as Sherman's troops. Mr. J.B. Ellis, a Pioneer Express Company messenger, said that he saw a Union soldier's cap "with a red ribbon around it, on which the words 'Mobile or Hell' were printed in large letters." It was Mr. Ellis's opinion that "the destination of the Yankees is undoubtedly Mobile."[4]

Alabama Governor Thomas A. Watts agreed with Mr. Ellis after McPherson's corps began moving down the M&O from Meridian. When they reached Quitman, Watts "issued a proclamation to the citizens of Mobile that the city is about to be attacked, and exhorting non-combatants to leave." He warned that the Federals were mistaken if they took too much comfort in the lack of opposition they encountered as they advanced southward on the railroad; Mobile would be a different story. Watts vowed the Yankees would "not be allowed to take Mobile without a desperate battle."[5]

The land defenses looked formidable. Beginning five miles outside the city, they consisted of three lines of earthworks connecting multiple installations, and there was plenty of artillery. A closer inspection revealed some weaknesses in Mobile's defenses, however. Adequate numbers of small arms continued to be a problem. Some of the defenders had only pikes to oppose the Yankees when they appeared. But the attack they expected on Mobile did not come. Instead, the attack came at Fort Powell.

On February 16, a fleet of eleven vessels approached and opened fire on Fort Powell, an earthen fort on Shell Island in Grant's Pass, on the west side of the entrance to Mobile Bay, thirty miles down from Mobile. They opened fire at 9:00 a.m. It was more of a loud demonstration than an actual threat, since all of the shots fell short of the fort. Similarly, the Federal fleet was in little danger, except for mishaps. In mid-afternoon, the Sawyer rifle on the *Jackson* "split in the vent, about five inches long, which rendered it useless," and the *Sebago* ran aground twice, but she was pulled off and moved safely down the sound. The bombardment ended about 7:00 that evening. The Federals opened fire again in the morning, fought all that day and the next, until foul weather forced them to retire. The action resumed on February 23. Hundreds of shells were fired over the next few days, a waste except for the practice it gave the gun crews. Neither the Union fleet nor Fort Powell suffered any serious damage from hostile fire. Farragut suspended the daily firing again about February 26. He said that he had been shelling Fort Powell for a week, "but have made but little impression on it, as we cannot approach nearer than 4000 yards." He had about expended his ammunition on the frustratingly ineffective fire and had no prospect of getting any more for at least two days. Also, the weather "became thick." The only advantage he could see from the noisy and expensive game was that "it assists General Sherman by keeping up the idea of an attack upon Mobile, which is looked for hourly by the Confederates." He added, "Would that were true; now is the propitious time."[6]

Farragut warmed to the theme, saying, "If we had only two or three thousand troops to make their approaches on the peninsulas the ships will run in, I think, easily. We might have done it long since.... I am ready the moment the army will act with me, but there is no doing anything with forts so long as their back doors are open."[7]

He planned to "recommence the work" the next morning, but said, "I have no hope of reducing the fort, as the steamers lie on the opposite side of it to take the people aboard, if necessary, or to relieve the garrison." When he did resume operations the next morning, he found that his luck had turned sour. The Sawyer rifle on the *Jackson* split again. The Confederate gunners' aim was suddenly improved and four 100-pound shells struck the *John Griffith*. But far more alarming was the March 1 appearance of the C.S.S. *Tennessee* "in full view in the bay opposite Grant's Pass." She was accompanied by three gunboats and two smaller ironclads, but all eyes were on the *Tennessee*. Farragut had believed that the ram was still being outfitted in Mobile. He had said that once the *Tennessee* came down, "it would be impossible to go in without an ironclad." He had none in his fleet, and now here was the *Tennessee*. The Federals fell back, and Farragut announced, "I will withdraw the forces from this place."[8]

"The situation of Mobile is undoubtedly critical," the Nashville *Daily Union* had said during Farragut's action against Fort Powell. But while the situation appeared dire at the southern terminus of the M&O Railroad, conditions farther north were improving quickly. Polk made plans to repair the railroad immediately after Sherman withdrew. He wrote to

President Davis on February 22, "I have already taken measures to have all the roads broken up by him rebuilt, and shall press that work vigorously." AAG Clifton H. Smith had promised that the government would pay for the repairs, so there was no reason that capital should be a concern. On February 25, General Polk, who was still at Demopolis, put the rebuilding effort in the hands of the capable Major George M. Whitfield, who was granted "discretion to impress all property and labor of every description necessary for the completion of the work and make requisition upon Chief [of] Subsistence for necessary supplies." Whitfield was also authorized to restore telegraphic service, a vital adjunct to railroads. The next day, Polk wrote to L.J. Fleming, saying that he had appointed Whitfield. Fleming knew Whitfield from the evacuation of Meridian, and he respected him. Polk told Fleming, "I desire the Mobile & Ohio RRoad rebuilt as soon as possible.... The cooperation of yourself and the whole force of your Corporation is expected and will be furnished."[9]

Collecting the work crew and traveling to the worksite took almost two weeks, and the reconstruction of the M&O did not begin until March 11. The first task was to rebuild the Quitman Bridge and the half mile of trestlework nearby. Compared to that, the work of spiking down sixteen miles of salvaged and straightened rails was simple. Citing the number of bridge carpenters and black workers on the road—finally over five hundred—who worked day and night "to keep the bridges in advance of the track," General Polk estimated the line could be in running order by April 1.[10]

On March 24, a week ahead of schedule, the crews repairing the destruction done by Hurlbut's men north of Meridian and by McPherson's men south of Meridian met in the ruined town and reconnected the broken ends of the Mobile & Ohio. The Memphis *Daily Appeal* said, "We think the repairing of the Mobile and Ohio road will compare with Yankee enterprise." Work on the tracks above West Point, that portion of the railroad that was destroyed William Sooy Smith's men, was expected to begin the next week. Rebuilt tracks did not mean a complete restoration of service, however. The *Daily Appeal* also reported, "The regular heavy freight train cannot be run until the water fixtures, and sidings are put in order."[11]

Compete restoration was the goal and not just to Okolona. They intended to make the railroad operational all the way to Corinth, a point they had not held since May of 1862. The Federals knew their enemy's weakness and knew that they no longer had to control every point in order to command the region. Plus, they understood that turning over the railroad would force the Confederates to deplete their dwindling resources maintaining it and to spread out their already thin manpower protecting it. They blew up their works and abandoned Corinth on January 24–25,

1864. The Chicago *Daily Tribune* ran an account of the Federal evacuation that said, "All our stores and other public property here have been moved to Memphis, and we leave Corinth a 'deserted village'; where secesh may hereafter lord it without fear of Provost guard or 'Yankee bayonets!' But there is nothing to live on in this region of the country, and as soon as we get away the few people remaining will find themselves without supplies and will follow our example by 'evacuating.' This section of the country is a woeful picture of desolation." The 12th Mississippi moved into Corinth on February 1. Now there was no obstacle to continuing railroad repairs to this once important railroad town. General Polk wrote Chief Engineer Fleming on April 2, "I desire you should push your work up to Corinth as soon as practicable." Three weeks later he followed up, "How soon will you reach Corinth?"[12]

The exact date the railroad was completed to Corinth is not known, but the Memphis *Daily Appeal* was able to report on May 18, "The cars on the Mobile and Ohio railroad are running through to Corinth daily." Some of the M&O cars had been taken for use by other railroads—a practice about which Fleming had bitterly complained to the directors and stockholders of the company—but now they were returned for use on their intended line, and Fleming was expressing hopes that the M&O could be pushed on to Tennessee. The Federals had been watching the restoration of the Mobile & Ohio with interest, but not alarm. Sherman wrote to Grant on April 19, 1864, "General Hurlbut [at Memphis] reports the Mobile and Ohio Railroad done from Mobile to Okolona, and that it will be finished to Corinth in a week. I don't believe it, but, even if true, when Banks strikes it near Mobile it will be worse than useless to the enemy." And he did not fear the results of abandoning places like Corinth, now rendered unimportant in his judgment. He wrote to General McPherson that the enemy would "of course, reoccupy Mississippi with his marauding cavalry. That can in nowise influence the course of the great war. I would heed his cavalry but little."[13]

There may have been more than a little bravado in Sherman's casual attitude about the Southern cavalry. Nathan Bedford Forrest commanded the Rebel horse soldiers in that area, and he had proven to the Federals time and again that he was not a man to ignore. He was up and down the Mobile & Ohio in the spring of 1864: Columbus, Okolona, Tupelo, and across the line in Tennessee. On April 14, General Polk wrote to Forrest, "At Jackson or elsewhere: I have been disappointed in not being frequently advised of your movements, and am therefore at a loss as to the orders proper to give you. I have not heard from you in two weeks. It is indispensable that I should be kept constantly informed of your situation and of all your operations."[14]

It happened that Forrest had been busy with more important matters than the filing of reports. He had been promised an independent command by President Davis, and, although Stephen D. Lee was his superior on paper, Forrest behaved as if he were the viceroy of the domain, and to do that effectively he had to build up his command and mount them on the best horseflesh available. On or about March 1, 1864, the 3rd, 7th, and 8th Kentucky Infantry were assigned to Forrest and ordered to report to him at Columbus, Mississippi, where they were joined with the 12th Kentucky Cavalry and organized into a new brigade to fight beside Tyree H. Bell's Tennesseans. Colonel A.P. Thompson commanded the Kentuckians, and although their formal designation was the 3rd Brigade in Forrest's cavalry, they soon began to earn their fame by a more familiar name, the Kentucky Brigade. However, there were not enough horses for Forrest's new brigade. The solution was a raid into Kentucky where they would find enough horses for all. They set out on March 15. They moved north along the route of the Mobile & Ohio. At Trenton, Forrest ordered two regiments to break off and make a demonstration on Union City, the station of five hundred Federals who could not be allowed to operate freely in their rear. Colonel W.L. Duckworth of the 7th Tennessee led his own men, the 12th Kentucky Cavalry, and Major Charles McDonald's battalion to Union City, where he briefly invested the town before demanding that Colonel Isaac R. Hawkins surrender his garrison, which he did a few minutes before noon on March 24. Duckworth's Rebels burned the Federal barracks and marched their prisoners back toward Trenton, Tennessee.

The main column had pushed on toward Paducah. On the night of March 24, they camped in Mayfield, Kentucky, and the next day they appeared on the outskirts of Paducah. Paducah was the largest city in western Kentucky and the northern terminus of a spur line of the M&O, the New Orleans & Ohio Railroad. The NO&O RR joined the main stem of the Mobile & Ohio just below the Kentucky line near Union City. In addition to its important railroad connections, Paducah was near the point where the Tennessee River joins the Ohio. It had been the staging area for the Fort Donelson Campaign. Paducah was also the site of a large earthen fort called Fort Anderson, where Colonel Stephen G. Hicks commanded between six and seven hundred men of the 8th United States Colored Heavy Artillery, the 16th Kentucky Cavalry, and the 122nd Illinois Infantry. Behind the powerful fort, two gunboats, the *Pawpaw* and the *Peosta*, prowled up and down the Ohio River.

Fighting in an urban setting against an entrenched enemy supported by two gunboats might have rightfully intimidated some cavalry commanders. Forrest was not intimidated, nor was division commander General Abraham Buford. General Buford ordered Colonel Bell to swing around and come in from the south, while Colonel Thompson approached Paducah from the west. The fighting began about three miles outside of town. The Confederates pushed Paducah's defenders steadily back to their works. Henry George said, "The Kentuckians were dismounted and moved in line of battle in the direction of the fort. The alignment was maintained until the more densely built-up portion of the city was reached, when it was broken by the buildings." The brigade advanced by "regiments or companies" along parallel streets "under a constant and withering fire from the fort by both small arms and artillery." Before they emerged into the open space before the fort, Forrest sent into Colonel Hicks a demand for surrender. When it was refused, the Kentuckians formed their lines and surged forward. As they charged, Colonel Thompson was struck by an artillery round. He died instantly. Some of the men may have continued to the moat surrounding Fort Anderson, but they got no farther and most did not make it that far. When Thompson was killed, Colonel Ed Crossland of the 7th Kentucky assumed command, and he ordered the men to retreat. They fell back to the protection of the buildings. From the upper stories of the homes and mercantile houses, they kept up a steady fire, making particular targets of the Union cannon crews.[15]

Colonel Thompson's death did not disrupt Forrest's plan. The Kentuckians kept to their work and pinned down the Federals while the rest of Forrest's men went through the city, collecting medical supplies and horses and destroying what they could not use. About 11:00 p.m., Forrest withdrew in the direction of Mayfield. There his men camped. They had secured four hundred horses and mules with equipage, plus quantities of hospital supplies and other stores. Some of the men were awarded a leave of absence at Mayfield, the rest continued south to Trenton, Tennessee. Paducah had not seen the last of the raiders, however. A follow up raid led by Brigadier General Abraham Buford on April 14 netted another 140 horses and assorted plunder. Buford's party returned to Tennessee and joined Forrest at Jackson. During their absence, they were fortunate to have missed taking part in Forrest's attack on Fort Pillow, one of the atrocities of the war.

Although Forrest seemed to prefer making his headquarters at Jackson, he was not permitted to remain there. He was needed more urgently in Mississippi. On May 1, Polk had "taken steps to have the works at Corinth put in order, or at least so much as may be held by a small force with light armament, and has determined to move the command of Major-General Forrest there, making it his headquarters and establishing it as a post." From Corinth, Forrest could threaten west to the Mississippi River, as far north as the Ohio River at Paducah. He would give continuing encouragement to and receive material aid from the people of west Tennessee, and "receive from the Tennessee River, via the military road build by Halleck from Pittsburg Landing, 18 miles, commissary and quartermaster's stores in exchange for cotton under existing contracts." Polk had thought as well about the blacks that Forrest had brought back as prisoners from his various operations in the spring. Polk wrote to Forrest, "Send the negroes captured by you to Maj. Gen. Maury at Mobile. Fleming has them at work on [the] Rail Road."[16]

It was one of the last communications between Polk and Forrest. Everything was changing in the command hierarchy in both armies. On March 18, Sherman had accepted command of the Military Division of the Mississippi and had gone to Georgia to lead a campaign against Atlanta. General Polk was called to Georgia to help oppose Sherman. The Fighting Bishop left with twenty thousand men and assumed command of the Army of the Mississippi, on May 12, 1864. Polk's successor as commander of the Department of Alabama, Mississippi, and East Louisiana was Major General Stephen D. Lee. Lee was not sure he deserved the elevation to departmental command. On May 9, he wrote, almost apologetically, to General Maury, "I assumed command of this department this morning, General Polk having left for Rome. I send you a copy of the order…. I asked to be relieved from the command and that you be assigned which was declined. I make you this statement, General, that you may see I thought of you and your rights." He vowed he would "always be pleased to co-operate with you, and know you feel the same toward myself. I would much prefer having a command in the active service, but soldiers must do as they are ordered."[17]

The changes at the highest levels of leadership were beneficial in a way; it gave everyone a brief period of relative inactivity while the new leaders settled into their unfamiliar positions. On May 20, 1864, General C.C. Washburn, head of the District of West Tennessee, wrote to Major General Edward R.S. Canby (commander of the Military Division of West Mississippi), "General Forrest, with from 10,000 to 12,000 men, is at Corinth and Tupelo. He has been resting for twenty days, and his horses and men are in fine condition. The cars run from Mobile to Corinth, and he is drawing supplies from that line of road." To the Federal commander, it all added up to one thing: Forrest was preparing for a new campaign. He wrote, "I think he means to cross the Tennessee River and ride roughshod over Middle Tennessee and Kentucky, robbing and stealing and breaking up railroads…. He ought to be attacked where he is at once and not allowed to carry out his plans, for, if not interfered with, he will do incalculable damage."[18]

General Sherman was thinking along those same lines. When William Sooy Smith failed to defeat Forrest, Sherman had disparaged him, but Uncle Billy himself lived in positive dread of the Wizard, and he feared that Forrest *would* slip across the Tennessee to attack his railroad lifelines that connected to Nashville and Louisville. It was the smart move, and was, in fact, exactly what Forrest was planning. He had already begun his move when department commander Stephen D. Lee called him back to Tupelo to meet a Federal threat to the Mobile & Ohio.

Two weeks earlier, Sherman had ordered Washburn to send forth an expedition against Forrest. Though it was, as Washburn said, "regarded as of the first importance to engage him [Forrest], and if possible to whip and disperse his forces, as also to destroy the Mobile and Ohio Railroad," he had to await the arrival of more troops at Memphis before he could issue his orders. Finally, on May 31, General Washburn gave General Samuel D. Sturgis an assignment. He was to keep Forrest in Mississippi by leading a column of infantry and cavalry in a destructive raid against the M&O. Washburn ordered Sturgis to march "directly to Corinth, via Salem and Ruckersville. After capturing Corinth, and destroying all supplies you cannot carry away, you will march your infantry down the line of the road [the M&O] to Tupelo. Your cavalry will also march to Tupelo, keeping as near to the railroad as practicable. The infantry will be ordered to effectually destroy the railroad as they pass down." Sturgis was to continue to Okolona, "destroying the railroad as you go." At Okolona, he would divide his forces to make the damage more widespread, but all elements would rendezvous at Grenada and begin the return march to Memphis. "Take your time," Washburn advised, "subsist on the country when you can." He was always to be on guard against Forrest. He was the major threat, and his whereabouts, Washburn said, "will, of course, have much to do in regulating your movements."[19]

General Sturgis moved out on June 1 with an infantry division under Colonel

General Samuel D. Sturgis.

William L. McMillen. The division consisted of three brigades: the First, under Colonel Alexander Wilkin; the Second, under Colonel George B. Hoge; and the Third, under Colonel Edward Bouton. Bouton's brigade consisted of two African American infantry regiments and Battery F, 2nd U.S. Colored Light Artillery. If the black soldiers felt queasy about going out to meet Forrest, in light of the recent massacre of black troops at Fort Pillow, they did not show it. Bouton's men wore a white badge on uniforms with the legend: Remember Fort Pillow. Also with Sturgis was a cavalry division commanded by Brigadier General Benjamin H. Grierson. His two brigades of horse soldiers were the First, under Colonel George E. Waring, and the Second, under Colonel Edward F. Winslow. All told, Sturgis had over eight thousand men and sixteen pieces of artillery. The number of men going out had left Memphis weak. General Washburn called Sturgis's command "my entire effective force."[20]

The infantry trained to near La Fayette, Tennessee, while the cavalry and artillery proceeded on parallel roads to the same point. It was from La Fayette that the expedition embarked. Grierson's cavalry was leading the way. On June 7, beyond Ruckersville, Grierson learned that the Confederates had left Corinth and gone south. When he relayed word of the evacuation back to Sturgis, the general ordered a change of course. Despite his specific orders to destroy Corinth and the M&O going south, Sturgis decided to follow the Rebels toward Ripley. As they moved in that direction, Grierson met a party of Rebels. He said, "The skirmishing was quite brisk for nearly two hours. We succeeded in driving the enemy until night, when they moved off in a southerly direction, and I fell back to a good position and encamped." It was a showery afternoon, and the roads were becoming "very bad."[21]

The rain continued the next day and the day after, June 9, when Sturgis detached and sent back to Memphis "400 sick and worn-out men and forty-one wagons." The rest moved on over increasingly difficult roads to Stubb's farm and camped. That night, Sturgis held a council of war. In the rainy darkness, in a close atmosphere of whiskey fumes, cigar smoke, and wet wool, the officers listened as their general explained why he had lost faith in their expedition. Sturgis later said, "I called their attention to the great delay we had undergone on account of the continuous rain and consequent bad condition of the roads; the exhausted condition of our animals; the great probability that the enemy would avail himself of the time thus afforded him to concentrate an overwhelming force against us in the vicinity of Tupelo, and the utter hopelessness of saving our train or artillery in case of defeat, on account of the narrowness and general bad condition of the roads and the improbability of procuring supplies of forage for the animals." Most of those present favored turning back. Grierson was in favor of proceeding, but recommended that they park the wagons at Ripley. The most vocal in favor of continuing was the infantry division commander, Colonel McMillen. According to Grierson, McMillen argued in a "rather contemptuous manner" against turning back. His argument was based less on their chances of success and more on the effect a retrograde movement would have on their reputations. A few weeks earlier, Sturgis had gone on a half-hearted expedition against Forrest, and, after one brief encounter, he returned to Memphis, pleading bad roads and poor forage—the same as now. McMillen said that, in view of the previous embarrassment, "it would be ruinous on all sides to return again without first meeting the enemy."[22]

McMillen's argument, plus Washburn's assurance to Sturgis that "there could be no considerable force in our front," settled the question. Sturgis said, "I determined to move forward, keeping my force as compact as possible and ready for action at all times, hoping that we might succeed, and feeling that if we did not yet our losses might at most be insignificant in comparison with the great benefits which might accrue to General Sherman by the depletion of Johnston's army to so large an extent." The next morning, June 10, the Federals pushed on toward the intersection of the Ripley—Guntown Road with the Pontotoc—Baldwyn Road. Ignoring Grierson's recommendation, they took the wagons along.[23]

Nathan Bedford Forrest had been waiting at Baldwyn, a depot on the M&O, watching the Federals struggle through the mud until he was sure of their destination. By the night of the 9th, the same night of Sturgis's fateful council of war, Forrest was sure he knew. With him in Baldwyn were his escort and Colonel William A. Johnson's small brigade. Johnson was not normally part of Forrest's Cavalry; he was of General Phillip D. Roddey's command in Alabama, and he had arrived, leading five hundred men, just that day. General Abraham Buford was at Booneville, with the brigades of Colonel Edmund W. Rucker and Colonel Hylan B. Lyon. Lyon had been assigned command of the Kentucky Brigade after the death of Colonel A.P. Thompson at Paducah, and this was his first action as part of Forrest's Cavalry. Colonel Tyree Bell's all-Tennessee brigade was at Rienzi, another depot town several miles north of Baldwyn. The night of the 9th, Forrest ordered Bell's return to Buford and ordered the whole division to move out at four o'clock the next morning. Forrest said, "I moved as rapidly as the jaded condition of my horses would justify, intending, if possible, to reach Brice's Crossroads in advance of the enemy."[24]

The heavy rain of the night before made the early going slow, but June 10 dawned clear and the morning sun was soon blazing hot. The roads were drying quickly in the heat, and the men moved through clouds of rising steam that made the march "almost unbearable for the men and horses." Forrest was leading the way with his escort and Lyon's brigade. At mid-morning, he learned that Grierson's cavalry was only four miles from the crossroads. He said, "I immediately sent forward Lieutenant [Robert J.] Black, temporarily attached to my staff, with a few men from the Seventh Tennessee Cavalry, who soon reported that he had met the advance of the enemy one mile and a half north of the crossroads and was then skirmishing with them. I ordered Colonel Lyon, whose brigade was in front, to move forward and develop the enemy." The shooting started at 10:30 a.m.[25]

Rucker's and Johnson's brigades remained well behind Lyon on the road, so the Kentuckian would have to do the heavy work by himself until they came on line. Even after the three concentrated they would have no cannon. Buford had begun the day with the farthest distance to travel, was expected to arrive last, and he had the artillery. Forrest ordered him to come up "as quickly as the condition of the horses and roads would permit," and he ordered Buford to detach one regiment of Bell's brigade to move forward by a different road "to gain the rear of the enemy or attack and annoy his rear or flank." The battle had not yet begun, but Forrest was already thinking ahead by several hours and about how to get the advantage over the enemy. Buford, or maybe Bell on Buford's orders, chose Colonel Clark R. Barteau and the 2nd Tennessee Cavalry for the assignment, and they broke off and disappeared to the west.[26]

The Union infantry, with Colonel Hoge's brigade in the lead, had started the day's march ninety minutes behind Grierson's cavalry. The infantry lagged even farther behind when, five miles out of the previous night's camp, they "found an unusually bad place in the road, and one that would require considerable time and labor to render practicable." It was there that Sturgis learned Grierson's horsemen had bumped into the Confederates at Tishomingo Creek bottom, near the crossroads. More information followed. Grierson had followed them across the bottom, over the creek bridge, and up the road to the ridgetop. Beyond the spot where the roads crossed, Grierson's scouts found the enemy in force—Lyon's men— coming down the Baldwyn Road, "and brisk skirmishing ensued." Grierson sent Colonel Waring's brigade forward and a portion of Winslow's, which took position on Waring's right flank. Grierson held the rest, about six hundred men, in reserve.[27]

Lyon's men advanced on Grierson's cavalrymen in line of battle, but Forrest did not intend for the Kentuckians to bring on a general engagement until more of his men and the artillery arrived. Instead, Lyon's job was to hold the Yankees in place with a strong demonstration. He pushed them enough to earn their respect and enough to arouse their fighting spirit so that they would not retire, and then he dug in behind the usual barricade of logs and the rails of some unfortunate farmer's fence. When

Rucker came up, Forrest directed him to Lyon's left. Johnson arrived and was ordered to the right. When everyone was in place, Forrest ordered a charge. Three times they charged, and twice they were repulsed. On the third attempt, Lyon broke the Federal line. Grierson's men limbered their field pieces and retired toward the crossroads, trying to hold back the Confederates with their pistols. Their rifles were empty. Both their wings were being bent back "until they formed a tight semi-circle around the tiny cluster of buildings where the roads crossed." Grierson had told Sturgis earlier that "his position was a good one, and he would hold it," but the Rebels were taking a terrible toll on him with nothing but small arms; their artillery had not even arrived. The Federals had their cannon at the crossroads, though, and that saved them.[28]

Bell and Buford (with Forrest's cannon) arrived about 1:00 p.m. Bell was sent to Rucker's left while Buford positioned the big guns and went to work. Forrest ordered another charge. Captain H.A. Tyler said, "Think of it, a little heroic command about one third the size of its adversary, not only attempting to retard the march of the enemy, but actually prepared and determined to become the aggressor." Forrest left Buford in command of the right wing while he rode to the other end of the line to lead the left. Forrest said, "In a few seconds the engagement became general, and on the left raged with great fury." But something had gone wrong—there were no sounds of battle coming from the right. Forrest said, "Fearing my order to General Buford [to attack] had miscarried, I moved forward rapidly along the lines, encouraging my men, until I reached General Buford ... and finding but two pieces of artillery in position and engaged, I directed my aide-de-camp, Captain Anderson, to bring up all the artillery, and ordered General Buford to place it in action at once, which was promptly done." Buford's unaccountable mishandling of his field pieces corrected, the Confederates pushed on with a fury, and the battle settled into a grim two-hour contest for the crossroads.[29]

McMillen and the Federal infantry were still slogging forward, many falling out because of the breathless heat of the afternoon. Colonel Hoge and the Second Brigade led the strung out column. Wilkin's First Brigade was in the middle, and Bouton's U.S. Colored Infantry brigade was in the rear, escorting the slow-moving wagons. Sturgis rode on ahead to the crossroads with his escort and the 19th Pennsylvania Cavalry. He said he "found the battle growing warm." It was an afternoon of peculiar mishandling of the artillery on both sides. He was surprised to find that Grierson's four pieces had fallen silent. He ordered a two-gun section to begin firing. He said, "The enemy's artillery soon replied, and with great accuracy, every shell bursting over and in the immediate vicinity of our guns." The cavalrymen were being "hotly pressed," nearly out of small-arms ammunition and still no sign of the infantry. As a stop-gap, Sturgis ordered the 19th Pennsylvania to shore up Colonel Waring's brigade, but Grierson noticed that the general seemed strangely disconnected. Grierson said, "I judged he did not, even then, realize the fact that the rebels were in large force in our front." Another hour elapsed before the first of the infantry began arriving, at 2:00 p.m. Colonel Hoge reported that he had not been apprised of Grierson's situation; had not been urged to hurry forward until one o'clock, when "Colonel McMillen sent me word that he would move forward with his escort at such a gait as he thought infantry could march." He said to send word forward if the pace proved to be too much. It did. Hoge said that before the end of two miles, he lost five men to sunstroke. He sent an aide to McMillen to say, "That it was impossible to keep up that rapid gait." Then he halted at a stream for a rest before moving on at an easier pace. The Second Brigade went only a short distance before a rider came galloping back with an urgent order for the colonel. It said to "move forward as rapidly as possible, as the enemy were gaining ground, and the only thing that would save us was the infantry." The foot soldiers moved forward at the quick march.[30]

Three quarters of a mile from the crossroads, McMillen himself appeared. He ordered the Second Brigade to move to the line of battle at the double quick. The last bit was the hardest as they surged up the inclined road from the Tishomingo Creek bottom to the ridge where Grierson's defense was crumbling. Edwin C. Bearss says that, with the arrival of Hoge's brigade, "Grierson's fight was over. Now the defense of the crossroads was the responsibility of the ground-pounders." Hoge relieved Colonel Waring's cavalry on the left of the Federal line, where the fighting was the hardest. He placed his men between the Guntown and Baldwyn roads, facing Johnson and Lyon. Hoge set up his guns and they began firing shells with fuzes cut for five and three seconds. Colonel Wilkin and the First Brigade soon arrived and took position on Hoge's right. He placed his guns and opened fire.[31]

Last to arrive was the wagon train with its escort, Colonel Bouton's brigade. Bouton said that, although he had been hearing artillery fire for some time, he had received no orders, but as the teamsters reached the creek bottom and began "corralling the train," he sent back orders "to close up the troops and bring them forward at the double quick.... Many of them double-quicked two or three miles." Everything was happening at once. The main line was beginning to buckle under the relentless pressure from the Rebels. Sturgis said he was endeavoring "to get hold of the colored brigade, which formed the guard to the train," when the main line collapsed. "Order soon gave way to confusion, and confusion to panic," Sturgis later remembered. Bouton was moving forward at this moment.

He saw "our cavalry falling back, soon followed by infantry and artillery, and judging somewhat of the enemy's strength and position by the fire he was delivering, I saw that my brigade must be thrown forward into action at once to save a total defeat." Without orders, he began to feed the men into the fight where they were needed, even as the men who had been fighting on the ridge came streaming down to the bridge across Tishomingo Creek. General Grierson called Bouton's calm service at this moment and, indeed, his conduct through the rest of the afternoon, "gallant and timely."[32]

But nothing could stem the tide. Confederate gunners were dropping shells among them, some fired "from cannon abandoned by General Sturgis, which were turned upon our own men." Adding to the panic of the bluecoats was the fact that Colonel Barteau and the 2nd Tennessee had appeared. After a winding cross-country march, they emerged from the woods in the Federal left rear, in perfect position to cut the enemy off from the bridge. They attacked. The Federal retreat from the ridge was well under way. The rush was on to get across the bridge before that one means of escape was closed. Some of the teamsters had foolishly been allowed to take their wagons across the creek, and now they were caught up in the general retreat, trying to turn panicked teams in the midst of a mob of men and get across the muddy creek bottom. They "sank axle-deep into the mud and became inextricable," presenting another obstruction to men whose only desire was to escape. One of the wagons made it to the bridge where it somehow overturned, blocking the way entirely and creating an even greater desperation in the retreating troops. Some stopped at the roadblock and were killed, others jumped into the creek to wade across. They raced across the bottom on the far side of the creek and up the slope of the distant ridge. They came to the battle line formed by Bouton and seven companies of the 55th U.S. Colored Infantry, who parted to let them through and then closed ranks to meet the Confederates, who had cleared the bridge and rushed forward to press their advantage.[33]

Bouton said his men "opened a steady and well-directed fire on the enemy, which for a time seemed to hold in check his right and center." However, the Confederates refused to be stopped by men whom they considered to be no better than runaway slaves. They opened a murderous fire that no men could have stood for long. The 55th fell back half a mile to the next battle line. Waiting there were the 59th U.S. Colored Infantry, a section of Battery F, U.S. Colored Light Artillery, and about half of Colonel Wilkin's brigade. Bouton reported that his artillery began throwing "2½ and 3 second fuse-shells over our retreating men into the woods through which the enemy were advancing in great numbers." When the 55th had passed through, the artillerymen lowered their aim and sprayed "the open ground in front with canister." The Rebels charged through the sheets of canister and forced the Federal artillery to retire. Bouton said the Rebels "came forward in great numbers, engaging my entire line, and moving forward on the road in solid column under the fire of the battery." Some of the companies on Bouton's line held their fire until the Rebs came perilously close. Then they opened up with a blaze of musketry. The slaughter was terrible, but the attackers stepped over the dead and came on. Bouton's blacks and Wilkin's whites fell back when about to be flanked on the right, but they went in good order, for the most part, turning and firing, "and holding our position at every ditch, ridge, or skirt of timber."[34]

Bouton and Wilkin deserve great credit. They kept their men fighting when all the rest had fled, from Sturgis down to the lowliest private, and though they fell back at the end, some breaking and running (the black troopers tore off their "Remember Fort Pillow" badges and threw them away), most stood, retired, and formed to fight again until sundown. Their fidelity to duty saved Sturgis's army from annihilation.

There was some sporadic fighting through the night. Bouton and Wilkin remained in the rear. Wilkin remembered halting in mid-evening to give his men a rest and seeing campfires burning ahead. It was a confusing sight; surely the army was not stopping to camp with the Confederates breathing down their collars. An officer commanding a cavalry squadron appeared and explained that the fires "were built by him under orders from the general commanding, in order to deceive the enemy." It was one of the last intelligent orders Sturgis gave that day. About midnight, there was another traffic jam at that boggy stretch of road that had delayed them in the morning. Bearss says, "Many teamsters panicked, cut loose their teams and abandoned their wagons. The road became choked and the panic spread.... Ambulances filled with wounded were mired in the road along with hundreds of other wagons, and soldiers on foot sank knee deep in the mud." This is where Bouton caught up with the column. He was dismayed at the collapse he saw all around him. He found Sturgis astride an artillery horse; he had lost his warhorse, another indignity on this day of humiliations. Bouton went to him and said, "General, for God's sakes, don't let us give up so." He vowed that he would re-form his men and buy time for the train and the artillery to be saved "if you will give my blacks the ammunition the whites are throwing in the mud." By now, Sturgis was utterly unstrung. He cried, "For God's sakes, if Mr. Forrest will let me alone, I will let him alone. You have done all you could, and more than was expected of you, and now all you can do is save yourselves." The retreat continued with no effort at defense, and two hundred more wagons were abandoned, along with fourteen field pieces. Farther back in the jam, and more vulnerable to a dash by Forrest's cavalry, Wilkin ordered "the animals remaining with the rear of the train to be taken out and the wagons abandoned. The train was not burned, as I thought it probable that our line of battle had been reformed beyond, and that it might yet be saved." Besides, a conflagration of wagons would guide the Rebels to the Federal position. So the wagons were left, their cargoes intact, a further bounty for the Confederates.[35]

After a harrowing night, the Federals began arriving at Ripley on the morning of June 11. From there, Sturgis sent a dispatch to Major General Washburn that bounced between mendacity and the miserable truth. Sturgis reported, "Yesterday we had a very hard fight near Guntown. The enemy was a very large force. Our loss in killed and wounded is very heavy. We have lost most everything, including a number of wagons and artillery, with ammunition." He begged for a brigade of infantry and a supply of forage and commissary stores. They continued from Ripley to Collierville, where, the following day, Sturgis sent another wire which revealed the heavy toll of his failed campaign against the M&O. He asked for "25,000 rounds Sharps cavalry ammunition, 10,000 rounds Spencer, and 3000 rounds Colts revolving rifle, and one day's rations for, say, 4000 men." At noon that day, a train from Memphis arrived with reinforcements and supplies. The next day, June 13, the infantry, the dismounted cavalry, and the artillerymen who no longer had any artillery, boarded the trains at White's Station and rode back to Memphis. They arrived that evening. Their condition was shocking. Wilkin said, "Nearly all were barefooted, their feet badly blistered and swollen, and in some cases poisoned. Most of them had eaten nothing for three days and all had suffered for want of food."[36]

"We have lost most everything," Sturgis had said. Included in what was lost was his own career. General Sherman was blunt in his disapproval. He said, "I will have the matter of Sturgis critically examined, and, if he be at fault, he shall have no mercy at my hands." A board of inquiry convened in Memphis on June 27, and although its findings were never made public, its condemnation of Sturgis's conduct and leadership can be inferred by his reassignment to Covington, Kentucky, where he remained without a command for the rest of the war. Grierson said, "May God for the future keep such men from our army."[37]

That Sturgis had suffered a notable defeat was undeniable, but he *had* inflicted over four hundred Confederate casualties when the South was dying for lack of manpower, and, more important strategically, he had succeeded in keeping Forrest off of Sherman's communications in Tennessee while the armies of the Cumberland, the Tennessee, and the Ohio moved ever closer to Atlanta.

The Battle of Brice's Crossroads was Forrest's greatest victory. Winning against three-to-one odds, he had kept the Federals away from the

Mobile & Ohio Railroad, when its destruction was a specific object of Sturgis's written orders, and he had sent his enemies flying back to the protection of Memphis. He was universally celebrated for his performance and he, in turn, praised his brigade commanders and men in an exuberant message dated June 28. Referring to the battle by its other name, Forrest said, "Tishomingo Creek is the brightest leaf in your chaplets of laurels.... Victory was never more glorious, disaster never more crushing and signal." He assured them the final victory was nigh. He said, "Be true to yourselves and your Country a little while longer, and you will soon be enabled to return to your desolated homes, there to collect together once more your scattered household gods."[38]

Forrest almost certainly did not compose the congratulatory message himself, but it truthfully conveyed his pride in his men, his recognition that the war was not yet over, and his determination to fight to the end. Whether or not his men shared that determination was soon to be tested, for as Forrest said, "the enemy is again preparing."[39]

CHAPTER TEN

Tupelo and Memphis

General Leonidas Polk was killed by an artillery shell atop Pine Mountain near Marietta, Georgia, on June 14, 1864. Sherman mentioned it fleetingly in a wire to Secretary of War Stanton the next day, but his mind was on the death—the potential death—of another Confederate general. Sherman said that he was going to order a force to go out and "follow Forrest to the death, if it cost 10,000 lives and breaks the Treasury. There never will be peace in Tennessee till Forrest is dead." He wanted Major General A.J. Smith, who commanded the right wing of the XVI Army Corps, to lead the latest effort to bring Forrest to bay. Sherman described Smith as one officer who "will fight all the time."[1]

On July 5, 1864, Smith's expedition left La Grange, Tennessee, with orders to destroy the Mobile & Ohio Railroad at Tupelo and to kill Forrest, if possible, but at the very least to keep him in Mississippi. The safety of Sherman's rail connections to the north was still paramount to the success of the Atlanta Campaign. General Washburn wrote to General Canby, "If, as is alleged, there are 15,000 to 20,000 men on the Mobile and Ohio road, 12,000 of whom are mounted men, it is our object *to hold them there*." (Emphasis added) To accomplish that, General

General A.J. Smith.

153

Smith had about fourteen thousand men. The First Division was led by another of Sherman's favorites, Brigadier General Joseph A. Mower. The Third Division was commanded by Colonel David Moore, and there was a brigade of USCT commanded by Colonel Edward Bouton, who was one of the heroes of Brice's Crossroads. General Grierson was again in charge of the cavalry division. Sherman ordered that the force going out after Forrest should proceed with the intention of "devastating the land over which he has passed or may pass, and make him and the people of Tennessee and Mississippi realize that, although a bold, daring, and successful leader, he will bring ruin and misery on any country where he may pause or tarry. If we do not punish Forrest and the people now, the whole effect of our past conquests will be lost." The Federals convened in the vicinity of Ripley, arriving by different roads on July 8. They set fire to the town and continued in the direction of Pontotoc.[2]

Forrest's scouts had reported General Smith's movements to Ripley and beyond, and he ordered General Abraham Buford "to pursue him, to hang upon his flanks, and to develop his strength" (without bringing on a battle) once the enemy column turned toward Pontotoc. Forrest at this time was suffering from an outbreak of boils that "greatly depleted even his iron constitution," and he had asked for permission to take temporary leave of his responsibilities during the coming campaign. His request was denied. Instead, department commander General Stephen D. Lee traveled north to be with Forrest and to take a more hands-on role in opposing the Federal column. However, Lee came with a distracted mind. As was their usual practice when a land campaign was getting underway, the Federals were making ominous moves outside of Mobile, an effective diversion from their true intentions. It seems obvious that they did not really want to attack and conquer Mobile because garrison duty there occupied hundreds of soldiers that might otherwise be active in the field and because it was too useful as a source of confusion; the Northerners repeatedly feinted toward the city, pretending to be about to attack when their actual purpose was to distract and divide the Confederates. Still, no one could tell when a genuine attack would come; perhaps it was now. So it was that when General Lee arrived at Forrest's headquarters, he was torn by the need to meet two perils. While Smith was advancing toward Pontotoc in the north, Mobile was facing a double threat in the south; Rear Admiral Farragut was poised for action at the mouth of the bay, and General Canby had sent an oversized cavalry force from Baton Rouge to cut the M&O RR just above the city. On July 9, from Forrest's headquarters at Okolona, Lee warned of Canby's move against Mobile in a wire to General Braxton Bragg, now a military advisor to President Davis in Richmond. Lee said, "All I can do is dismount a part of Forrest's cavalry and put them at Mobile.... I deem it of vital importance that an infantry force be put at Mobile at once." The next day he added more information about his troubles; Maury needed six thousand men to fill Mobile's works but had only two thousand. Lee said he could send two thousand men south when the fight with Smith was over, but not until then. Obviously, a quick conclusion to the crisis in northern Mississippi was imperative.[3]

The Federals marched into Pontotoc on the morning of July 11, after a march that David W. Reed of the 12th Iowa remembered as "the hottest sun and the deepest dust that we found in all our marching." The fully-equipped Federal infantryman carried more than fifty-four pounds of weight: the knapsack, with contents and blanket weighed almost fifteen pounds; the haversack and rations almost seven; a full canteen weighed almost four pounds; the rifle and accouterments about thirteen pounds; forty rounds of ammunition weighed four pounds; and the uniform, including hat and brogans, weighed twelve pounds. The overburdened, overheated foot soldiers staggered into Pontotoc in less than prime condition to face Colonel Robert McCulloch's brigade (of Brigadier General James R. Chalmers's division), who held the town. Luckily, the Federal cavalry saved the weary infantry from having to fight. The 7th Kansas occupied the Rebel's attention to the front while Grierson's cavalry moved around to hit them from the rear, compelling the enemy "to evacuate precipitously and in some confusion, leaving several dead and wounded in our hands."[4]

The Confederates were preparing to meet Smith at Okolona, but the Federals stopped at Pontotoc. The afternoon passed with no forward move. The next morning, Smith sent out three scouting parties: the one on the road to Okolona was turned back by Colonel Lyon and the Kentucky Brigade; a second one on the road to Houston was successfully blocked by Colonel McCulloch; and a third one on the road to Tupelo was driven back by Colonel Edmund W. Rucker. During the day, Forrest and Lee finished their arrangements. Everything was ready to meet the Federals at Okolona, and the Wizard ordered that no attempt be made to block them if they again moved in that direction, but they did not. They remained in Pontotoc, and Forrest said, "The delay of the enemy at Pontotoc produced the impression that he designed to fall back toward Memphis, and after a short consultation it was determined to accept battle wherever he offered it and to attack him if he attempted to retreat."[5]

Paul Ashdown and Edward Caudill observe that General Smith "was proving a more wily opponent than Sturgis." He had done a masterful job of keeping Forrest and Lee off balance, and they were caught by surprise again the next morning, July 13, when their patrols found the Federal camps empty. Captain William Pirtle of the 7th Kentucky Mounted

Infantry made the discovery that the Yankees had stolen a march. Pirtle "noted something was amiss in the Union camps and was soon joined by General Chalmers. Both came to the same conclusion: the enemy … was headed off to the east." Chalmers carried the word to headquarters.[6]

Forrest said, "Lieutenant-General Lee ordered me, with Mabry's brigade, my escort, and Forrest's old regiment, to attack and press upon the rear of the enemy. At the same time Lieutenant-General Lee moved forward, with Chalmers's and Buford's two divisions on the right [that is, south of the Federal column], with the view of attacking the enemy's flanks at every vulnerable point." Forrest easily caught up with the slow-marching Federals and attacked their rear guard only one mile out of Pontotoc. Colonel Edward Bouton was in the rear, just behind the train, with his African American brigade. With him was "a portion" of Colonel Thomas Herrick's 7th Kansas Cavalry. The Kansans and Company A of the 61st U.S. Colored Infantry had been skirmishing with Forrest for about a mile when Colonel Bouton picked a site for an ambush and ordered two companies of the 61st to spring it when the Rebels appeared. They soon did. The black infantrymen held their fire until Forrest's horsemen were within twelve paces. Then they fired a "well-directed volley which emptied 15 or 20 saddles and threw his column back in confusion." Colonel Bouton laid a second ambush a mile farther down the road. He called the second ambuscade a partial success, "not so complete" as the first, but it nevertheless staggered the graybacks, who gave the Federals a respite of five miles before they again appeared.[7]

Just after Bouton's men forded a small stream, the Confederate riders made a dash on them. They drove in the bluecoat flankers and the artillerists shelled them from an overlooking hill. Bouton said, "I moved forward under this fire until I gained the ridge on [the] opposite side of [the] bottom, where I put my battery in position and answered them at about 800 yards range." The 59th U.S. Colored Infantry supported the battery on the right, the 61st on the left, and the 68th was held in reserve. The fighting at the creek settled into a contest of dangerously long duration. The main column was moving without stopping and the gap between it and Bouton was becoming wider with each quarter hour, putting both the wagons and their increasingly distant defenders at risk. Finally, Bouton began to disengage. He sent the 68th to catch up with the train, then the 61st, and then two of his guns. Only one section of artillery and the 59th were left. One wing of the regiment was hidden by a screen of thick brush. The concealed troopers remained behind when Colonel Bouton gave the order for the last two guns and the visible half of the 59th to withdraw. The others waited to surprise the Rebels, the third ambush of the morning. Parson says the ploy had "worked time after time, and for the first half of the day Forrest was kept at bay." Bouton was gambling it would work again. It did. When the graybacks were at a distance of only fifteen yards, the half-regiment fired "a deadly volley, quickly followed by others, which seemed to tell on them with terrible effect, throwing them back in confusion." The Confederate setback was only temporary. They recovered and began to fire on the black troopers, and Bouton saw Confederates gathering in strength on both his flanks. He knew it was more than his men could handle, and he sent an orderly with a request for aid from General Mower. Mower ordered Colonel Lyman Ward to hurry one regiment of his brigade back to support Bouton. Ward picked Colonel F.S. Lovell and the 33rd Wisconsin. They marched to the rear at the double quick. They expected a fight, but the action that followed was light and of short duration.[8]

Forrest said that the enemy "was driven from his position and made a rapid retreat across an extended field, while my artillery poured upon him a concentrated fire." And with that, the fight with the Federal rear guard ended. Forrest was satisfied with his own morning's work. He had become concerned that he was not hearing any fighting from Buford and Lee up ahead. Their part of the plan was to attack the enemy's flanks, but it was after noon and Forrest could hear no battle sounds but his own. His cocksure self-confidence began to work against him. He said, "I had now driven the enemy ten miles, and as his flanks had not yet been attacked I was afraid that he was driven too rapidly." In other words, his own great success had upset the battle plan of the day because men of lesser skills had failed to keep up. "I therefore halted my command," he said, "and awaited the attack upon his flanks." An hour passed before the clamor he had been listening for came echoing through the heavy July air.[9]

The delay had not been Lee's fault. "The roads upon which Chalmers's and Buford's divisions had to advance were narrow gaps through dense woods, in large part, very unfavorable for the rapid movement of cavalry." Therefore, Chalmers's division, with General Lee accompanying, were slow in getting into position to strike the Yankee flank. They chose a speck on the map called Bertram's Shop as the place to attack. At about 2:00, as the blue line passed, Colonel Edmund Rucker's brigade hit the Federals hard. They broke through the column and the surprised bluecoats of Colonel Lyman Ward's brigade suddenly found themselves in a deadly box. W.H. Tucker of the 14th Wisconsin said, "We were penned in, rebs to the front, rebs on the right, and in the rear and heavy timber on the left, nothing but fight and fight it was." Parson says, "Through pure luck, Rucker had struck the gap between [Colonel Joseph J.] Woods' and Ward's brigades." He continues, saying that Rucker's men enjoyed their breakthrough only briefly. "The threat to the Colored Brigade had passed and Ward, with the 33rd Wisconsin, was already on the way back to its place in the column."

The 33rd, with the help of the 7th Minnesota and 12th Iowa, turned the tide. Now it was the Confederates who found themselves "hemmed in." They began to back out of the fight the best way they could. Ninety minutes after the attack began, the Southerners managed to extricate themselves, losing heavily as they went. Once the fighting ended, Mower took inventory and counted twenty-seven mules dead or so badly wounded that they had to be put down. Seven wagons wrecked beyond repair were unloaded and burned, and the column passed on. General Smith said, "Immediately after this attack, I learned from General Grierson that he had possession of Tupelo." The day was nearly done, but not quite.[10]

At Camargo Crossroads (sometimes called Calhoun's Crossroads), General Abraham Buford waited with Colonel Tyree Bell's brigade. The Kentucky Brigade of his division was further back; Buford had only Bell's men, but he thought they were enough to commence the fight and the Kentuckians would soon be up. So confident was Buford of success that he warned his men not to shoot the Union mules but to herd them back so that they could become Confederate mules. Still, Buford knew the Federals would not be easy to knock over. He said, "At no time had I found the enemy unprepared. He marched with his column well closed up, his wagon train well protected, and his flanks covered in an admirable manner, evincing at all times a readiness to meet any attack, and showing careful generalship." At five o'clock, Colonel Barteau and the 2nd Tennessee Cavalry, who had done such good service at Brice's Crossroads, burst out of the woods on the Federal right. No one was yet ready to support them; they rushed toward Colonel W.L. McMillen's brigade alone. What should have been a full-fledged attack in brigade strength was being made by one regiment. A second regiment, the 15th Tennessee, came up to join the attack, but it was too little too late. The Yankee infantry and artillery turned to meet the attack with a cool efficiency that sent the Tennesseans reeling back down the narrow road after only fifteen minutes. The Federals followed, crowding the two regiments back into the rest of Bell's brigade, "which had been hurrying up to the sound of the guns." The Tennesseans were tangled up in a knot of confusion. It was Captain Morton's artillery that prevented a disaster. His guns began blasting the attackers and held them back "until the Tennesseans could remount and ride back to Buford's defensive line." Buford said, ""The Kentucky Brigade having by this time arrived at the scene of action, I formed the two brigades to repel any attack that might be made." The Federals chose not to attack. They returned to the main road, retrieved their wounded, and continued toward Tupelo.[11]

A few more miles brought Smith's expeditionary force to the end of its day's labors. Part of the general's mission had already been accomplished; Grierson's cavalry had reached the target and was dismantling the

Mobile & Ohio Railroad in Tupelo, but the infantry column did not continue that far. Instead, it stopped two miles west at an abandoned village called Harrisburg. The population of Harrisburg had picked up and relocated to Gum Pond (later given the more dignified name of Tupelo), when the M&O reached the area in 1859. The battle line General Smith laid out was, according to a New York *Times* correspondent, a sign of his "superior generalship and good judgment." It was "in the centre and most elevated part of an area of partly open and partly wooded ground that the eye could take in within a radius of from one to two miles." Beyond that, continuous woods blocked the view. The Rebels would be able to form up under concealment, but the ground in front of them, over which they would charge, was mostly open, rising in gentle undulations toward the Federal position on the high ground. It was, said the correspondent, "A magnificent position in which to receive the attack of the enemy."[12]

A position naturally powerful was improved by General Smith's informed placement of his troops. General Mower's division was on the north of the Pontotoc—Tupelo Road. South of the road was Colonel Moore's division. The Federal line generally faced west, with Tupelo at its back. Colonel Edward F. Winslow's brigade was on the extreme right and refused so that it faced north. Colonel Bouton's Colored Infantry brigade was on the extreme left and refused so that it faced south. Elements of Grierson's cavalry were posted on each flank, just beyond the ends of the infantry line. Artillery batteries were placed at intervals all along the ridge. The men worked into the night erecting barricades and then settled down in line of battle for a short night's rest.

When Smith had finally come to a halt, so had the Rebels, a short distance west. When morning came, Buford's division was on the C.S.A. left, north of the Tupelo Road. Chalmers's division was in the center, south of the road. Brigadier General Philip D. Roddey's division, traditionally not a part of Forrest's cavalry, was the farthest south, on the far right and slightly in front of the others. There was a fourth Confederate division at Harrisburg, as well. When General Lee arrived at Okolona, he had brought with him two thousand unmounted men. Forrest had no horses for about eight hundred of them, and there was no time for a Paducah-like raid to obtain any additional mounts, so the horse-less soldiers were formed into a small infantry unit. On July 12, Brigadier General Hylan B. Lyon had been removed from command of the Kentucky Brigade by order of General Lee and reassigned to command the new-born infantrymen. Colonel Edward Crossland took Lyon's place at the head of the Kentuckians. Crossland was a brave and capable man, but to elevate him to be a replacement for Lyon, one of Forrest's most "professional and experienced" brigade commanders, and to remove Lyon from the brigade he had led with notable success, and all of this practically on the eve of a major battle, was a reckless rotation of talent. Lyon's infantry was held in reserve athwart the Tupelo Road, some distance behind the cavalry, and would have no part to play in the coming battle.[13]

In the early hours of July 14, Lee and Forrest had a council of war. General Maury recalled in his memoirs the Wizard's "peculiar sensitiveness when under control" and said that "he could never brook the dictation of any commander." He had a history of quarreling with his commanders, often to the verge of insubordination and sometimes, as in the case of Braxton Bragg, almost to the point of demanding satisfaction. His truculence was on full display during the council of war at Harrisburg. True, he was exhausted by a day of riding and fighting in the soul-sapping heat, followed by a midnight reconnaissance of the Federal position, and he was in agony from those painful boils. One of his staff officers later said that "when sick or wounded he was the most restless and impatient men I ever saw." But, considering his past relationships with superior officers, one can imagine that, even under the best of circumstances, he would have been difficult and uncooperative in Lee's presence. Certainly, he was sulky at the pre-dawn conference on July 14. Lee explained his battle plan, expecting that Forrest would carry it out. To his surprise, Forrest "declined to take command on the field, citing Lee's superior rank as the reason." He would command the right wing only. Lee urged him to reconsider; since the units out there in the dark had fought and won battles under him and had confidence in him, he should absolutely take command. Forrest refused, and Lee accepted his decision. Then, when it came down to specifics, the alignment of the troops, Forrest again got his back up—a peculiar reaction from one who had moments earlier refused to lead. James Hancock, an officer in Roddey's division, heard the exchange between Lee and Forrest. Lee indicated that he wanted to place Roddey's division on the left for the attack and Buford's on the right. Forrest bluntly opposed him. He said, without elaboration, "No, I want Buford's division on the left and Roddey's on the right." Lee explained the reason for his preference, but Forrest dug in. "No," he said, "I want Buford on the left." Lee again acceded to Forrest and said, "Very well, have your own way then." It was a bad start to the day that was going to settle the fate of Smith's campaign, one way or the other. And Forrest's insubordination was not at an end.[14]

Hours later, about 7:30 a.m. on that same July 14, Colonel David Moore, commander of the Federal Third Division, saw a brigade of dismounted cavalry emerge from the shade of the trees in the valley below. This was the Kentucky Brigade, and they were moving against the center of the Union line, Colonel Moore's First Brigade, commanded by Colonel C.D. Murray. But, in a larger repeat of Colonel Barteau's mistake of the day before, Crossland's men had begun their charge before anyone else was ready; they advanced without support on either flank. The Union cannon began firing long range rounds at them. The Federal infantry just waited and watched them come charging at the double quick across a half mile of open ground as the shells exploded among them. Colonel Moore said they "were permitted to advance in solid columns upon our line through an open field. Our lines being concealed from their view by the brow of the hill, we were not discovered until the enemy had reached a point about twenty paces distant." By the time the attackers came that close, their line was being shredded by oblique fire from the batteries left and right; those gunners, with no foe to face on their own front, had turned their pieces pigeon-toed and began pouring canister and grape into the Kentuckians. Men fell all around. The survivors of the storm stepped over their comrades and marched on among strangers. Their regiments were tangled and intermixed. They still had not seen the hidden line of infantry when the men of Colonel Murray's brigade "sprang to their feet, and, with a yell like that of demons, raced forward, pouring into the ranks of the advancing foe a desperate volley of musketry, causing them to flee in the utmost disorder, exclaiming 'My God! My God!'"[15]

As Crossland's decimated ranks struggled back toward the trees, the Yankees added to their casualty lists by firing into their backs. General Smith said that Moore's soldiers killed "even more as they were running than they did in the first volley." Crossland afterward remembered the fight as "the most severe and destructive ever encountered by the troops of this brigade, who are veterans in the service. Their loss was unprecedented."[16]

The Federals saw that the enemy, despite the carnage, was not finished. New lines of graybacks came out of the trees, headed toward Mower's section of the line. These were the brigade of Colonel Hinchie P. Mabry, followed at an interval of several minutes by Colonel Tyree Bell and his Tennesseans. General Smith said the Confederates "started from the edge of the timber in three lines, at the same time opening with about seven pieces of artillery. At first their lines could be distinguished separately, but as they advanced they lost all semblance of lines and the attack resembled a mob of huge magnitude." The expanse of open ground the attackers had to cross was so wide that, once again, the Federals had the leisure to watch before they had to go to work. Someone remembered a verse from his schooldays and quoted William Cullen Bryant aloud: "Leaden rain and iron hail, Let their welcome be!" General Smith said, "They were allowed to approach, yelling and howling like Comanches, to within canister range, when the batteries of the First Division opened on them." They charged through it, and then came the musketry. For two and a half hours the Confederates and Federals grappled. Smith said, "They would come forward and fall back, rally and forward again, with the like result." The attackers died by the score. The Federals on the battle line fired and reloaded as fast their muzzle loaders would allow, and when the guns became fouled and the men had to fall back to clean them, others moved forward so that there was no let-up in the slaughter.[17]

Federal casualties were few, but one of them was lamented throughout the service. Colonel Alexander Wilkin, who commanded Moore's Second Brigade, had just led two regiments forward to the battle line when a Southern bullet pierced his heart and killed him on the spot. Lieutenant John K. Arnold, his adjutant, was near him when he was killed. He said in a letter that was reprinted in the Minnesota newspapers, "The bullets and shells were flying thick and fast. Colonel Wilkin sat on his horse and when he was struck he was giving orders as cooly as he ever did on dress parade." As Wilkin gestured, a rifle ball struck him beneath the left arm, passed through his body laterally, and came out under the right arm. Arnold said, "He never spoke after being hit, but fell from his horse, and was dead before reaching the ground." Wilkin was "universally mourned by the army," said Arnold, and it seems to have been true. General Washburn in Memphis said, "He was the bravest of the brave, and his fall is mourned by the entire army." Wilkin was the highest ranking officer to die at Tupelo.[18]

General Smith said the Confederates' "determination may be seen from the fact that their dead were found within thirty yards of our batteries," and when Mower's men emerged from their works to push the enemy, "270 of their dead were counted on the field immediately in his [Mower's] front." From the precipitous charge of the Kentucky Brigade to the tardy and uncoordinated attack that went forward afterward, it had been a morning of Confederate mistakes. However, the day was young, and there was still time to make some more. Parson says that General Lee "had observed the piecemeal attacks with frustration and anger. His plan for a simultaneous attack by four brigades had evolved into three separate charges, each by a lone brigade." To try to salvage something out of the calamity, Lee decided to send in General James Chalmers's division to strike the Federal right. Chalmers intended to obey, but he was intercepted by General Forrest as he moved his men to the front. And where had Forrest been during the morning's battles? By his own insistence, he had been in command of the Confederate right wing and was with General Roddey. When the attack began, he was supposed "to swing the right around upon the enemy's left," but when the Kentucky Brigade stepped off, albeit earlier than expected, Forrest held Roddey's troops in position. When he saw the Kentuckians come tumbling back down the hill, he rode over to meet them. He was not altogether welcome. Colonel Crossland was bitter about the failure of the right wing to support his charge and said, "The failure of Roddey's division to advance, and thus, draw the fire of the enemy on my right flank was fatal to my men." The Kentuckians were not even in Forrest's sector; they were in Lee's, yet here was Forrest, seizing their colors and ordering them to form a new line. It was simultaneously a failure to attend to his own duties and an outrageous interference in a superior officer's sphere. Herman Hattaway calls it "meddling" and points out that, at the very moment he was treading on Lee's toes, Forrest was "expected to be leading Roddey's flank movement." Instead, they all fell back and made a new line.[19]

Now Lee was sending Chalmers's division into action, and once again Forrest interfered. He stopped Chalmers and ordered him to support Roddey, who had no need of support. He was still sitting motionless on the right. At about the same time, Chalmers received an order from Buford to come relieve him in the center and one from Lee to move to the left and support Mabry. Chalmers said, "Major-General Forrest being my immediate superior, I obeyed his order and moved to the right, but before I had reached the desired position another order from General Lee in person divided my command." McCulloch's brigade was to stand in reserve, Lee ordered, while Rucker's brigade moved left to attack. Chalmers was with Rucker's men as they "passed over plowed ground and through a cornfield, in full view of the enemy, for 2000 yards, under fire of three pieces of artillery and small-arms from the enemy.... Before we reached the position to charge many of the men fainted from exhaustion." When they came into the open they were immediately under a deadly from the ridge. By the time they got halfway to the Federal works, one-third of them had fallen, and Chalmers called them back.[20]

By now, Lee himself had ridden over to the right to see what had gone wrong. He met General Forrest, who was largely responsible for the magnitude of the day's defeat. Parson recounts their conversation, which Lee wrote down many years later. Lee asked Forrest, "Why did you not carry out the plan of the attack?"

"Buford's right had been rashly thrown forward and repulsed. In the exercise of my discretion I did not move Roddey forward but I have moved him to the left and formed a new line."

"In doing as you did, you failed to carry out the plan of battle agreed upon, and have caused the loss of many men in the left wing."[21]

Forrest did not flare up. He merely indicated that he had not intended it. Of course, mistakes *had* been made, some of them growing out of a conscious disregard of military propriety, but Forrest was not alone in his culpability. General Lee had dismissed what appears in hindsight to have been some splendid advice before the fight began. The night before,

General Buford had "modestly expressed the opinion that the attack should not be a direct one, but the majority of the forces should be thrown on the Verona and Tupelo road, and a vigorous assault made on his left flank; that a direct charge was what the enemy most desired, and for which he was strongly posted both by nature and art." Lee ignored the suggestion and also brushed off the recommendation of Captain Morton, Forrest's prize artillery officer, who "made the suggestion that he be allowed to concentrate all of the artillery in the left center and make a breech in the Federal lines, creating confusion in their works, which would give the Confederates easy work." Morton said that, to his great disappointment, Lee instructed him instead "to send one battery to support the Kentucky brigade on the right of the Harrisburg road, another to support Bell's brigade on the right of that road, and a third to support Roddey's brigade [sic]."[22]

Lee had confidently stuck to his own conception of the battle, a plan that showed little finesse and undoubtedly resulted in a bloodier defeat. But even Lee's flawed plan might have been better executed, and the responsibility for that failure rested upon his subordinates with the braid on their sleeves. Wyeth, General Forrest's admiring biographer, says that July 14, 1864, was "a battle tragedy for a parallel to which the historian will search the records, without co-ordination or concert of action between the different portions of the assailing line, and without proper control even of the separate commands, one brigade after another, in isolated rashness, precipitated itself against the exceedingly strong position." Like the waves rushing in to a rocky shore, they were "dashed to pieces."[23]

It was the Yankees who, in Morton's phrase, had the "easy work." At very little cost to themselves, they had destroyed the Rebels in detail. A Southern prisoner later told his captors that "he had been in seventeen battles, but was never under such a heavy musketry fire before as that they had encountered from us." Now, the day's victors emerged from their works to retrieve the wounded from the bloody slope for transport to the hospitals in Tupelo and to break up the abandoned small arms, for which there was no transportation. An officer in the 7th Minnesota, who called himself "E," wrote a letter to the St. Paul *Weekly Pioneer and Democrat* describing the ghastly scene in the last hours of daylight after the battle. It said, "The very trees bear evidence of the strife. They are scarred and broken by the storm of shot and shell…. The cannon are now silent, and there before them is the field of death, a long, grassy slope, skirted with straggling bushes…. Scattered at intervals over the field of a few yards, are dull gray blotches, half shaded by the grass. These are the rebel dead." Some appeared to be asleep, some smiling, and "E" noticed one with a band of white around his finger where a pilfered ring had been. Or maybe the ring was taken by his widow.

Women from the town and the surrounding farms moved over the field, raising a "piteous cry" when they discovered the remains of a loved one.[24]

No one got much sleep that night. The Federals burned the ghost town of Harrisburg and thirty-five buildings in the living town of Tupelo. The left wing fought off an attack by Forrest and Rucker's brigade (which was led on this nighttime excursion by Colonel William Duckworth). General Smith had adjusted his lines on the left, which the Confederates did not know until they attacked. They drove in Bouton's pickets and then ran into the bulk of Colonel Moore's Third Brigade. The Second Brigade "pushed forward in quick time" to help repel the attack. Forrest said they "opened on me one of the heaviest fires I have heard during the war. The enemy's whole force seemed to be concentrated at this point." It was remarkable that no one was killed, but the fire of the enemy was nonetheless daunting enough that the Rebels discontinued the attack and returned to camp.[25]

In spite of the boils that weakened him, Forrest had been constantly active and without rest for nearly thirty-six hours. During that time his designs had been repeatedly foiled by a surprisingly obstinate enemy, and the smothering heat continued to be a torment. Added to this was his unhappy situation; he was, against his will, made to share command on the field with an officer for whom he had little professional respect. When summoned that night to attend the council of war at Lee's headquarters, an occasion he had intended to skip, Forrest was described as "so mad he stunk like a polecat." As the easy-going department commander went around the room, giving his officers the chance to offer suggestions about how best to proceed after such a grim day, Forrest folded his arms and brooded. When it was his turn to contribute ideas, he used it to attack Lee. He said, "Yes, sir, I've always got ideas, and I'll tell you one thing, General Lee. If I knew as much about West Point tactics as you, the Yankees would whip hell out of me every day." He added, "I've got five hundred empty saddles and nothing to show for them." Forrest's behavior had been insufferable since the beginning of the campaign at Pontotoc, and such an outburst might have been the final straw in another man's command, but General Lee was of a tolerant nature and, once again, Forrest was to suffer no repercussions for his insubordination.[26]

The next morning, July 15, the Confederates made another attempt on the Federals. Buford sent Bell's Tennesseans and Crossland's Kentuckians forward. They pushed the Federals back about a mile before Mower and Bouton repulsed them, a job made easier by the weakened state of the attackers. They suffered more from the heat than the enemy's bullets. Forrest said, "But few men were killed or wounded in this engagement, but I found the road strewn with men fainting under the oppressive heat, hard labor, and want of water." Buford said he had eighty men struck down by heat stroke and carried to the rear, "perfectly exhausted, most of whom were insensible."[27]

The Confederates apparently did not know that the Federals were in motion, retreating in the direction of Memphis. Smith had discovered that he was low on artillery ammunition, and his bread rations, which he had believed to be abundant, had spoiled. He was down to one day's ration per man. He decided that it was "a matter of necessity" to end his campaign and return to Memphis. The damage Grierson's men had done to the Mobile & Ohio would have to be enough. General Lee later scoffed at Smith's reason for retiring, at least as far as the matter of rations was concerned. Lee said that Smith "was in a corn region and his troops killed, wantonly, enough cattle to have furnished beef for his command." Be that as it may, Smith was leaving his works, and Buford had been fighting what amounted to an infantry screen for the withdrawal. Shelby Foote says it was a "curious spectacle," to see a winning army "retreating from a field on which it had inflicted nearly twice as many casualties as it suffered and being harassed on the march by a loser reduced to less than half the strength of the victor it was pursuing."[28]

And harass them on the march they did. Lee turned command of the pursuit over to Forrest, who, when unleashed, experienced a wonderful return of his usual zeal. He sent Buford after Smith, with McCulloch's brigade of Chalmers's division following. Once again, Roddey had the lightest duty of the day. He and his division, augmented by Rucker's brigade, "were left behind to guard Tupelo from an enemy they believed to be retiring in the opposite direction." All afternoon, Buford's horsemen fought Grierson's troopers, the Federal rearguard.[29]

The Federal cavalry had not been heavily engaged at Tupelo, but they had been busy; they had destroyed nearly twenty miles of the Mobile & Ohio Railroad between Verona and Saltillo. Major F.M. Malone and a detachment of the 7th Kansas had destroyed the bridges and water tanks north of Tupelo and Colonel Datus E. Coon led a separate detail that the burned bridges and trestles south of the town. Until now, neither they nor any of their mounted comrades had seen any real fighting, but on this day they fought a running skirmish with Rebel cavalry to Old Town Creek, where, though his army had come only four miles and it was still afternoon, Smith had decided to bivouac for the night. Mower and the First Division had crossed the creek when Buford's artillery began lobbing shells from a hill above. As the shells flew, Buford sent Bell's and Crossland's brigades charging down the hill. Parson says, "In those brief, fleeting minutes, Lee's army came closer than at any point in the campaign of repeating the successes of Brice's Crossroads. And just as quickly it was over—the Federals refused to panic." General Mower re-crossed the creek to help Moore meet the threat. They formed a battle line, a Union battery set up, and the contest was on.[30]

After thirty minutes of fighting a more determined foe than expected, Buford was on the point of retiring. Then some of Chalmers's men began to arrive. They quickly deployed. Forrest came up on their heels and said he "found General Chalmer [sic] and General Buford hotly engaged." He was riding across the field, giving orders, adjusting the placement of regiments and batteries, when a bullet struck him in the right foot, inflicting one of the most painful of the many wounds he suffered during the war. He went down and word spread among the men that he had been killed. Chalmers took command while Forrest was helped to the rear to have his wound cleaned and wrapped. Knowing the disheartening effect the rumor of a general killed could have on fighting men, he did not take time to rest at the field station. As soon as his wound was dressed, he remounted and joined them for the retreat. Robert M. Browning says that when the Wizard appeared among his men with a bandaged foot but alive, the effect was "indescribable. They seemed wild with joy at seeing their great leader was still with them."[31]

The next day, Smith continued in the direction of La Grange, the Confederates following. His men were on short rations, perhaps because foraging was left so poor by their earlier passage, during which, Chalmers charged, the Yankees had killed cattle from "mere wantonness," leaving the carcasses to rot "in private yards and on the public thoroughfares." It did not end with that. Chalmers said, "Every species of vandalism was committed. Not only were non-combatant citizens maltreated, their homes rifled of clothing, money, and other valuables, besides the theft of every pound of bacon and every ounce of meal, but the same course of rapine and cruelty was shown toward unprotected widows and orphans, who were stripped of their all, and in many cases turned out of doors, with nothing left them save the wearing apparel upon their persons." Forrest also mentioned in his report "the desolation and ruin which everywhere marks the invader's tracks," and he took note of a greater sorrow. He said that the battles with General Smith had "cost the best blood of the South."[32]

To be exact, it had cost the blood of 1326 Southern men killed and wounded. Buford's division accounted for forty percent of the casualties. Crossland lost 306 out of eight hundred engaged, Bell lost 400, and Mabry 291.

The Federals had lost 674, almost exactly half that of the Confederates. They had burned Ripley, much of Tupelo, and what was left of Harrisburg. They had destroyed almost twenty miles of the M&O Railroad and had picked the country bare. They had kept Forrest in Mississippi for a few more weeks, and, more importantly, they had permanently broken his power. Edwin Bearss says, "Although Forrest would rally his force and make a number of daring raids, never again would his corps be able to stand and fight Union infantry."[33]

In his report, General Smith cited his division commanders for their gallantry and ability and specifically named General Mower, who was "more fortunate than the others in being in the exact position where the hardest fighting occurred, and nobly bore the brunt and deserves the bays." He paid a similar honor to one brigade commander and his men. Smith said, "The colored brigade, under Colonel Bouton, fought excellently well, and showed the effect of discipline and drill, and I am free to confess that their action has removed from my mind a prejudice of twenty years' standing." The general also referred to the death of Colonel Wilkin, saying, "He died as a soldier may, at his post on the field of battle ... his many noble traits had endeared him to all."[34]

Smith's opposite number never wrote a report of Tupelo, and that was unusual and perhaps revealing. Lee's biographer, Herman Hattaway, notes that "this was the only engagement on which Lee wrote no official report." Years passed before Lee did finally speak and write of the battle. When he did, he detailed the "blunders and mistakes that complicated matters." First, Forrest "should have had supreme command." Secondly, "the precipitate charge of the Kentuckians; they drew on themselves the fire of both wings of the Union army before the troops on right and left of them were up." Thirdly, "Gen. Forrest changed the plan of battle by withdrawing Roddey [which] caused all the artillery in the Federal third division, several batteries in all, and most of the infantry, to fire continuously into the flank of the brigades of the Confederate left wing."[35]

General Forrest did write an after-action report, and, as has been seen, he put the best face on things throughout and in the end claimed credit for saving more of Mississippi from the ravages of Smith's army. The "greatest soldier of his time" showed an unsavory smallness of character in the days following Tupelo. He never had the grace to admit his many contributions to the disaster. Instead, as he wheeled around the Confederate camp, his slow-to-heal foot resting on the dashboard of his buggy, he shifted all responsibility for the Confederate defeat at Tupelo onto the shoulders of others. To all who would listen Forrest said, "This [was] not my fight, boys."[36]

Despite his efforts to shed the blame, Forrest surely knew that his performance at Tupelo had been far below his usual standards. His personal pride was bruised, and his patriotism must have burned to think that the Yankees had handled Southern troops so roughly. However, there soon came a sequel to the Tupelo Campaign in which Forrest removed some of the tarnish that had attached to his record after Tupelo.

A story was circulating that Forrest had died of lockjaw, a result of his foot wound, but General Sherman did not quite believe it. He ordered General Washburn to send Smith back out. Uncle Billy had been unhappy with the sudden termination of the Tupelo expedition, and now he said that Smith must take to the field again, pick up Forrest's trail, and "keep after him till recalled by me or General Grant." It was an open-ended assignment, the goal of which was to run Forrest to ground or, failing that, to keep him out of Tennessee, an objective of "vital importance" to Sherman.[37]

The order was issued, General Smith informed his subordinates to prepare their brigades to march, and long blue columns soon began converging on the staging area, Holly Springs. Smith had ten thousand infantry and four thousand cavalry behind him. Their destination was Columbus, Mississippi, that town on the end of an M&O spur line that had so often been the safe depository for equipment and papers when the Yankees threatened. By August 10, they had forced the Confederates south of Oxford. Forrest realized he could not outfight Smith with the depleted numbers at his command, but he could out-strategize him and in that way defeat his expedition. The plan he developed was three-fold: he would leave Chalmers and Buford to occupy Smith, he would send a small strike force of two regiments to destroy infrastructure in Smith's rear, and he, Forrest, would lead a picked group of men around Smith's flank and make a raid on Memphis.

On the evening of August 18, Forrest set out with 1600 men. At 3:00 a.m. on August 21, he and his raiders entered the southern edge of Memphis. Hours of mayhem followed. By the time they rode out at 9:00, they had captured a herd of three hundred horses and mules, taken four hundred prisoners, and thrown such a scare into the Union high command that, when word of the raid reached General Smith, he terminated his expedition and turned back toward Memphis.

Forrest had won a great game of bluff. The Wizard had saved the Mobile & Ohio Railroad by attacking in the opposite direction. He soon after received a message from Major General Maury, who had temporarily succeeded General Lee as head of the Department of Alabama, Mississippi, and East Louisiana. Maury wired Forrest, "You have again saved Mississippi. Come and help Mobile."[38]

CHAPTER ELEVEN

Grierson and Hood on the M&O

Forrest started down the M&O for Mobile, as General Maury instructed, but he had barely begun his journey when he learned that Lieutenant General Richard Taylor had succeeded Maury as chief of the Department of Alabama, Mississippi, and East Louisiana, and Taylor wanted to see him in Meridian. Forrest detrained there and went to Taylor's headquarters. Mobile was safe enough for the time being, Taylor told him, but his help was needed at once in Tennessee.

A little background is in order. General Sherman had occupied Atlanta on September 2. Three weeks later, General John Bell Hood, sitting with the Army of Tennessee outside of Atlanta, slipped away and raced north in an attempt to draw the Federals away from the city and, if things went well, out of Georgia. Sherman was taken completely by surprise, but he quickly recovered to give chase, always a little behind as Hood moved up the Western & Atlantic Railroad, picking off one prize after another.

To cripple the opposing Yankees and aid Hood in his ambitious campaign, Taylor wanted Forrest to commence his long-looked-for chance to raid along Sherman's railroad supply lines in Tennessee. Forrest returned north, assembled his command, and struck out in late September. He spent the next two weeks gobbling up blockhouses and their garrisons one after the other and tearing up all the railroad, bridges, and trestles in between.

Sherman claimed not to be overly alarmed at either Hood's or Forrest's activities, but he knew that he could not allow them to roam at will, especially Hood, who had 35,000 men. He sent General George H. Thomas to Nashville to deal with the danger on that end while he pressed Hood from behind, following him north over the same route he had followed south a few months before. He later explained, "I had little fear of the enemy's cavalry damaging our roads seriously, for they rarely made a break which could not be repaired in a few days; but it was absolutely necessary to keep General Hood's infantry off our main route of communication and supply."[1]

It was necessary, but it was an annoyance. Sherman had proposed making a destructive, punitive march from Atlanta to the seacoast, and this was interfering with his preparations. He learned while following Hood through northern Georgia that his colorful scheme had been approved, and he became even more eager to return to Atlanta. When the Confederates veered west into Alabama in the third week in October, Sherman followed only a short distance more before breaking off the pursuit. Hood appeared to have made a self-defeating detour into a country where he could do no harm, and if his Confederates turned again and went north, General Thomas would meet them at Nashville, where he was gathering what would finally be an aggregate of forty thousand men. Tennessee was safe. Sherman returned to Atlanta, where he had his own business to attend to.

Hood continued west. He moved farther into Alabama than originally intended, looking for a place where General Forrest could cross the flooded Tennessee River to join him. It was not until he reached the area of Florence, Alabama, that he called a halt. Sherman was glad to see Hood land there. He wrote to Grant, "The country round about Florence has been again and again devastated during the past three years, and [the Confederates] must be dependent on the Mobile and Ohio Railroad, which has been broken and patched up to its whole extent." As Uncle Billy predicted, supplies soon became a problem for the Confederates. Over the next month, Hood divided his time between Florence and Tuscumbia, which he intended to be his supply base. On October 30, he wrote to Lieutenant General Taylor, "I am here, and need at once twenty day's supply of breadstuffs and salt, with some forage for the supply train animals…. Can't the cars on the Mobile and Ohio Railroad run directly to Cherokee so as to avoid reshipment [on the M&C] at Corinth?" The next day he sent almost identical messages to L.J. Fleming and to the quartermaster at Meridian, Major George Whitfield. Their answers, apparently lost to history, are revealed by Hood's next message to Taylor, dated November 1: "The Mobile and Ohio Railroad refuse to send rolling stock enough to supply the wants of the service on the road from Corinth here. It is most important that this should be at once attended to. General Beauregard desires that you will take measures promptly to put the Mobile and Ohio and Memphis and Charleston Railroads to work together and secure enough cars and motive power."[2]

General Beauregard had become the superior of both Hood and Taylor in October, when President Davis appointed him commander of the Military Division of the West, a command that encompassed Alabama, Mississippi, as well as parts of Louisiana, Georgia, and Tennessee. In spite of past failures, Beauregard's return was well received by the men. Charles

Todd Quintard, a chaplain in the army said, "The General was very popular with his troops and his name was a tower of strength." Restored now to command, Beauregard had to balance the demands against the abilities of two armies and the two railroads that served them. All complaints landed on his desk. On November 1, M&O superintendent L.J. Fleming wrote to General Beauregard regarding the demands Hood was making on his railroad. Fleming said, "I fear you have greatly over-estimated the capacity and condition of this railroad to transport the supplies for General Hood's Army." The Mobile & Ohio was in a rickety condition. Fleming explained that the bridges to Okolona had been destroyed by the enemy "and recently only patched up to pass a few trains of supplies for General Forrest, and are liable to be swept away by freshets which we may soon expect." In addition, the cross-ties on the M&O "are so much decayed that three trains ran off yesterday, and the track will be still worse in rainy weather." He concluded, "I have called upon General Taylor for additional labor, and will use every effort to forward the supplies, but deem it due you to advise you of the true condition of the road."[3]

Hood's campaign was stalled, and while he waited on the south bank of the Tennessee the chances became even more remote that his expedition into Tennessee—once it got off—would result in permanent gains. Abraham Lincoln was re-elected on November 8, 1864. The North had spoken and the last hope of the Confederacy to achieve separation from the United States disappeared except in the hearts of the most militant. The hopes for a negotiated peace were dashed, and the Southern states no longer had the strength to win the ultimate victory on the field of battle. As the President said in another context, the Confederacy was being "extinguished by mere friction and abrasion—by the mere incidents of war." The only choice before the military and political leaders of Dixie was whether to fight on in the name of honor or to surrender in order to preserve Southern lives.[4]

The Southern leaders decided to fight on. Manpower was critically short in their dying country, but Southerners continued to produce and stockpile a surprising amount of foodstuffs. W.H. Dameron, Chief Commissary of Subsistence for Mississippi, had reported at different points along the Mobile & Ohio Railroad back in August: 1104 beeves; 227,617 pounds of bacon; 63,108 bushels of flour; 59,664 pounds of meal; 41,444 pounds of beans; 9585 pounds of rice; 1319 bushels of wheat; 31,158 pounds of sugar; 10,288 bushels of corn; 327,512 pounds of salt; 120 bushels of peas; 151 bushels of oats; 12, 650 pounds of hard bread; and 104 gallons of whiskey. The problem was not so much a lack of sustenance, but the impossibility of keeping the supply lines functional, and this was proving to be the greatest stumbling block to Hood's invasion of Tennessee. He said, "I was constrained to await repairs upon the railroad before a sufficient amount of supplies could be received to sustain the Army till it was able to reach Middle Tennessee."[5]

As important as the M&O Railroad still was as a lifeline, it was not receiving the necessary support from the government. In July, after Smith's expedition to Tupelo, L.J. Fleming wrote to Lieutenant Colonel F.W. Sims, the Chief of the Railroad Bureau in Richmond. Fleming protested the removal of the officer who had been responsible for "auditing and paying Rail Road accounts," and he added, "Please say to the Quartermaster General also that this Company has not been paid for several months, and as nearly our whole earnings are for Government transportation, and the large expenditures and small receipts consequent upon the Sherman Raid made it necessary to borrow money to pay the expenses of operating the road."[6]

While Richmond neglected the railroad, General Beauregard was doing all he could locally to solve the railroad's disabilities so that it could meet Hood's needs. From his headquarters in Tuscumbia, he assured Hood on November 2 that "General Taylor has been instructed to impress the number of laborers required by Major Fleming, chief engineer and general superintendent Mobile and Ohio Railroad." The shortage of skilled workers was particularly sharp. The railroad advertised in the local papers for blacksmiths, boiler makers, and machinists, and Fleming was even given authority to obtain the release of prisoners who had been mechanics. On the 15th, Beauregard wired Hood, "All orders for completing the defenses of Corinth, repairing and prosecuting vigorously the work on the M. and C. RR to this place, and for repairing the M. and O. RR from Okolona to Bethel, have been given, and are being carried out as rapidly as the limited means of the engineer and quartermaster's departments will permit. It is at present reported that the railroads referred to will be completed in from fifteen to twenty days; but it is not unreasonable to suppose that the prevailing unfavorable weather will delay the work one or two weeks longer."[7]

Hood did not have to wait one or two weeks longer before the metaphorical logjam at Florence was broken. General Stephen D. Lee's corps arrived, and Forrest managed to cross the Tennessee River at last. His cavalry corps came up on November 18, and the next day Hood's columns stepped off for the bountiful region of middle Tennessee. They drove hard. Beauregard was pushing Hood because of events in Georgia. Sherman had marched eastward from Atlanta on November 15, and Beauregard sent his general in the field an urgent dispatch on November 24: "Sherman's movement is progressing rapidly towards Atlantic Coast, doubtless to re-enforce Grant. It is essential you should take offensive and crush enemy's force in Middle Tennessee soon as practicable, to relieve Lee." Two disastrous battles followed. Franklin on November 30 and Nashville on December 15–16, ended all hopes for Hood. After the second day at Nashville, the Army of Tennessee ceased to exist as a cohesive fighting force. The survivors stumbled and staggered in disorganized clots of men along the winter roads south, hammered repeatedly by the Federals as they ran.[8]

What remained of Hood's command crossed the Tennessee River on December 27. They were making for Corinth, that poor, battered town that had seen so much of the war. For the past month, Corinth had been built up as "one of the main depots of this army." Beauregard had ordered Colonel William B. Wade, commanding there, to "prepare Corinth for a desperate defense against any force of the enemy which may attack it," to hold it "to the last extremity," and to "give all the assistance possible in guarding the Mobile and Ohio and Memphis and Charleston Railroads." At the same time, the Federals were determined to sever Hood's source of provisions. Even before his withdrawal from Nashville, they began thinking of ways to foil his retreat. On December 5, 1864, General Thomas at Nashville wrote to General Halleck, "If an expedition could be started from Memphis against the Mobile and Ohio Railroad, and thus cut off Hood's means of supply, he will run the risk of losing his whole army, if I am successful in holding him back." The next day, Halleck wrote the commanding officer at Memphis, "You will immediately endeavor to cut the Mobile and Ohio Railroad so that Hood's army cannot be supplied by that route." Two weeks later, the commanding officer at Memphis, Major General Napoleon J.T. Dana, wrote to Halleck, "In obedience to your orders I have today sent all the effective cavalry, without a wheel accompanying them to strike the Mobile and Ohio Railroad above Tupelo." The leader of the expedition was a familiar figure along the M&O RR, General Benjamin Grierson.[9]

Grierson led three brigades—about three thousand men—out of Memphis on December 21. They carried 120 rounds of ammunition per man and twenty days' rations on pack animals; no wagons would hinder or delay this raid. The traveling conditions were enough of a hindrance, even on horseback. Grierson said, "For several days after leaving Memphis the ground was frozen enough to form a crust to the deep winter mud, but not sufficient in strength to bear up the horses and pack-mules. The march was therefore tiresome, and much impeded near the streams and bottom lands. Many shoes were pulled from the feet of the horses and mules by frozen mud and the ice. The legs of animals were frequently cut, sprained, and otherwise injured." Those animals that were too injured to continue were abandoned and replaced by horses and mules stolen from the locals along the line of march.[10]

They reached Ripley on December 24. From there, Grierson sent two detachments out. The first, 150 men of the 2nd New Jersey Cavalry under

Major Philip L. Van Rensselaer, went to strike the Mobile & Ohio at Booneville, while the 4th Illinois, under Captain A.T. Search, went to tear up the M&O at Guntown. Between them, they destroyed "4 bridges, 8 or 10 culverts, several miles of the track and telegraph, and a large quantity of army supplies," before rejoining the main column en route to Tupelo. The riding became easier now. Grierson said that beyond Ripley "the rains were not so heavy or continuous, the mud was not so deep, the sun occasionally shone out, and the clouds were not so thick and dark."[11]

On Christmas Day, at Old Town Creek, Grierson learned that there was a Rebel camp and supply dump at Verona. The general ordered Colonel Joseph Kargé to lead his brigade there to disperse the enemy and destroy the stores. Grierson said, "Our movements thus far had been rapid, and the indications were that the enemy had no knowledge of our presence," so he did not expect Kargé to run into any difficulties. It was raining again the night that Kargé and his brigade set out on their mission. They kept to the road, finding their way by the flashing lightning. About one mile from their destination, they came upon the enemy's picket line. They drove the pickets back and charged into town, but "owing to the darkness of the night, the enemy, numbering from 200 to 300 men, made his escape." Kargé's men went to the work of destroying Confederate stores right away. They found "450 English carbines; 500 Austrian rifles; 200 boxes of ammunition for carbines and rifles; a large amount of fixed ammunition for artillery and shells, the explosions of which commenced at 10 p.m. and did not cease until 5 o'clock the next morning." They discovered two hundred wagons marked "U.S.A." (some of the captured vehicles from Sturgis's defeat at Brice's Crossroads) loaded with "provisions, clothing, and other supplies" and waiting to be sent to General Hood's army, which was falling back after its defeat outside of Nashville. Kargé's raiding party also found and destroyed a train of twenty cars and eight large warehouses filled with "a large quantity of saddles, quartermaster's and commissary stores." They cut the Verona telegraph line and uprooted some lengths of railroad track and turned back toward Harrisburg the next morning.[12]

Grierson had made camp on Christmas night between Old Town Creek and Tupelo. He ordered the 11th Illinois to destroy the M&O bridge over the creek and the track from there to Tupelo. They worked through the rainy night and by morning had rendered the railroad between the two locations "a complete wreck." On the 26th, with all the different detachments returned, the whole column moved south along the M&O. Grierson said, "The destruction of the railroad between Tupelo and Okolona was especially assigned to Colonel [Embury D.] Osband's brigade. Nearly two days were occupied in accomplishing that important work, besides which two trains of twenty-three cars, one wagon train of twenty wagons all loaded with army supplies, and two storehouses filled with quartermaster, commissary, and ordnance stores were captured and destroyed at or between those stations." They had come sixty-five miles from Ripley when Grierson called a halt at a point just south of Okolona.[13]

The Confederates had known since December 22 that the Federals were moving toward the Mobile & Ohio. On December 24, Major General Franklin Gardner, commanding the District of Mississippi and East Louisiana, issued orders to his scattered troops in the field to begin concentrating their troops on the M&O in the vicinity of Tupelo. Major John S. Hope, Assistant Inspector General of the Department of Alabama, Mississippi, and East Louisiana, was sent by Lieutenant General Taylor to take overall command of the defense.

Major Hope traveled to Meridian and was waiting there on December 26, when a troop train arrived from the south with seven hundred infantry and one battery. Hope discovered, to his dismay, they had come with no ammunition. He drew seventeen boxes from the chief ordnance officer in Meridian and moved by the cars up the Mobile & Ohio toward Tupelo. They arrived at West Point late on the afternoon of the 26th. Major Hope learned there that the enemy were nearer than he expected; they were moving down the railroad toward Okolona. He wired the information to General Taylor, who ordered him to continue north; more men and ammunition would come on the railroad to join him tomorrow. His force augmented by these reinforcements from Mobile, Hope would check the enemy in the vicinity of Okolona until General Gardner could arrive.

Hope and his command left West Point about 11:00 p.m., but the unrepaired damage the enemy had done to the M&O in earlier raids became a factor in his advance. The railroad agent informed Hope that there was no water tank north of West Point, so someone "would have to bail water in order to get to Okolona." Hope spoke to the local officer in charge, who provided a bailing detail. The water tank was filled or nearly so, and they proceeded up the track. When the engine ran short of water in spite of their efforts, the engineer uncoupled the cars and took the locomotive alone to Okolona to get water and then return. Apparently, there was enough water to power an engine that was not straining against the weight of a train of cars behind. Major Hope accompanied the engineer and learned at Okolona that the Federal cavalry, numbering upwards of 2500 men, was camped only a few miles north. Nothing was between the invaders and Okolona except a meager force under General Samuel J. Gholson, and they were reduced to the role of mere observers because they had no ammunition. Hope sent a courier to inform Gholson that he and his troops were nearby. While waiting for a reply, he ordered the removal of fourteen railcars south to Egypt; they "were of more value to the company than the defense of the track." Hope went with them, reported what he had learned at Okolona, and then dispatched 270 men to a bridge about two miles south of Okolona with orders to fall back to Egypt Station "should the enemy make a demonstration on either flank." Hope had decided that Okolona was not the place to make his stand.[14]

Grierson's raiders advanced without opposition to Okolona, where they destroyed the Mobile & Ohio depot and five other buildings filled with supplies. While his men went about their work, Grierson tapped into the telegraph line and intercepted messages from General Taylor and General Gardner to Major Hope. At the same time, some deserters from Egypt Station came into the Federal lines. They were former prisoners of Andersonville who had agreed to fight for the South in return for their release from the Georgia hellhole. At the first chance, they had abandoned their new army and come back to their first with important information. From these sources, the telegraph and the prodigal sons of the North, Grierson developed a picture of the Confederate deployment and learned that reinforcements were on their way to join Hope, five hundred infantry coming up from Mobile and expected to arrive no later than 5:30 the next morning, December 28. Grierson, knowing army ways, had no fear that they would arrive that early, but he did intend to attack Major Hope before the reinforcements appeared.

He advanced on the morning of the 28th with Colonel Kargé and the First Brigade leading the way. About 7:30, they bumped into the Confederate skirmishers a half mile north of Egypt. Kargé ordered the reliable 2nd New Jersey Cavalry to charge, which they did with such "impetuosity" that they drove not only the first but also the second skirmish lines back through the town to the enemy's works at the M&O depot. They saw that the Rebel line was arrayed around a fort "and flanked by railroad earth embankments." The fort Kargé saw was the house of the railroad section master which was enclosed by a stockade. The Mobile *Register and Advertiser* described the odd arrangement, "For want of rails for a fence in his lot, the section master had collected the partially decayed cross-ties and set them endwise in the ground, about two feet deep, which left them about six feet above the ground." The Federals also saw on the tracks nearby a train that included a platform car on which there was a four-gun battery.[15]

Kargé arrayed his men in line of battle and charged. He said, "I ordered Captain [Joel H.] Elliott to take the 7th Indiana Cavalry and 4th Missouri Cavalry to capture the train, which was about to move off, and which annoyed my line by opening with shell and solid shot from a battery." Grierson appeared at the front while Kargé was fighting. He took charge of the right wing while Kargé moved to oversee the action on the left. The left dislodged the Rebel defenders from their position, but the five hundred graybacks inside the stockade had not budged. Kargé sent four mounted and three dismounted companies to flank the fort on either side and drive them out. They pushed forward through the continuing fire from the battery on the platform car and poured "such a galling fire ... upon the enemy that he surrendered."[16]

The Mobile *Register and Advertiser* made no admission of Kargé's claim that the Confederates surrendered because they were outfought. It said instead that the men inside the stockade poured "destructive volleys into the enemy until the last cartridge was shot away." The defenders had lost only because they run out of ammunition (a plausible explanation, considering what Major Hope had reported earlier). The newspaper did admit that the section master's house was "perforated with balls," but said the "inmates of this house, Mrs. Kellian and Mrs. Brown, remained in-doors all the time, and strange to say received no injury."[17]

While the fight at the stockade was going on, Colonel Osband and the Third Brigade had come up on the right. Colonel Gholson was in front of them. The platform car battery was still firing and Gholson and his men "were inflicting great loss to the Fourth Missouri Cavalry from the shelter of a railroad embankment, without danger to themselves." The 4th Missouri and the 4th Illinois prepared to charge and drive Gholson away. Osband said, "The revolver and saber were freely used by our men, 15 or 20 of the enemy being either killed or wounded, including Brigadier-General Gholson, mortally wounded." The enemy was routed and the victors moved to join the fight against the stockade, but it surrendered before they could engage.[18]

Numerous reports besides Kargé's claimed that Gholson had been killed or had suffered a mortal wound, all of them wrong. He did suffer a wound that cost him his right arm, and he became one of the five hundred Confederates captured at the end of the battle; the number killed is undetermined. The Federals lost twenty-two killed, 101 wounded, and "about 100 horses disabled or killed in action, which however were replaced by those captured from the enemy." None of the losses came from Colonel Edward F. Winslow's Second Brigade, which had come up too late from the rear of the Federal column to take part in the battle. General Grierson threw open the supply house doors and "the poor people of the place were allowed to help themselves to necessaries from the rebel government supplies, which they did with great alacrity; the remainder was entirely destroyed." The defeated Rebels were falling back toward West Point along with what was left of the railroad train. It had found itself unable to move until it abandoned eight cars, along with their passengers, who soon became prisoners. As the short little train steamed south, it was pursued by Grierson's chief of staff, Captain Samuel L. Woodward of the

6th Illinois, "a young officer but brave and cool." The Memphis *Bulletin* reported, "For two miles the gallant gentleman and his men held up to the train, [in] spite of the battery in the platform cars, which was plentifully used. Horseflesh, however, could not hold out against steam, and the train escaped."[19]

About five miles south of Egypt Station, the retreating Confederates came upon the long-awaited reinforcements, Lieutenant Colonel William W. Weir and about 350 infantrymen of the 1st Confederate Volunteers. Like Hope's men, they had been delayed "by being obliged to supply water for the engine at Prairie Station by means of buckets." Colonel Weir reported that he "immediately moved up the railroad at a double quick to an eminence about half a mile in front. When I gained this position the enemy were formed and moving down upon me, my skirmishers already firing on them. They then moved around my right flank, causing me to change my front. From this position they bore down upon me at full gallop. My men were steady and cool, and with a well-directed fire scattered them in every direction. They then fell back to their former position near Egypt, but in full view." Both sides dug in and glared at the other across the way for two hours before the Federals faded back.[20]

The enemy appeared to be building up in Grierson's front, and that concerned him, but that was not all. There was a force of 350 infantry under Colonel J.C. Cole coming up behind him from Corinth. They had set out by train the day before, December 27, and got to within a mile of Tupelo before they were brought to a halt by a burned railroad bridge and a half mile of "turned over" track—some of Grierson's handiwork. They continued the next morning on foot along the route of the railroad, finding very little additional damage until they reached Shannon. From there to Okolona, the M&O was "very badly damaged, thirteen bridges and culverts burned; some of the bridges (and very important ones) are very severely injured." They were slowed, but still coming, and Hope and Weir remained in front, and it did not take an imaginative mind to conclude that others must be on their way. Until now, Grierson had planned to continue south along the Mobile & Ohio, but the increasing numbers of Confederates converging on Egypt persuaded him, as Ballard says, "that he must forget Alabama and head for Vicksburg." In his report, Grierson gave no hint that he was intimidated by the numbers of the enemy gathering against him. He merely said, "Having secured about 500 prisoners, cared for the dead and wounded, and destroyed all Government property, I moved due west to Houston."[21]

General Grierson also did not mention what was later reported, that he left behind thirty-five wounded when the column left Egypt on the afternoon of December 28. Three days later, on December 31, Dr. F.H.

Evans and at least part of his medical staff arrived in Egypt to remove the wounded. He had left West Point the day before, "carrying with me one acting assistant surgeon, three hospital stewards, and sixty litter-bearers." They had had an easy trip on the M&O until they came upon a break about a mile and a half south of their destination. Everyone was learning that travel on the Mobile & Ohio had become a slow proposition; the tracks were like a line of disconnected dashes. Dr. Evans ordered fifteen of his litter-bearers to begin repairing the damage while he and the rest hiked into Egypt. There, they found thirty-five Federals, most of them seriously wounded, and seven Confederates quartered in nearby homes turned into temporary hospitals. A Federal surgeon named Krauter was in charge of the Northern soldiers. The Confederate surgeon, Evans, began removing the wounded of both sides to the train, the worst of them carried on litters. They were placed aboard the cars and made as comfortable as possible for the trip, but there was a delay before they could begin their return south. Evans said, "The engine having exhausted its supply of water, and there being no tanks between Egypt and this point [West Point], we had to bail water, and were six hours *in transitu*." They arrived at West Point so late in the night that it was decided after a consultation that included the Yankee doctor to leave the wounded on the train overnight; it would cause them more suffering to try and move them than to leave them where they rested. Stewards fed the convalescents and put fresh dressings on their wounds. The next morning they were removed to another train and transferred to the hospital in Columbus, Mississippi. Dr. Krauter went along to oversee the care of the wounded of his own army.[22]

By that time, Colonel J.C. Cole's column had crews of impressed slaves repairing the damage to the Mobile & Ohio near Okolona. He and his men had entered on December 29. He found that the railroad water tank was burned, "but otherwise no serious injury to the railroad was done"; a dubious claim considering that the town itself had certainly felt the Yankees' wrath. "All the business portion of the town was burned, and one private dwelling." Reviewing what he had seen between Tupelo and Okolona, Cole reported, "I cannot form my estimate of the length of time it will take to repair the railroad, but I consider the damage done to it very serious … every effort should be made to push it through as rapidly as possible." To that end, he had set the slaves to work. He added that his information was that the enemy was headed west.[23]

While the Confederates were repairing damage that Grierson had left behind on the Mobile & Ohio, he was inflicting even more pain along the Mississippi Central. He sent detachments to feint toward Pontotoc, West Point, and other stations along the M&O, but his direction was west astride the MC. The skirmishes that broke out along the way did not significantly hinder the horse soldiers' progress. They reached Vicksburg on January 5, 1865. Grierson said he arrived "with my entire command in good condition with about 600 prisoners, 800 head of captured stock, and 1000 negroes, who joined the column during the march." Grierson's Third Brigade commander, Colonel Edward F. Winslow, observed, "The labor of destroying railroads is quite severe," but Grierson's men had overcome the severities to destroy: "20,000 feet of bridges and trestle-work (cut down and burned); 10 miles of track (rails bent and ties burned); 20 miles of telegraph (poles cut down and wire destroyed); 4 serviceable locomotives and tenders and 10 in process of repair; 95 railroad cars," as well as "over 30 warehouses filled with quartermaster, commissary, and ordnance stores; large cloth and shoe factories (employing 500 hands); several tanneries and machine shops; a steam pile-driver; 12 new forges; 7 depot buildings; 5000 stand of new arms; 700 head of fat hogs; 500 bales of cotton (marked 'C.S.A.'); immense amount[s] of grain, leather, wool, and other Government property, the value and quantity of which cannot be estimated." Summing up, he gave a self-evaluation of his December adventure as "one of the most successful expeditions of the war."[24]

The Northern press agreed with that appraisal. The New York *Times* lauded the destruction of wagons, weapons, and equipment earmarked for the use of Hood's army and especially the demolition of the Mobile & Ohio, "forty miles ... so badly damaged that Hood's whole army cannot repair it in months." The Chicago *Tribune* lavished praise on Grierson and said his expedition was "most brilliant and successful and in results must prove most disastrous to Hood's army, inasmuch as he procured his supplies over railroads destroyed by the expedition."[25]

To the east, John Bell Hood's hungry army was down to half-strength, something between fourteen thousand and eighteen thousand men, and he was calling for reinforcements, but manpower was desperately lacking, and Beauregard had to refuse him. Along with his refusal came a warning: "The enemy's cavalry has cut the Mobile and Ohio Railroad, and a large force is now moving on Corinth. This movement may possibly cut you off from your retrograde march via Corinth, and force you to adopt another route."[26]

The danger was exaggerated and Hood did not have to choose another course. He directed his tattered men to continue toward Corinth. Their suffering was intense. The hardworking nurse Mrs. Ella Palmer, who had traveled the length of Mississippi from Corinth to Fort Morgan to tend the Confederate sick and wounded, was working in the hospital in Iuka at this time. She remembered that a winter storm had hit northern Mississippi after Christmas, "the worse storm in years," and the sleet-covered snow was agonizing to the defeated army staggering toward Corinth. The men, she said, "were all in rags, and many without shoes; some had taken parts of their blankets and wrapped their bare, bleeding, frost-bitten feet to keep them off the ice-covered ground." Many of the men had not eaten in days. Mrs. Palmer "saw many officers walking along in tears because they were so discouraged, cold, and hungry. The hospital could not help them, as they had but very little food for the sick. The hospital supply of food was reduced to corn meal, coffee, rice, molasses, and bacon, and very little of these articles." Captain James L. Cooper of the 20th Tennessee remembered that they arrived in Corinth, soaking wet and half starved, on or about New Year's Day, 1865. He said, "The army was thoroughly demoralized, and only the semblance of discipline maintained."[27]

In Corinth, General Hood headquartered at the Verandah House, and his supplies were stockpiled in the Tishomingo Hotel. Some of the men were furloughed and went home, the rest camped east of town. The Federals did not expect Hood's army could remain in Corinth long, "as General Dana has broken the Mobile and Ohio Railroad for some distance below that point," and they did not. During the third week in January, said Cooper, "we received the welcome order to march, and through rain and mud started another retreat.... The infantry marched the greater part of the way on the railroad track, which was very hard on the feet." Many of the men remained shoeless. R.N. Rea, captain of the 13th Mississippi, remembered years later that he had marched barefoot all the way from Franklin, 250 miles. "I certainly came near freezing to death. I had no blanket, nothing but my sword and pistol." He added, "This part of my life as a soldier is so sad that I do not care to describe the retreat of the army from Nashville to Tupelo." He did remember, as did others, that he got a pair of shoes at Tupelo. Aside from that, Tupelo was not a particularly pleasant memory for anyone. Tennessean James L. Cooper said, "At Tupelo we found the whole country filled with soldiers.... My mess had no tent, and the greater part of the time nothing to eat, and we were altogether in a miserable fix."[28]

When General Beauregard saw the scraps of Hood's army at Tupelo on January 15, he "looked at the tattered, shattered ranks, the shot-torn flags and gunless batteries, and could scarcely recognize what he himself had once commanded." General Taylor, too, was at Tupelo to meet Hood's survivors. He said, "This was my first view of a beaten army ... and a painful sight it was. Many guns and small-arms had been lost, and the ranks were depleted by thousands of prisoners and missing. Blankets, shoes, clothing, and accoutrements were wanting ... it was now near [sic] January. Some men perished in frost; many had the extremities severely bitten. Fleming, the active superintendent [of the M&O] strained the resources of his railway to transport the troops to the vicinity of Meridian, where timber for shelter and fuel was abundant and supplies convenient, and every energy was exerted to reëquip them."[29]

The army was dispersed at Tupelo. According to Hood (who was relieved of command at his own request and left Tupelo on January 23), about nine thousand of the men deserted, about five thousand were sent to General Joseph E. Johnston in North Carolina, and about four thousand went to join General Maury at Mobile. These last made at least a part of their journey by rail. Captain R.N. Rea said, "Having secured transportation for my men and myself, we got on top of a box car (on the Mobile and Ohio Railroad) and, after having ridden one hundred and thirty miles in very cold weather, disembarked at Meridian." It was not only a cold ride, but also a sooty one. Smith Powell of the 36th Alabama said that his regiment traveled south on the cars to Mobile "where our first colonel, Robert Smith, met us at the depot. We were a sight to behold, black, begrimed with smoke and dust from the boxcars and from fires in the cars made out of pine plank."[30]

Thus ended the year of 1864, the most challenging year in all the troubled history of the Mobile & Ohio Railroad. So tumultuous was it that the board of directors issued the following statement: "The matter of holding an annual meeting of Stockholders and an election was the subject of conversation at the Board and the opinion was universally expressed that under present circumstances it was inexpedient to hold such a meeting." Consequently, there was no convention in the spring of 1865 and no report made for the year 1864. Stockholders had to wait until the next report, in April 1866, to learn how their company had fared. The result may have surprised them. The report gave a rudimentary summary of the figures for 1864 and showed that, even amidst the corporate, political, and military rubble, the railroad emerged with a profit, tiny though it was. The report said, "Our earnings for 1864, including express and mails, were $3,674,498.99. Our expenses, $2,281,596.38, leaving a net revenue of $1,392,902.11." This was on paper, of course, and did not include any calculation of debt or depreciation for the year. Nevertheless, that the M&O had earned any profit at all was a testimony of the vigor of an American corporation, even one that was trying to do business in an insurgent nation on the verge of defeat.[31]

Its physical damages notwithstanding, the Mobile & Ohio Railroad Company seemed at the moment to be in better condition that the government it served. But the endgame had begun and the question remained: could the railroad survive?

CHAPTER TWELVE

Last Stop
The Fall of Mobile

The Confederates' end had not yet come, but it was only a matter of time. The Federals could raid freely along the length of the M&O RR, break it at almost any point, and there was hardly any Rebel force north of Mobile worth supplying. The Federals controlled long stretches of the railroad, and, ironically, citizens depended on Northern stewardship of a Southern rail line for help in returning Confederate lives to some semblance of normalcy. In January 1865, General George H. Thomas, from headquarters of the Army of the Cumberland in Eastport, Mississippi, granted permission for the citizens of Tishomingo County "to run the Mobile and Ohio Railroad and the Memphis and Charleston Railroad within the limits of the county, strictly for the convenience of the citizens thereof. This privilege to be conditional on the roads being used solely for the private interests of the citizens of this county, to be void and null when this condition is broken."[1]

General Forrest replied to Thomas. He said that he would operate the trains in "good faith" with the Union general's conditions. "No Confederate soldiers or officers will be authorized or allowed to go upon these trains," he said. But he warned, "At the same time you are fully aware that the border is infested by lawless bands of deserters from both armies and in case they should force themselves upon the train I hope you will not act hastily in the matter." Forrest proposed that a "sufficient guard" be placed upon each train "to enforce a strict observance of the agreement." This, Thomas refused.[2]

Defending their remaining segments of the railroad had become nearly impossible for the Confederates. When, in January 1865, General Beauregard asked "whether the block-houses and small field-works for the protection of the bridges and trestles on the Mobile and Ohio Railroad have been constructed?" Major D. Wintter, engineer in charge of the military district, replied that "no block-houses or small field-works have been erected."[3]

Keeping the railroad functional was becoming nearly impossible for the government and the corporation alike. There was not only a lack of workers and mechanics, but also a shortage of funds. Most of the M&O's business was with the government, and the government was not paying its fares. In addition, the government was not honoring its commitment to pay for the repairs of war-related damage. On January 21, 1865, railroad president Milton Brown submitted to Brigadier General Alexander R. Lawton, the Quartermaster General in Richmond, a claim for damages incurred during Sherman's expedition, almost a year before, and Grierson's more recent raid. The accompanying cover letter said, in part, "The rebuilding of the destroyed portion of the road was ordered by Gen. Polk who under authority conferred on him from Richmond assumed the payment of all expenses. The rebuilding of the destroyed portion of the road was deemed essential to the operations of the Army, but was not expected to yield, and has not yielded any material benefit to the Company. Hence the agreement of the Government to pay the expenses."[4]

Brown said to Lawton, "You will confer a special favor by aiding us in having these accounts settled by the Government. As I explained to you in person, we are nearly run down, and cannot run the road six months longer without relief from the Government." He concluded with a mild admonition, "In payment of amounts due from the Government we have been constantly compelled to take bonds when we were not able to pay our expenses & keep up repairs of the road. We are reduced by repeated raids of the enemy and the immense destruction on our road, so that we must be paid promptly in Cash for amount due us. We have run the road almost entirely for the benefit of the army & have nearly sacrificed the road."[5]

The only secure stronghold left on the M&O was Mobile, and even its security was tentative. A Union spy reported conditions in Mobile, saying that there were no more than seven thousand defenders there, and perhaps as few as six thousand, not including the cavalry force east of the bay. Many of them were young boys and old men. "They are much dissatisfied, being mostly conscripts," he said. The thirty thousand civilians in Mobile were likewise dissatisfied, the spy said, and watched anxiously "for the Union force to take the city."[6]

Mobile had been under almost unendurable strain since August of the year before, when a joint operation of the Federal army and navy resulted in the loss of the forts guarding the entrance to the bay. The Union plan had first been developed on July 8, 1864, when Rear Admiral Farragut met on his flagship, the *Hartford*, with Major General Edward R.S. Canby and Major General Gordon Granger. Farragut's fleet would slip by Fort Morgan, which guarded the eastern side of the bay, while Granger's land forces (from Canby's department) moved forward to invest Fort Gaines, on the tip of Dauphin Island on the west.

Granger landed on Dauphin Island with upwards of two thousand men on the night of August 3 and immediately moved on the rear of Fort Gaines. When Fort Gaines's call for help arrived at Mobile, "every available man" was hurried forward. The reinforcements were a sacrificial offering, for unfolding events would soon leave them cut off and isolated and finally prisoners of war. Maury might have handled the emergency differently if he had been in Mobile, but his duties as department commander had called him up the M&O RR to Meridian. He later said of the men sent down from Mobile city, "They were too few to make the proposed [counter] attack, but were too many for the proper siege garrison of Fort Gaines."[7]

Farragut made his assault on August 5. The scene before him: "On the left, some three miles distant, was Fort Gaines, a small brick and earth work, mounting a few heavy guns, but too far away from the ship channel to cause much uneasiness to the fleet. Fort Morgan was on the right, one of the strongest of the old brick forts, and greatly strengthened by immense piles of sand-bags, covering every portion of the exposed front. The fort was well equipped with three tiers of heavy guns.... In addition, there was in front a battery of seven powerful guns, at the water's edge on the beach. All the guns, of both the fort and water battery, were within point-blank range of the only channel through which the fleet could pass." The approach was limited to this one useable channel because the Confederate engineers had arranged rows of pilings "which extended to deep water in the main ship channel. From this piling rows of torpedoes had been planted, extending nearly across the ship channel, their eastern limit being marked by a large [red] buoy. The channel between this buoy and Fort Morgan was left open for blockade runners, but being but a few hundred yards wide, forced every vessel using it close under the fort." Three Rebel gunboats and the ram *Tennessee* augmented the defenders' power.[8]

Shortly before 6:00 a.m., the Federal fleet was underway, the wooden ships moving forward in pairs, tethered side by side with sandbags piled on deck above the engines to protect them from plunging fire and a veil of chains draped over their vulnerable sides. The four Union ironclads took position "on the starboard side of the wooden ships, or between them and Fort Morgan for the double purpose of keeping down the fire from the water battery and the parapet guns of the fort, as well as to attack the ram *Tennessee* as soon as the fort was passed." At the last minute, Farragut yielded the lead position to the *Brooklyn*, "as she had four chase guns and an ingenious arrangement for picking up torpedoes."[9]

The ironclad *Tecumseh* fired a shot that exploded over Fort Morgan at a quarter to seven. Twenty-five minutes passed before the fort's gunners returned fire. The morning was soon "lively" with Confederate iron.

The flotilla continued forward through the fire of fifteen Rebel guns when the fast moving *Brooklyn* suddenly cut her speed; she was about to pass the ironclads. Farragut ordered her to proceed, but before she could, the *Tecumseh* struck an underwater mine and went straight to the bottom, along with Captain T.A.M. Craven and ninety-one men of her crew. Farragut sent the *Metacomet* to pick up the survivors. The *Brooklyn* was stalled, holding up the progress of the fleet, making it a stationary target for the gunners of the fort and of the Rebel boats that had come to join the fight. John Coddington Kinney wrote, "It was during these few perilous moments that the most fatal work of the day was done to the fleet." On Farragut's flagship, the *Hartford*, "men were being cut down by the score." Blood made the deck too slippery to stand upon and parts of men were strewn about. One man was decapitated. Another lost both legs and both arms. Farragut ordered the *Hartford* to steam forward into the lead position. He judged that plowing through the mine field was less dangerous than remaining abreast of Fort Morgan. Every crewman and officer of the squadron had seen the tragedy of the *Tecumseh*, but they followed the lead of the *Hartford*, "believing they were going to a noble death with their commander in chief." As the *Hartford* passed the *Brooklyn*, a warning was called out to Farragut to beware of the torpedoes. "Damn the torpedoes," he yelled, and the fleet continued forward at full steam.[10]

In order to see the action better, Farragut had climbed aloft. Secured by a rope in his perch, Farragut directed the course of the wooden ships through the mine field. Going forward was a calculated risk. Farragut said, "Believing that from their having been some time in the water, they were probably innocuous, I determined to take the chance of their explosion." Still, the danger from them was not zero. Witness the *Tecumseh*.[11]

Before the ships had cleared the fort, the Rebel ram *Tennessee* steamed close and sent two rounds into the *Brooklyn*. The

Rear Admiral David G. Farragut.

ships in position fired back at the *Tennessee* and some tried to ram her, but she was as invincible as the rumors had said. It was a surprise, then, when she broke off the attack and slipped behind Fort Morgan. Valuable time had been lost by the inertia of the *Brooklyn* and the attack of the *Tennessee,* but by eight o'clock the fleet was past the fort. A final, successful exchange of fire with the Confederate gunboats *Morgan, Gaines,* and *Selma,* seemed to put an end to the combat. Farragut ordered the squadron to anchor. The crews began washing the decks and clearing the debris while the cooks started breakfast and the surgeons treated the wounded. Then someone saw the *Tennessee* approaching. The Federal fleet raised anchor once more and steamed forward to meet her, "and then began one of the fiercest naval combats on record."[12]

Captain Miles D. McAlester of the Union navy said the *Tennessee* "was rammed six or eight times fairly, at good speed, by our heaviest ships, without effect. Whole broadsides of 9-inch and 11-inch shot were thrown upon her, producing no apparent injury, except the bending of some of her port shutters (made to slide up and down outside) and carrying away her smoke-stack." Another shot cut her rudder chain. After an hour of combat, the invincible *Tennessee* was in trouble.[13]

Aboard the *Tennessee,* Captain James D. Johnston took an inventory of his damages: "the two quarter-post covers had been so jammed by the fire of the enemy as to render it impracticable to remove them, and the relieving tackles had been shot away and the tiller unshipped from the rudderhead. The smoke pipe, having been completely riddled by shot, was knocked down close to the top of the shield by the concussion of vessels running into the ship. At the same time, the three [Federal] monitors were using their 11 and 15 inch solid shot against the after end of the shield, while the largest of the wooden vessels were pouring in separate broadsides" from only a few feet away. The Federal fire was incessant and the *Tennessee* could not reply, "as it was impossible to change the position of the vessel, and the steam was rapidly going down as a natural consequence of the loss of the smoke stack."[14]

Johnston went below to report the condition of his ship to Admiral Franklin Buchanan, who was lying wounded with a broken leg. Returning topside, Johnston "observed one of the heaviest vessels of the enemy in the act of running into us on the port quarter." This was the *Ossipee.* At the same time, "shot were fairly raining upon the after end of the shield, which was no so thoroughly shattered that in a few moments it would have fallen and exposed the gun-deck to a raking fire of shell and grape." Johnston said, "Realizing our helpless condition at a glance, and conceiving that the ship was now nothing more than a target for the heavy guns of the enemy, I concluded that no good object could be accomplished by sacrificing the lives of the officers and men in such a one-sided contest." Johnston hoisted the white flag, and the Battle of Mobile Bay came to an end.[15]

The army also won a small prize that day and set itself up to win a second, larger one. General Granger had opened fire in the morning as Farragut's fleet was beginning its action. His guns silenced the water batteries on Dauphin Island, and, that night, the Confederates evacuated Fort Powell. The garrison escaped to Cedar Point, but they left behind eighteen serviceable guns. Fort Gaines, still waited, but two days later, on the morning of August 7, the commander, Colonel C.D. Anderson opened negotiations for the surrender of his post. Farragut and Granger consulted and then informed Anderson that their only offer was: "First. The unconditional surrender of yourself and the garrison of Fort Gaines, with all of the public property within its limits. Second. The treatment which is in conformity with the custom of the most civilized nations toward prisoners of war. Third. Private property, with the exception of arms, will be respected."[16]

Since August 4, Brigadier General Richard L. Page, commander of Fort Morgan, had been urging Colonel Anderson of Fort Gaines and Colonel James M. Williams, commanding Fort Powell, to defend their side of the bay at all costs, but they let him down. Williams abandoned Fort Powell without a fight on the night of August 5 and now Anderson had, without authorization, begun a conversation with the enemy. Page tried continually and without success to learn what was happening until the morning of August 8, when he looked across the bay to see the United States flag flying over Fort Gaines. The next day, General Canby reported to the Chief-of-Staff in Washington, "Fort Gaines, with 46 commissioned officers and 818 enlisted men, with its armament, 26 guns intact, and provisions for twelve months, has surrendered unconditionally. It was occupied by our forces at eight o'clock yesterday morning."[17]

Only Fort Morgan remained. Canby expected General Granger to keep the pressure on, to maintain "the state of uneasiness now felt there." The land forces began the tedious work of besieging Fort Morgan, primarily a job of digging "approaches" under the supervision of the engineers. The Union sharpshooters were a constant menace to the cannon crews inside the fort. (Page said that "our guns had to be served with much care and under great difficulty.") Meanwhile, the fleet bombarded the fort at intervals, demonstrating that its "brick walls were easily penetrable to the heavy missiles of the enemy, and that a systematic, concentrated fire would soon breach them." One of the vessels firing on the fort was the captured *Tennessee*.[18]

A hurricane on the night of August 19–20 hindered the Federals' preparations temporarily, but by the evening of August 21 they had extended their works to within two hundred yards of Fort Morgan. August

21 was the day, incidentally, that Nathan Bedford Forrest made his raid on Memphis, a victory whose small size and scope did not offset the loss the South was about to suffer.

General Granger had twenty-two guns and sixteen mortars in position to blast Fort Morgan from behind while Farragut's ironclads and wooden gunboats assaulted it from the front. The commencement of what Farragut called a "magnificent fire" came at dawn on August 22. The bombardment continued through the day and "disabled all the heavy guns save two … partially breached the walls in several places, and cut up the fort to such extent as to make the whole work a mere mass of debris." Even after nightfall the Federal fire did not diminish, and "the wood-work of the citadel was fired by the mortar shells and burned furiously for some hours."[19]

The men inside Fort Morgan fought the fire and kept it from spreading, but they could not extinguish it. Fearful that his magazine would explode, Page had eighty thousand pounds of gunpowder carried out and drenched with water to ruin it. The Yankee guns kept firing. More fires broke out, and reports reached Page that the walls had become so weakened that they were in danger of collapsing. Continued resistance was useless. General Page sent forward to Granger a request for terms of surrender.

General Granger notified Farragut of Page's message and informed the Rebel general that he would suspend hostilities until Farragut arrived and they discussed the matter. Later that day, August 23, they informed Page of their terms. They were the same as those given to Colonel Anderson at Fort Gaines. Page accepted the conditions and the surrender took place that afternoon.

General Granger had overcome his doubters, General Grant among them, and now it was his pleasure to inform General Canby of Page's capitulation. He said, "Fort Morgan is ours. After a furious bombardment of twenty-four hours it surrendered unconditionally, leaving in our hands [about six hundred] prisoners and a large number of cannons and materials of war, etc. Thus ends the campaign for the opening of Mobile Bay." Rear Admiral Farragut was more effusive in his announcements of victory. "Page did not make us wait as long as I expected," read one. "We will cheer our flag and salute it when hoisted with one hundred guns by the fleet." He was very pleased with the "harmonious" co-operation he had experienced in this joint operation. Between General Granger and himself there had been "no ambition to excel each other but in the destruction of the enemy's works, which was effectually done by both Army and Navy."[20]

General Maury, twenty-seven miles north in Mobile, recognized that the fall of Fort Morgan constituted a disaster and an immediate threat to his city. He began sending wires the next afternoon after the surrender. To

General Samuel Cooper: "Attack of Mobile may commence at once. Need much more and good troops and ammunition." And to General John Bell Hood, who had succeeded Joseph E. Johnston outside of Atlanta: "Fort Morgan is gone. Expect early attack on city." He asked for some infantry, and Hood replied, "Send you a brigade, though I cannot spare it. It goes at daylight."[21]

However, what had been true before was still true. Mobile had considerable value to the Federals so long as it remained in Confederate hands. Sherman proposed to Halleck that Mobile should not be attacked for the time being, and Halleck broke down the argument for Grant. He explained that "the capture of Mobile will only weaken our active forces by the garrison required to hold it, whereas garrisoned by the enemy and threatened by our gunboats, Hood's forces are weakened to the amount of that garrison." Devoting troops to keeping the Confederates on station and at the ready at Mobile presented no hardship at all to the more powerful Federals.[22]

So, Mobile was neutralized without being conquered. It was sealed off from the life-giving Gulf by the Federal navy. Blockade runners like the *Cuba, Heroine Mary,* and *Red Gauntlet* no longer brought rum, tobacco, dry goods, and medicine into the city, and the Mobile & Ohio Railroad could not make up the deficit. The lack of medicine was especially lamented, and there was not enough food. Benjamin B. Cox remembered in his article for *Confederate Veteran* that "Soup houses were established throughout the city, and every day those who were in need were furnished bread and soup. This means of relief was continued until the end."[23]

In General Grant's opinion, the end should have come well before this. He said, "I had tried for more than two years to have an expedition sent against Mobile when its possession by us would have been of great advantage," but he had been continually refused. Even as his fame and reputation grew, he could not get his way. General Halleck ordered in November 1864, "No further military operations on the coast will be undertaken at this time. Troops in Mobile Harbor will be required solely for holding the harbor defenses." This was contrary to Grant's thinking, but he let it go until January 1865 when he wrote to General Canby to urge action. He was somewhat disdainful of Canby. He said that he was "deliberate in all of his movements," and compared him to General George H. Thomas, which was not a compliment, coming from Grant, but a criticism. He now ordered Canby "to move against Mobile, Montgomery, and Selma, Alabama." A month passed, and Grant wrote again to Canby, expressing his frustration that the campaign had not begun. Grant was aggravated, moreover, that Canby had assigned General Granger to command of a corps, despite Grant's blunt warning to him that "he must not put him in command of troops." Neither did Grant approve of Granger's choice of cavalry chief, Brigadier General William W. Averell. He ordered General Grierson to Mobile to take command of the cavalry in Averell's place.[24]

By the third week in February, Canby had given in to Grant's urging, and preparations were under way. A.J. Smith's XVI Corps of thirteen thousand men had arrived in theater, fresh from helping General Thomas defeat Hood at Nashville. While the infantry organized and provisioned itself for a new campaign, Canby planned a number of diversions. Columns of cavalry would ride out from Baton Rouge, from Memphis, and from Vicksburg to strike the railroads. General Grierson said, "The Confederacy had already become a skeleton almost as pitiable as some of our martyred heroes in their Southern prison hells," and the raids against the M&O demonstrated just how pitiable the South had become. The expedition that originated in Memphis was led by Colonel John P.C. Shanks. His raiding party left Memphis on March 3 and struck Ripley on March 6. From there, fifty men of the 4th Illinois cavalry under Lieutenant Colonel Abel H. Soley went south to Booneville. Their orders were to destroy the railroad between Booneville and Baldwyn and then return to Ripley. Soley reported, "On arriving at Booneville, I learned that the railroad track had been washed away at points both above and below, and that it would require some time to repair it." In addition, this was part of the railroad covered by General Thomas's special agreement to let citizens operate the railroad for their own, peaceful purposes. Soley said, "Under these circumstances, I did not feel justified in destroying the road." He arrived back at Ripley on March 8, having fought no rebels, having destroyed no railroad at all, and having captured a total of eight mules and horses. The whole First Brigade captured only sixteen horses and sixteen mules. Clearly, the bountiful days of raiding along the Mobile & Ohio Railroad were over.[25]

Everything was at Mobile, and that was the Federals' primary objective. Three lines of

General Edward R. S. Canby.

works stood on the western skirt of the city, so Canby decided to attack the opposite side: Spanish Fort and, a short distance north, Fort Blakeley. To reduce them, Canby had 4500 cavalry and two infantry corps, about 45,000 men, commanded by General Gordon Granger and General A.J. Smith, plus artillery, engineers, and escorts. In addition to Granger's and Smith's corps, there was a smaller third column of three divisions led by Major General Frederick Steele on its way from Pensacola. Rarely described as a corps; it was simply referred to as Steele's column or, by Canby, as the Column from Pensacola. The navy, which had had its moment back in August, would play a role "transporting and conveying troops and supplies and covering the operations of the army by water." The naval squadron was commanded by Rear Admiral H.K. Thatcher.[26]

The campaign stepped off on March 17. General Granger's XIII Corps led the way "with ten days' subsistence, five days' forage, and 100 rounds of ammunition per man," each man carrying fifty rounds and four days' subsistence, the rest in the train "of 321 regimental, battery, and general supply wagons." The train and artillery were hard to move over ground left mushy by "heavy rains that drenched the coast almost every day," but they began arriving at the concentration point, Danley's Mills, on the 22nd. General Smith's XVI Corps had traveled by water and were waiting there.[27]

When they resumed their march on the 25th, Smith led the way. They moved only eight miles before stopping at Deer Park. The two corps diverged from there when the march continued the next morning. The XVI Corps moved to Sibley's Mills, which would put it between Spanish Fort and Fort Blakeley, in good position to threaten both. Granger moved directly toward the first target, Spanish Fort. Brigadier General C.C. Andrews, in his postwar *History of the Campaign of Mobile*, described Spanish Fort not as a single edifice, but as "a line of field fortifications." The fort itself was "a bastioned work, nearly enclosed and built on a bluff whose shape projects directly to the water. Its parapet, on the bay side, was partly natural, being made by excavating the earth from the side of the bluff, and was thirty feet in thickness.... Extending around that, in a semicircle, was a continuous line of breastworks and reboubts." In front of the breastworks was a ditch five feet deep, rifle-pits for sharpshooters, and a "line of abatis fifteen feet wide." It was a formidable sight that lay before them, but about noon on the day of their arrival, Granger's men went to work. They drove in the enemy pickets and established themselves "on the southeast front of Spanish Fort, and communicated by pickets with the left of the Sixteenth Corps." The Federals sent a skirmish line to within a mile of the enemy works, and both blue and gray settled in for the night.[28]

The morning of March 27, Smith moved with two divisions on Spanish Fort, drove in the Confederate skirmishers, aligned with Granger's XIII

Corps, and "advanced to within about 400 yards of the enemy's works, at which distance the first parallel was made." A scientific investment in the classic mold was shaping up. Smith said from the first parallel "saps were worked forward by each brigade, and these again connected by trenches at a distance of about 200 yards from the enemy's works. From the second parallel saps were again worked forward by each brigade to distances varying from twenty-five to seventy-five yards, depending on the nature of the ground." As the men dug, heavy artillery was dragged forward and placed. Batteries of siege mortars came next. All the while, Granger's men suffered "a well-directed fire of musketry and artillery," and the Third Division of Smith's corps was enfiladed by fire from the two main forts and two gunboats on the river behind the forts. Both Smith's and Granger's corps took numerous casualties, but the siege artillery forced the Rebel gunboats back and silenced the musketry and artillery from the two forts.[29]

Inside Spanish Fort were Brigadier General Randall Lee Gibson and about 2500 men (soon to be reinforced by General Maury to a strength of four thousand), and in the Tensa River four gunboats, the *Nashville, Morgan, Huntsville,* and *Tuscaloosa.* Over the next two weeks, both land and sea forces poured heavy fire into the Federals, but every new sunrise revealed that the besiegers had "crept up a little, so that our people found dirt breastworks a little nearer each morning." William Lochiel Cameron, a young officer on the flagship *Nashville,* said, "Even in daytime they approached, using hogsheads filled with sand, which they rolled in front of them for protection. By this method they secured an advanced position." But it was not without cost. The hogsheads were proof against musket fire only, not against Rebel gunners, particularly a section of the Washington Artillery. Their rounds frequently struck the hogsheads, "which, with men, tools, guns, etc., went up in a cloud of smoke and dust." The Washington Artillery was also a deadly menace to the Federal pickets. Philip Daingerfield Stephenson remembered the cohorn mortars to be the most useful weapon they had against the Yankees in the trenches. He said, "It was one of our diversions to watch the cohorn shells plump exactly into those pits and look for coats, hats, etc. to rise into the air after the explosion."[30]

General Canby had hoped that the Federal navy would be more of a factor in the siege, that it would eliminate the fire of the Confederate gunboats, at least, and move close enough on the waterways to complete his investment of the fort. C.C. Andrews says, "Could this have been done the hours of Spanish Fort would have been brief." But it was impossible. The "shallow water, the elaborate obstructions, and the torpedoes prevented" a close approach. The torpedoes were especially intimidating; some of these vessels had been part of Farragut's flotilla in the battle at the mouth of Mobile Bay, and everyone remembered the *Tecumseh.* On March 28, their fears became a reality. The *Milwaukee* struck a torpedo. Andrews says her "stern sank in about three minutes, but the forward compartments did not fill for nearly an hour afterward" and the crew was able to escape with "most of their effects." The next day an undetected torpedo sent the *Osage* to the bottom, and on April 1 the tin-clad *Rodolph* was sunk by a torpedo that opened in her hull a gaping hole ten feet across.[31]

Two days later, Admiral Thatcher set a dispatch to the Secretary of the Navy, saying that he had had the water "thoroughly dragged" for mines before entering the mouth of Blakeley River, "and many were removed." He said, "We continued to drag until no more could be found, and it was believed that we could successfully advance upon the forts, but the result has proved the impossibility of doing so without endangering the loss of all our light-draft vessels." He added, "These hidden instruments of destruction abound everywhere in these shallow waters." That same day, Thatcher began additional torpedo removal operations. Sweeping in pairs, each boat took the end of a weighted net and drug the bottom "in parallel lines up or down the channel." When a torpedo was pulled up, it was dragged to the shore where it was "pierced with a rifle-ball or augur, to admit water and drown the charge." Twenty boats took part in the operation, moving cautiously up and down the river and also across from bank to bank, and in this way they "found and destroyed about 25 torpedoes."[32]

The siege dragged on. Stephenson said, "We had no rest day or night. The picket fights waxed hotter and hotter." When not on duty at the front, some of the butternuts used their time to gather spent bullets "and other forms of lead" to send into Mobile to be remanufactured into cartridges. It was a worthwhile occupation, for every man "who gathered a certain amount got a furlough for a day or so into the city. The boys did not hesitate to risk their lives while not in action roaming around in the exposed open ground behind us gathering bullets. A furlough was a furlough." Andrews says that a sense of despondency pervaded in Mobile, "but it was not much shown." The citizens "cooked and sent over provisions to the garrison, bestowed every attention upon the wounded, and manifested a devotion well calculated to keep up the resolution of their defenders. The daily newspapers were prohibited from publishing details of the operations and casualties, and confined what they published to general statements," which praised the strength of their defensive works and the "valor of our soldiers."[33]

And the siege continued. On March 29, General Steele's divisions arrived and took their place in the line in front of Fort Blakeley. His horsemen gained some ground in front of the Rebels on April 1, and on the 2nd the Rebels tried to take it back. Some of Steele's troops repelled them. These troopers were part of an all-black division, nine regiments in three brigades of United States Colored Troops, commanded by Brigadier General John P. Hawkins. Noah André Trudeau calls them the "largest single organization of Western black troops ever assigned to a combat role in the Civil War."[34]

On April 4, Steele's men received their entrenching tools and they joined their brothers in the XIII and XVI Corps as burrowers. Andrews said, "It was by no means smooth work; for in some places the ground was rocky, in others it was filled with stumps and roots, and covered with large logs." Still, they kept at it, to the wonder of the Rebels. General Randall L. Gibson wrote to General Maury, "I never saw such digging as the enemy does—he is like a mole." There was daily firing between the Union and Confederate skirmishers, sometimes growing so fierce that "to show a limb was to lose it," according to the chaplain of the 51st U.S. Colored Infantry, but worse than the musket fire was the fire from the Confederate vessels on the water behind the fort. Trudeau says, "With the right flank of Hawkins's line resting within range of the Tensaw [sic] River, the U.S.C.T. units also had to endure periodic visits from Rebel warships, whose shelling extracted a human toll." Brigadier General Hawkins called the fire from the gunboats "particularly annoying and destructive." Digging, skirmishing, and ducking were all that was expected of Steele's men at this time. They were not to make an assault upon Fort Blakeley until Spanish Fort was taken.[35]

That was accomplished on April 8. The Federals had kept the pressure on Spanish Fort over the preceding days, creeping ever closer in their parallels and saps under the cover of the pounding guns that subdued the enemy while the trenchers dug. The firing was incredible. Andrews said, "A ten-inch mortar-shell is a fraction under ten inches in diameter, and weighs very nearly ninety pounds. An eight-inch shell is nearly eight inches in diameter, and weighs about fifty pounds. Some idea can be formed of the noise they produce in exploding." Their destructive effect, too, can be imagined. The shells could pierce the earth to a depth of six feet and go through the roof of the sturdiest bomb-proof shelter man could build—and they came plummeting into the Confederate works by the score. The firing did not cease after dark. Some individual batteries threw more than fifty shells a night. Granger said the U.S. pieces barked through the evening "from five o'clock to 7 p.m., at the rate of three minutes' interval for each gun, and during the night at thirty minutes' interval."[36]

By the day of the assault, General Canby had arrayed against Spanish Fort "fifty-three siege guns (including ten 20-pounder rifles and sixteen mortars) and thirty-seven field pieces. Of these, ten siege rifles and five siege howitzers on our left center enfiladed the enemy's left and center, and five siege howitzers close in on our extreme right enfiladed his center."[37]

At 5:30 in the afternoon on the 8th, the guns all opened, "every piece that could throw iron into the fort." Covered by the bombardment, two companies of skirmishers from the 8th Iowa (of the Third Brigade, Third Division, XVI Corps) moved toward the left of the enemy line. They gained a position from which they could enfilade the Rebels with small arms, and when the rest of the Third Brigade came up in support, "they took about 300 yards of the enemy's main line of works, capturing many prisoners in them." They seized the enemy's guns and turned them to fire on the men who had abandoned them. Canby was encouraged by the light resistance the XVI Corps had faced so far. He ordered Smith "to put his whole force to the work and press it on to completion." Support from other parts of the line poured in to the scene of action, and by midnight Spanish Fort was in possession of the Federals. Part of the garrison escaped, but the victors netted two miles of entrenchments, "540 prisoners, 46 pieces of artillery, including three 7-inch Brooke in the water battery, and two 8-inch columbiads in front and 4 stand of colors." Granger's role in the fight was artillery support for Smith. He said, "all batteries and light batteries on my line opened at 5:30 p.m., continuing it for one hour, under cover of which the left of the enemy's line was carried by the troops of Major-General Smith by assault." Steele's artillery had also taken part in the attack. His guns on the right wing drove off the Rebel gunboats and covered "the redoubts and the steam-boat landing at Blakely."[38]

Since the beginning of the siege, the Confederates has been watching for General Forrest to come and join in the defense of Mobile, but Forrest had been defeated by General James H. Wilson at Selma on April 2, and he was trying to save himself and what was left of his command. Forrest was not coming. Spanish Fort had fallen and Fort Blakely was next. General Canby said, "Early on the morning of the 9th, and soon after the fall of Spanish Fort was assured, Smith was ordered to move the First and Third Divisions of his corps to the left of the line at Blakeley" where he would begin the assault. Three brigades from Granger went to join Steele. Twenty-eight siege guns and sixteen mortars were moved to the front. General Canby himself went to the right wing "and found that the prospects of a successful assault were promising." He said that "the resistance of the enemy was less spirited than on previous days."[39]

At 4:00 p.m., Smith wired Canby that everything was ready. Steele was informed and ordered to "time his movements with those on [his] left, to advance his line strongly supported, and if possible to carry the enemy's works." From one end to the other, the Federal line was four miles long. In front of them, the enemy "had a development of two miles and a half. It consisted of nine strong redoubts connected by rifle-pits and palisades, and was covered in front by slashings and abatis, and in some places by outworks of telegraph wire and by torpedoes or subterra shells." Half past five approached. The men took a breath and stepped off, and what is famously called the "last infantry battle" of the Civil War began.[40]

In accordance with General Smith's precise orders, General Kenner Garrard led the assault behind two double lines of skirmishers while Generals John McArthur and Eugene A. Carr moved in support. The main line was ordered "to charge as soon as the advanced line reached the works." The first skirmish line took the worst of it, advancing under a heavy fire of musketry and canister, but "covered by a sharp fire from the main line, soon reached the main works, and a cheer was given as a signal to charge." The three brigades of the XIII Corps and General Steele's command took up the charge, but, Smith said, "I am certain that the advance line of General Garrard was on the parapet with their colors at the time the other commands started."[41]

The C.S.S. *Nashville* was at anchor just off of Fort Blakeley. Lieutenant J.W. Bennett was in command. He received an order from General St. John R. Liddell about the time the Federal skirmishers began their charge to move into a position in the Blakeley River where he could open fire on the Union right flank. Bennett said, "This could not be complied with because of the current at that point and the absence of holding ground, and also for the reason that I should much endanger the men of our extreme left from the uncertainty of our shells." He had learned the night before that his ammunition was faulty; some shells shattered at discharge and turned into deadly pieces "like canister or grape" and fell short of their target. Others became "tumblers," and they, too, fell "far short of the desired aim." Still others had fuzes that would not burn. For these reasons, any rounds that the *Nashville* fired would likely rain down on the Confederates and endanger them more than the attacking Yankees. While Lieutenant Bennett pondered the situation, he heard "a continuous discharge of artillery and small arms mingled with loud cheers." The first wave of the enemy were atop the Rebel parapets.[42]

Bennett understood what the cheering meant. He moved the *Nashville* closer to Fort Blakeley and began rescuing "such of the garrison as were able to float themselves off." Soon, General Liddell appeared on the beach. Bennett sent a gig to rescue the general, "but, unhappily, before the boat could reach the shore the enemy's sharpshooters were at the water. It was inexpressibly painful to me," said Bennett, "to abandon the attempt of his rescue." Other boats of the squadron had more success in the rescue operation. They carried to safety upwards of two hundred of the men who had fled the fort.[43]

William Lochiel Cameron of the *Nashville* wrote vividly about the attempt to save the garrison of Fort Blakeley. He said, "And then there came with a rush our poor fellows, closely followed by the enemy. Our men jumped into the water. Many could not swim, and those who could were an easy mark for the negro soldiers, who fired at them from the bank and at us in the boats. We picked up all we could and quickly retired to our respective vessels, where we landed them and returned for more. I do not know how many were rescued, but many were drowned, some killed in the water and some on shore, and the rest surrendered."[44]

The killing apparently went on even as the Rebels put down their weapons and raised their hands. Throughout the war there were stories of atrocities committed against a defenseless enemy, killed after they had lain down their arms, killed even killed while lying wounded. Fort Pillow is the most notorious example of such crimes, but it was not the only one on the black-bordered list; there were Saltville, Poison Springs, Mark's Mill, Jenkins Ferry, not to mention innumerable guerrilla actions like that at Centralia. And, if numerous witnesses are to be believed, Fort Blakeley should be added. Stephenson of the Washington Artillery said, "Blakely was the Yankee Fort Pillow." Cameron of the *Nashville* remembered the black soldiers, crying "Remember Fort Pillow!" as they shot down the Confederates who had given up fighting. Trudeau points out that "relatively few prisoners were taken" on Colonel Hawkins's front, and Lieutenant Walter Chapman, 51st United States Colored Troops said, "The niggers did not take a prisoner. They killed all they took to a man." Trudeau also quotes the Confederate artillerist E.W. Tarrant, who said the black soldiers brandished "their guns in great rage" and went on shooting and clubbing, and Private Ben H. Bounds, 4th Mississippi, who said that "he was one of a group of forty to fifty men who were shot at after they gave up; only by keeping a white Union guard between him and the infuriated U.S.C.T. soldiers did he save himself from being killed." Some white officers received their wounds while trying to save surrendered Confederates. C.C. Andrews says the black Louisiana troops "made an attack on the prisoners and were with difficulty restrained from injuring them." Some officers of the black regiments later denied that any such slaughter had occurred, but Trudeau concludes that, "While there was no wholesale massacre of white Rebel prisoners at Fort Blakely, the evidence suggests that a small number of Confederate POWs were probably killed by black soldiers after raising their hands." Neither side, neither race, could claim clean hands in the dirty war that was ending.[45]

General Canby claimed that 3700 Confederates surrendered at Fort Blakeley. His men also captured dozens of artillery pieces and quantities of ordnance and subsistence stores. They were the prizes of only twenty minutes work on the afternoon of April 9, 1865. It was a grand afternoon, and to cap it off, the men later learned that General Robert E. Lee had surrendered to General Grant at Appomattox Courthouse, Virginia, that same, glorious day.

General Canby put Colonel Henry Bertram's brigade of the Second Division, XIII Corps, in charge of holding the enemy's works and collecting the captured property on the east side of Mobile Bay. Some of the many artillery pieces they inventoried had come from the other end of the line, Columbus, Kentucky; brought down on the Mobile & Ohio Railroad when Fort De Russey was evacuated in 1862. The rest of Granger's corps marched down to transports at Starke's Landing on the east shore of the bay on the evening of April 11. They crossed to the western side and landed at Catfish Point, a few miles below Mobile. From there, Granger and Admiral Thatcher composed a message and sent it by their emissaries to Mayor R.H. Slough in Mobile. It said, "Sir: Your city is menaced by a large land and naval force. We deem it proper to demand its immediate and unconditional surrender." In his reply, Mayor Slough opened with the usual courtesies and then said, "The city has been evacuated by the military authorities and its municipal authority is now under my control. Your demand has been granted, and I trust, gentlemen, for the sake of humanity, all the safeguards which you can throw around our people will be secured to them."[46]

Granger sent a dispatch to General Canby, saying, "Mobile was evacuated last night. Our troops are now moving into the city. The citizens are more than happy at our arrival and give us every information required." Later that day, he ordered his men not to disturb the property or the people of the city. Many of the citizens were "strongly Union," he said.[47]

The citizens were no doubt grateful that they had not been burned out by their own army. General Maury had vowed he would put the city to the torch "if he was compelled to abandon it." He had waited and watched, considered his options and their probable outcomes, and after taking careful stock of the situation, he had reached the inevitable conclusion. He realized that his "effective force was now reduced to less than 5000 men, and the supply of ammunition was nearly exhausted." He knew that the defenseless citizens "were entirely exposed to the fire which would be directed against its defenses" and feared that the consequences of the city "being stormed by a combined force of Federal and negro troops would have been shocking." So, he had decided in the end to abandon Mobile, but he reconsidered his threat to burn the city. In his haste to escape, Maury did not even burn the twenty thousand bales of cotton that waited on the platform at the Mobile & Ohio Railroad station "for transportation to the interior as soon as the rebels should become convinced of their inability to hold the place." And now the Federal army was in charge of a city that was battered but unburned, and the remnants of the city's defenders were refugees.[48]

Maury and 4500 men had gone north on the Mobile & Ohio Railroad, perhaps surprised and certainly relieved that the Federals had not swung around to attack it. Maury said, "We always feared lest he might intercept us on the Mobile and Ohio railroad, by which we ultimately moved away unmolested." The train crews had to be forced to remain on duty during the evacuation. General Taylor was in Meridian, and he sent a dispatch to General Maury in those last hours, saying, "You should place guard over each train on its arrival to prevent hands deserting. They must not be allowed to leave their trains for a moment unless vouched for by the Superintendent." Taylor knew of Lee's surrender, which "left us with little hope of success." However, General Joseph E. Johnston was still in the field and President Davis's administration, though driven from Richmond, was still intact. That being the case, Taylor said, "We owed it to our own manhood, to the memory of the dead, and to the honor of our arms, to remain steadfast to the last."[49]

As General Maury evacuated Mobile, falling back in the direction of Meridian, Colonel Philip B. Spence remained behind with the 16th Confederate Cavalry to cover the retreat. Maury had complete confidence in him. Spence had opposed the Federal advance on Mobile "with excellent skill and courage," and Maury later remembered him as one who was "devoted, active, brave and modest, and did his whole duty to the very last day of our existence as an army." General Randall L. Gibson ordered Spence on April 11, "Do not let any part of your command be captured, but remain in the city as long as you can safely. When you quit the city take the road leading to Meridian and cover the troops and trains."[50]

The moment came that Spence could not safely remain came the next afternoon when he received an order from General Maury, at Chunchulla but *en transit.* The general was heading north to Citronelle. He ordered Spence was to follow and destroy the M&O RR bridges and trestles from Mobile as he came. Ninety minutes after the order, a second one arrived from Maury, who had by then arrived in Citronelle. The order read: "You must keep close to the enemy and not give up ground unless forced to do so. Send news to Citronelle of the enemy's force, etc." The general emphasized again, "Burn all the trestles and bridges between this point and Mobile as the trains pass over." He must put his artillery on its way to Meridian and then move with his "whole force to serve as a guard for wagon train and keep the wagons moving as fast as practicable." A postscript was added: "All troops and railroad trains will be off from here by 12 m[eridian]." Maury later said he "reached Meridian with my army unopposed." That was due, in no small part, to the efforts of Colonel Spence and his cavalry.[51]

Colonel Spence established himself in Citronelle with a force of eighty men. He kept an eye on the Federals, maintained a line of couriers to Meridian, and kept the wagons moving. He counted on Meridian to keep him supplied via the Mobile & Ohio until he was forced out by the enemy. The Federals in Mobile tolerated Spence in Citronelle until April 24, when Granger sent Brigadier General W.P. Benton to proceed north with 250 horsemen, surprise and take into custody Spence and his command, and capture the four M&O locomotives and railcars that the Confederates had been using to communicate with Meridian. Granger added, "I do not wish the railroad destroyed unless it should be absolutely necessary to save the command, prevent the escape of the rebels, or save the railroad property captured." General Taylor called the action that followed "the last engagement of the Civil War." That was not quite true, but there was considerable exaggeration concerning the last days of Taylor's command in Mississippi. It was also claimed by Judge R.C. Beckett of West Point, Mississippi, that "the last man killed in the war" met his end in one of the small actions fought along the M&O Railroad during this time. Judge Beckett said in 1903 that his regiment of Mississippi cavalry was in a skirmish with "the advance guard of the Federal army, which was following us, and one man in our regiment was killed. This was about the 4th or 5th of May, 1865, and I remember talking about it after we surrendered that our regiment had the last man killed that was killed in the war, and I think it is a fact." It was not a fact, and neither was it true that the skirmish between Spence and Benton was the last engagement of the war, but the war in the West was sputtering to a strange end. That was a fact.[52]

By this time, Taylor had only about fifteen thousand men in his department. He intended to lead them east from Meridian and join General Johnston in North Carolina. They had barely started when, on April 18, Johnston surrendered to Sherman. It was a broad agreement, applicable to all the armies remaining in the field. It touched upon civil issues as well. At news of the surrender, Taylor led his men back to Meridian. He and Canby agreed to meet on the last day in April at a place called Magee's Farm, a few miles above Mobile.

Taylor arrived with his aide, Colonel William Levy, aboard a Mobile & Ohio handcar powered by two black men. Taking the white officers to surrender as the last flicker of life left the Confederacy was one final task of servitude, but one that the blacks may have quietly relished. Taylor found Canby waiting for him with a contingent of officers in full regalia and a band. Taylor said, "General Canby met me with much urbanity." They went into a room and emerged in just a few minutes with an agreement— Sherman and Johnston had provided the template by their agreement in North Carolina—with the provision that it could be "terminated after forty-eight hours' notice by either party." They repaired with the other officers to a table where, in Taylor's recollection, "a bountiful luncheon was spread, of which we partook, with joyous poppings of champagne corks for accompaniment, the first agreeable explosive sounds I had heard for years." And the band played.[53]

Two days later, a notice arrived from Canby "that the truce must terminate, as his Government disavowed the Johnston-Sherman convention." All the armies in the field were back at war. Taylor would have to surrender again under the same terms Grant had given Lee at Appomattox. The two Kentuckians met again on May 8 at Citronelle, at the home of a Dr. Borden, and in his house the Department of Alabama, Mississippi, and East Louisiana became a thing of the past. The Southerners met its end with something more than mere acceptance, partially a conse-

General Richard Taylor.

quence of General Canby's courtesy to the vanquished. Taylor said, "He was ready with suggestions to soothe our military pride. Officers retained their side arms, mounted men their horses ... and public stores, ordnance, commissary, and quartermaster were to be turned over to officers of the proper departments and receipted for." As for the men themselves, Taylor said paroles "were to be signed by their officers on rolls made out for the purpose, and I was to retain control of the railways and river streams to transport the troops as nearly as possible to their homes and feed them on the road."[54]

The New York *Times* reported that the Rebels "frankly expressed themselves fairly beaten, but no bitterness seemed to remain with them," and said they expressed "loathing and detestation of the fiend who committed the assassination of Pres. Lincoln" on April 14. The paper said, "A return once more to their homes and peaceful pursuits seemed the only thing they desired." Their officers encouraged them in that desire. In his farewell order, General Maury told his men to conduct themselves "with the dignity of veterans who are the last to surrender." Addressing the Federal officers, General Canby said that their conduct and that of the men "must be such as to inspire the people with confidence and respect and no depredations, however slight, nor interference with the citizens in their lawful pursuits, must be permitted." Maury and Canby helped set the example. Before taking his leave, Maury went to bid Canby farewell, and the two friends of the Old Army days parted, "after the long contested battles of Mobile, with mutual respect for each other."[55]

Taylor's surrender left no regularly organized troops of Confederates east of the Mississippi River. The Nashville *Daily Union* observed that Edmund Kirby Smith's command in the Trans-Mississippi "is all that is left of the splendid armies of the Confederacy." The paper said, "It is generally believed that his good judgment and humanity will cause him to follow the example of Lee and Johnston and Taylor. If he should do this, the war may be regarded as closed, and the future will be left to the resources of statesmanship."[56]

General Smith surrendered on June 2, 1865. The war was over.

Epilogue

On May 5, 1865, General Canby returned partial control of the Mobile & Ohio Railroad and others to their civilian officers. He said they would be "put in possession of the offices, depots, locomotives, rolling-stock, and all other material and property pertaining to said roads, so far as they may be under the control of the U.S. military authorities within the limits of this command." For the next few months, the railroad officials essentially functioned as agents of the United States Army. It was an uncomfortable relationship. Once again, President Brown was forced to weigh the needs of his railroad against the demands, conditions, and restrictions of a more powerful authority, this time the U.S. government. To ease the pressures both corporate and political, Brown and his board of directors took the U.S. oath of allegiance on May 17, and "after the May 29 Amnesty Proclamation, he [Brown] also took the oath required by it." This opened the door for the next step. In order to remove all obstacles to obtaining the credit he needed to put the M&O back in operating order, Brown "humbly" requested "a full pardon for the railroad and himself, declaring, 'If we have sinned, we will sin no more.'" Three days later, Brown was pardoned.[1]

The way forward grew easier afterward, but the situation in the first summer after the war was unprecedented, and occasional friction between the corporation and the authorities was inevitable as both sides tried to find answers to never-before-asked questions. In his August report about conditions on the western railroads, Captain F.J. Crilly acknowledged the tension between military and civil officials and explained that they clashed because of the lack of "precedent or regulation to govern anomalous cases that constantly arise." He added that the railroad superintendents sometimes ignored the military authorities.[2]

President Brown and Superintendent Fleming of the Mobile & Ohio struggled under the unwieldy system for only a few months before they were given unfettered control of the railroad on August 25, 1865. The line's six-month-long status as a U.S. military railroad undoubtedly contributed to the decision not to hold an annual convention until the spring of 1866.

On April 17 of that year, at Irving Hall in Mobile, the stockholders assembled to hear the analysis and summary of their chief officers and to learn where the corporation stood at war's end.

The tables distributed to the Mobile & Ohio stockholders showed that in the year of 1865, twelve months inclusive, the railroad had earned a net revenue of $824,777. Two-thirds of that was earned after the surrender. The railroad possessed only fifteen locomotives in running order, eleven passenger cars, three baggage cars and 231 freight cars. L.J. Fleming added the caveat, "The stock designated as in running order on the 1st [of] May [1865] would not have been used before the war, but the pressure of business forced its use notwithstanding its bad condition." As for the condition of the tracks, the company was rebuilding as quickly as possible but had had to order from manufacturers in New York five hundred tons of light rails for temporary use and from manufacturers in the United Kingdom 3500 tons of heavy rails, only some of which had arrived.[3]

Superintendent Fleming's report continued, "The war has been as disastrous upon the railroads in the southern States as upon any other interest." Some pre-war lines had been built at low cost and were free from debt. "Where, however, railroads were just completed, with a heavy bonded and floating debts, the larger part of which was held beyond the Confederate States and could not be paid during the war, the accumulated indebtedness for interest will bear heavily upon their prostrate condition for some years."[4]

That sum of accumulated indebtedness was not stated, but it was undoubtedly substantial, and added to it were other financial burdens. The "expenditures required for reconstruction and losses by the war," Fleming figured, amounted to more than $1,810,000. In addition, the railroad was owed in excess of $5,000,000 by the now defunct Confederate government, a sum that should probably be counted a dead loss. Though not hopeless, the forecast was dire.[5]

More uncertainty was thrown at the stockholders before the end of the convention by the resignation of Milton Brown as president. The delegates by unanimous resolution thanked him for his intelligent and energetic leadership through the years, and then they adjourned to contemplate the future.

As Superintendent Fleming predicted, the debts did bear heavily upon the Mobile & Ohio for years to come. Its plans to expand by linking to other rail lines in Missouri and Illinois were beset by delays and its finances faltered. The railroad went through a long era of receivership from the mid–1870s until the early 1880s. When it emerged, the railroad was on better footing. Profits increased and the value of its stock as well; the long awaited expansions were accomplished, and the company endured. The Mobile & Ohio Railroad continued operations under its own name until 1940.

Chapter Notes

Preface

1. Earl J. Hess, *Civil War Logistics: A Study of Military Transportation* (Baton Rouge: Louisiana State University Press, 2017), 238.

2. *Ibid.*, xi; Sun Tzu, *The Art of War*, trans. Lionel Giles (New York: Cosimo Classics, 2010), 22.

3. United States War Department, *The War of the Rebellion: A Compilation of the Official Records of the Union and Confederate Armies.* 129 Volumes. (Washington, D.C.: Government Printing Office, 1880–1901), series I, vol. 32, part I, 176 (hereafter cited as *ORA*); William G. Thomas, *The Iron Way: Railroads, the Civil War, and the Making of Modern America* (New Haven: Yale University Press, 2011), 70.

4. *ORA*, series I, vol. 7, 888.

5. *Ibid.*, 185.

Chapter One

1. "The Last Nail," Memphis *Daily Appeal*, April 28, 1861.

2. "Message of the Governor of Mississippi," Memphis *Daily Appeal*, January 23, 1861; Aaron W. Marrs, *Railroads in the Old South: Pursuing Progress in a Slave Society* (Baltimore: JHU Press, 2009), 192.

3. *ORA*, series I, vol. 1, 327.

4. *Ibid.*

5. *ORA*, series I, vol. 52, part II, 5.

6. "The M&O RR," Selma [Alabama] *Morning Reporter*, April 12, 1861.

7. "Letter from Wm. J. Sykes, Esq.," Nashville *Union and American*, December 23, 1861.

8. Hans L. Trefousse, *Andrew Johnson: A Biography* (New York: W.W. Norton & Co., 1989), 139, 141; John Keegan, *The American Civil War: A Military History* (New York: Vintage Books, 2009), 153.

9. E. Merton Coulter, *The Civil War and Readjustment in Kentucky* (Gloucester, MA: Peter Smith, 1966), 7–8.

10. *Ibid.*

11. *Ibid.*, 10; R.E. Banta, *The Ohio* (New York: Rinehart & Company, 1940), 469.

12. Coulter, 11–12.

13. Justin Lamb, "The South Carolina of Kentucky: The Jackson Purchase Secession Movement," B.A. thesis, Murray State University, Murray, KY, 2017 https://digitalcommons.murraystate.edu/bis437/108, Accessed August 16, 2019; Leslie Combs, letter to Abraham Lincoln, August 14, 1861. "The Abraham Lincoln Papers at the Library of Congress," http://memory.loc.gov/ammem/alhtml/malcap.html (accessed August 16, 2019). Hereafter cited as Lincoln Papers.

14. "Small Notes of the Railroad Companies," New Orleans *Times-Picayune*, January 4, 1862.

15. "Annual Report of the Mobile & Ohio RR, President's Report," May 7, 1861. David L. Bright, compiler, "Mobile & Ohio," www.csa-railroads.com. Accessed August 16, 2019. Hereafter cited as Bright, Mobile & Ohio, csa-railroads.com.

16. *Ibid.*

17. "Annual Report of the Mobile & Ohio RR, Chief Engineer's Report," May 6, 1861. Bright, Mobile & Ohio, csa-railroads.com.

Chapter Two

1. *ORA*, series I, vol. 52, part II, 53, 65. On May 1, Hardee's command was

extended to include Grand Bay, Horn Island, Ship Island, and the approaches.

2. *Ibid.*, 65.

3. Arthur W. Bergeron, Jr., *Confederate Mobile* (Baton Rouge: Louisiana State University Press, 2000), 115, 117.

4. *Ibid.*, 115.

5. Benjamin B. Cox, "Mobile in the War Between the States," *Confederate Veteran* (May 1916), 207.

6. Keegan, 204–205; "The Camp at Cairo," New York *Times*, May 8, 1861.

7. Untitled, The *Daily Nashville Patriot*, May 5, 1861.

8. *Ibid.*

9. "The War in the West," New York *Times*, May 8, 1861; "Important from the South," *Ibid.*, May 3, 1861; "From Kentucky," *Ibid.*, May 28, 1861.

10. *ORA*, series I, vol. 52, part II, 61–62, 94.

11. *Ibid.*, 94.

12. *Ibid.*, 95

13. United States Naval War Records Office. *Official Records of the Union and Confederate Navies in the War of the Rebellion*, Series I. 27 Volumes (Washington, D. C.: Government Printing Office, 1894–1917), Volume 22, 788 (hereafter cited as *ORN*); *ORA*, series I, vol. 52, part II, 94.

14. "Up River Travel," Memphis *Daily Appeal*, May 24, 1861.

15. William Howard Russell, *My Diary North and South* (Boston: T.O.H.P. Burnham, 1863), 336.

16. *ORA*, series I, vol. 4, 183.

17. "Extraordinary Development," Clarksville [Tennessee] *Chronicle*, July 5, 1861.

18. *ORA*, series I, vol. 4, 176–177, 178; "Miscellaneous Washington News," New York *Times*, August 30, 1861; Dan Lee, *The Civil War in the Jackson Purchase, 1861–1862* (Jefferson, N.C.: McFarland, 2014), 43.

19. Frémont, "In Command in Missouri," 284; *ORA*, series I, vol. 4, 179, 180; Hall Allen, *Center of Conflict: A Factual Story of the War Between the States in Western Kentucky and Tennessee* (Paducah: The Paducah *Sun-Democrat*, 1961), 19.

20. *ORA*, series I, vol. 4, 180.

21. *Ibid.*, 180–181; Huston Horn, *Leonidas Polk: Warrior Bishop of the Confederacy* (Lawrence: University Press of Kansas, 2019), 179–180.

22. *ORA*, series I, vol. 4, 182–182.

23. *Ibid.*, 185, 187; "Correspondence Between Hon. Jo. Holt and President Lincoln," New York *Times*, September 22, 1861; Jack Calbert, "The Jackson Purchase and the End of the Neutrality Policy in Kentucky," *Filson Club History Quarterly*, July 1964, 217.

24. *ORA*, series I, vol. 4, 191; 193–194.

25. Steven E. Woodworth, *Nothing But Victory: The Army of the Tennessee, 1861–1865* (New York: Alfred A. Knopf, 2005), 34.

26. Nathaniel Cheairs Hughes, Jr., *The Battle of Belmont: Grant Strikes South* (Chapel Hill: University of North Carolina Press, 1991), 36.

27. Sam Watkins, *Company Aytch*, edited by M. Thomas Inge (New York: Plume Books, 1999), 6; Keegan, 337–338.

28. Henry Morton Stanley, *The Autobiography of Sir Henry Morton Stanley* (Boston: Houghton Mifflin, 1909), 176.

29. Horn, 163–164.

30. John Milton Hubbard, *Notes of a Private* (Memphis: E.H. Clarke & Brother, 1909), 12; Berry F. Craig, "Northern Conquerors and Southern Deliverers: The Civil War Comes to the Jackson Purchase," *Register of the Kentucky Historical Society*, January 1975.

31. Henry George, *History of the 3d, 7th, 8th and 12th Kentucky C.S.A.* (Lyndon, KY: Mull Wathen Historic Press, 1970), 27.

32. Lee, *The Civil War in the Jackson Purchase*, 55.

Chapter Three

1. Shelby Foote, *The Civil War, A Narrative: Fort Sumter to Perryville* (New York: Random House, 1986) 151; Horn, 196.

2. Horn, 197.

3. *ORA*, series I, vol. 3, 325, 340.

4. Henry Walke, "The Gun-Boats at Belmont and Fort Henry," in *Battles and Leaders of the Civil War: The Opening Battles*, edited by Robert Underwood Johnson and Clarence Clough Buel (Edison, N.J.: Castle Books, 1995), 360.

5. "Statement of Sergeant Wilcox," Chicago *Daily Tribune*, November 15, 1861; Don Singletary, "The Battle of Belmont," *Confederate Veteran* (November 1915), 507; *ORA*, series I, vol. 3, 339, 340, 358.

6. *ORA*, series I, vol. 3, 323, 340, 358.

7. *Ibid.*, 341, 356, 358; Lee, *The Civil War in the Jackson Purchase*, 64.

8. *ORA*, series I, vol. 3, 362; Nathaniel Cheairs Hughes and Roy P. Stonesifer, *The Life and Wars of Gideon J. Pillow* (Chapel Hill: University of North Carolina Press, 1993), 201.

9. *Ibid.*, 363–364.

10. *Ibid.*, 353; Henry Walke, *Naval Scenes and Reminiscences of the Civil War* (New York: F.R. Reed, 1877), 36–37.

11. *ORA*, series I, vol. 3, 307, 344; Walke, 36–37.

12. Mark Twain, *Life on the Mississippi* (New York: Harper and Brothers, 1917), 217; *ORA*, series I, vol. 3, 344. From his own days on the paddle wheelers, Twain new these Kentucky river towns, Hickman and Columbus, and he knew the pilots who ferried men across the Mississippi during the battle of November 7, 1861.

13. Ulysses S. Grant, *Personal Memoirs of U.S. Grant* (New York: Library of America, 1990), 180.

14. *ORA*, series I, vol. 3, 344.

15. *Ibid.*, 308, 327–328, 344. Polk had been right about a Federal force east of Columbus. General C.F. Smith had moved from Paducah with two brigades and was prowling about in the Hickman County countryside. What Polk did not know was that Smith was under orders from General Frémont not to attack. Smith's demonstration lasted three days, but his men saw no action during that time except the mayhem which they themselves committed against citizens.

16. *Ibid.*, 306, 309; Horn, 200.

17. Horn, 202.

18. William D. Pickett, "The Bursting of the Lady Polk," *Confederate Veteran* (June 1904), 119.

19. *ORA*, series I, vol. 53, part II, 222. "The shells for Lady Polk had a slightly oversized flange around the bottom. They were difficult to cram in, even when the cannon was warm" (Lee, 87). When the cannon cooled and tightened around the shell, a dangerous plug was the result.

20. *ORA*, series I, vol. 7, 69, 71; Lee, 101; Hughes and Stonesifer, 196.

21. "Affairs in Kentucky: The Situation of Columbus," New York *Times*, February 9, 1862; "Columbus and New Orleans," Memphis *Daily Appeal*, February 15, 1862.

22. *ORN*, series I, vol. 22, 626.

23. *ORN*, series I, vol. 22, 651; George, 34. Some scholars believe that the evacuation of Columbus began two days earlier, on February 23, 1862.

24. *ORN*, series I, vol. 22, 653.

25. *ORA*, series I, vol. 7, 436–437.

26. *ORA*, series I, vol. 10, part II, 303; "Operations in Tennessee," New York *Times*, March 18, 1862.

Chapter Four

1. "Annual Report of the Mobile & Ohio Railroad, 1863: Chief Engineer's Report," Bright, Mobile & Ohio, csa-railroads.com.

2. Untitled, The Memphis *Daily Appeal*, February 4, 1862; "Famine in Mississippi," [Washington, D. C.] *National Republican*, May 3, 1861.

3. Untitled, Bright, Mobile & Ohio, csa-railroads.com. The rates were readjusted at a meeting of railroad executives in November 1863. In the new schedule, shipping rates for 1st and 2nd class articles more than doubled, the rate for 3rd class articles tripled, and the rate for 4th class articles more than tripled.

4. Untitled, Memphis *Daily Appeal*, October 11, 1861.

5. "Small Note Bill," Memphis *Daily Appeal*, December 27, 1861.

6. "Tennessee," New Orleans *True Delta*, January 16, 1862.

7. *ORA*, series I, vol. 6, 828.

8. *ORA*, series I, vol. 10, part II, 300–301.

9. *Ibid.*, 297–298.

10. Peter Cozzens, *The Darkest Days of the War: The Battles of Iuka and Corinth* (Chapel Hill: University of North Carolina Press, 1977), 22; Ben Wynne, Mississippi's Civil War: A Narrative History (Macon: Mercer University Press, 2006), 59; Michael Ballard, *The Civil War in Mississippi: Major Campaigns and Battles* (Jackson: University Press of Mississippi), 2011), 16; James M. McPherson, *Battle Cry of Freedom: The Civil War Era* (New York: Oxford University Press, 1988), 416.

11. O. Edward Cunningham, *Shiloh and the Western Campaign of 1862*, edited by Gary D. Joiner and Timothy B. Smith (New York: Savas Beatie, 2007), 122–123; *ORA*, series I, vol. 10, part II, 387.

12. *ORA*, series I, vol. 10, part II, 383; Cunningham, 123.

13. Mrs. F.A. Inge, "Corinth, Miss. In Early War Days," *Confederate Veteran* (September 1909), 444; Westley F. Busbee, Jr., in his book *Mississippi: A History* (Malden, MA: John Wiley & Sons, 2015) points out that Shiloh was "the single bloodiest battle ever fought in the Americas to this date." However, the tragedy was just beginning; Busbee adds, "by the time the Civil War ended three years later, the battle of Shiloh would rank seventh in casualty numbers" (137).

14. Cozzens, 23; Cunningham, 385–386; Shelby Foote, *The Civil War, A Narrative: Fort Sumter to Perryville* (New York: Random House, 1986), 381; *ORA*, series I, vol. 7, 888. L.P. Walker's quote is often given in reference only to the Memphis & Charleston, but his full statement plainly shows that he considered the M&O equal in importance to the M&C.

15. "Mrs. Ella Palmer: Reminiscences of Her Service in Hospitals," *Confederate Veteran* (February 1910), 72.

16. *Ibid.*, 72.

17. Foote, *Fort Sumter to Perryville*, 382.

18. Grant, *Personal Memoirs*, 249, 251; Sherman, *Memoirs*, 270.

19. W.J. Ross to P.G.T. Beauregard, April 12 [18], 1862; Robert B. Hurt to P.G.T. Beauregard, April 19, 1862; L.J. Fleming to Robert B. Hurt, April 18, 1862; L.J. Fleming to Hypolite Oladowski, May 7, 1862, Bright, Mobile & Ohio, csa-railroads.com.

20. Grant, *Personal Memoirs*, 251; *ORA*, series I, vol. 10, part II, 801–802; Cunningham, 389.

21. Cunningham, 389.

22. *ORA*, series I, vol. 10, part I, 809.

23. *Ibid.*, 784–785.

24. *Ibid.*, 814.

25. *Ibid.*, 715, 784; Ballard, 27.

26. Ballard, 18–19.

27. *Ibid.*, 29; Sherman, *Memoirs*, 273.

28. Palmer, 73.

29. Watkins, 38.

30. Sherman, *Memoirs*, 274; *ORA*, series I, vol. 10, part I, 862, 863–864.

31. *ORA*, series I, vol. 10, part I, 865.

32. Frederick Ingate, letter to P.G.T. Beauregard, June 3, 1862. Bright, Mobile and Ohio Railroad, csa-railroads.com.

33. *ORA*, series I, vol. 10, part I, 863.

34. Oscar L. Jackson, *The Colonel's Diary: Journals Kept Before and During the Civil War by the Late Colonel Oscar L. Jackson; Sometime Commander of the 63rd Regiment O. V. I.*, edited by David Prentice Jackson (Sharon, PA, by the editor, 1922), 59.

35. *ORA*, series I, vol. 10, part I, 765; Philip B. Spence, "Services in the Confederacy," *Confederate Veteran* (November 1900), 500. McPherson, *Battle Cry of Freedom*, 402. McPherson says Beauregard was a man of "Napoleonic plans and Lilliputian execution," and his conduct had grown tiresome to President Davis. His self-indulgent vacation to a health resort was the final straw (McPherson, *Battle Cry of Freedom*, 417).

36. *ORA*, series I, vol. 10, part I, 786.

37. *Ibid.*, 781, 783; "Peace. From the Mobile Advertiser," New York *Times*, August 1, 1864.

38. *ORA*, series I, vol. 10, 785.

39. *Ibid.*, 784.

40. *Ibid.*, 785; *ORA* 17, part II, 626; Cozzens, 38.

41. Ballard, 34.

Chapter Five

1. *ORA*, series I, vol. 10, part I, 795.

2. *Ibid.*, 796, 797.

3. *ORA*, series I, vol. 10, part II, 72.

4. *ORA*, series I, vol. 10, part I, 668.

5. Andrew F. Lang, "The Perils of Occupation," *The Civil War Monitor*, summer 2019, 65.

6. "A Rebel Operator Reads Gen. Halleck's Dispatches for Four Days," Memphis *Daily Appeal*, August 9, 1862.

7. *Ibid.*

8. Untitled, The Memphis *Daily Appeal*, August 4, 1862; "From Jackson—Guerrilla Depredations—Hanging of a Citizen of Jackson," Memphis *Daily Appeal*, August 4, 1862; Untitled, The Memphis *Union Appeal*, August 1, 1862.

9. Lang, 60.

10. *ORA*, series I, vol. 17, part II, 192.

11. *ORA*, series I, vol. 52, part II, 379, 380, 389.

12. Cozzens, 42.

13. *Ibid.*, 57, 59–60; *ORA* 17, part II, 696–698, 700; W.P. Helm, "Close Fighting

at Iuka, Miss.," *Confederate Veteran* (April 1911), 171.

14. *ORA*, series I, vol. 17, part I, 118, 119. Ord later blamed contrary winds for his inability to hear the sounds of Rosecrans's battle.

15. Cozzens, 120; *ORA*, series I, vol. 17, part I, 122.

16. Cozzens, 122; *ORA*, series I, vol. 17, part I, 122, 139–140.

17. W.P. Helm, "Close Fighting at Iuka, Miss.," *Confederate Veteran* (April 1911), 171; Cozzens, 133.

18. *ORA*, series I, vol. 17, part I, 68.

19. William B. McCord, "Battle of Corinth, The Campaigns Preceding and Leading Up to This Battle, and Its Results," in *Glimpses of the Nation's Struggle, Fourth Series: Papers Read Before the Minnesota Commandery of the Military Order of the Loyal Legion of the United States, 1892–1897* (Saint Paul: H.L. Collins Co., 1898), 573.

20. "Vivid War Experiences at Ripley, Miss.," *Confederate Veteran* (June 1905), 262; Robert George Hartje, *Van Dorn: The Life and Times of a Confederate General* (Nashville: Vanderbilt University Press, 1967),

21. Frank A. Montgomery, *Reminiscences of a Mississippian in Peace and War* (Cincinnati: The Robert Clarke Company Press, 1901), 91.

22. Cozzens, 174.

23. *ORA*, series I, vol. 17, part I, 252.

24. Cozzens, 203.

25. *ORA*, series I, vol. 17, part I, 256, 273; Augustus L. Chetlain, "The Battle of Corinth, October 3 and 4, 1862," in *War Papers Read before the Michigan Commandery of the Military Order of the Loyal Legion of the United States, Volume 2* (Detroit: James H. Stones & Co., Printers, 1898), 269. General Hackelman was P.A. Hackelman, who commanded the 1st Brigade in Davies's division; Colonel Baldwin was Silas D. Baldwin, who commanded the 3rd Brigade; and General Oglesby was Chetlain's own 2nd Brigade commander, Richard J. Oglesby.

26. ORA, series I, vol. 15, part I, 205, 206, 227.

27. *Ibid.*, 177; S.H.M. Byers, *With Fire and Sword* (New York: The Neal Publishing Company, 1911), 34–35; Horace Wardner, "Reminiscences of a Surgeon," in *Military Essays and Recollections: Papers Read Before the Commandery of the State of Illinois, Military Order of the Loyal Legion of the United States, Volume III* (Chicago: The Dial Press, 1899, 189.

28. David S. Stanley, "The Battle of Corinth," in *Personal Recollections of the War of the Rebellion: Addresses Delivered Before the Commandery of the State of New York, Military Order of the Loyal Legion of the United States, Volume II*, edited by A. Noel Blakeman (New York: G.P. Putnam's Sons, 1897) 274.

29. *ORA*, series I, vol. 17, part I, 169, 379, 398–399.

30. Stanley, 274.

31. *ORA*, series I, vol. 17, part II, 238, 259–260.

32. *ORA*, series I, vol. 17, part I, 291, 379, 399; Cozzens, 267.

33. *ORA*, series I, vol. 17, part I, 169, 180, 206.

34. Captain George A. Williams, in Rosecrans, "The Battle of Corinth," 750.

35. *Ibid.*; Cozzens, 262; Jackson, *The Colonel's Diary*, 86.

36. J.H. McClay, "Defense of Robinette," in *Civil War Sketches and Incidents: Papers Read by Companions of the Commandery of the State of Nebraska, Military Order of the Loyal Legion of the United States, Volume I* (Omaha: by the Commandery, 1902), 171.

37. Cozzens, 273; *ORA*, series I, vol. 17, part I, 380; McClay, 170; Hartje, 234.

38. Rosecrans, "The Battle of Corinth," 753.

39. *ORA*, series I, vol. 17, part I, 380; Hartje, 234.

40. *ORA*, series I, vol. 17, part I, 380.

41. J.R. Perkins, "Gen. Sterling Price," *Confederate Veteran* (January 1904), 16; Cozzens, 300; "Vivid War Experiences at Ripley, Miss.," *Confederate Veteran* (June 1905), 262–263; Frank A. Montgomery, *Reminiscences of a Mississippian in War and Peace* (Cincinnati: The Robert Clarke Company Press, 1901), 94.

42. Cozzens, 303; "Vivid War Experiences at Ripley, Miss.," 264

43. "Vivid War Experiences at Ripley, Miss.," 264.

44. Cozzens, 319; Jackson, 64–65.

45. The Memphis *Daily Appeal*, October 11, 1862; The Winchester [Tennessee] *Daily Bulletin*, October 15, 1862.

Chapter Six

1. Sherman, *Memoirs*, 284.

2. Grant, *Personal Memoirs*, 283; Arthur B. Carter, *The Tarnished Cavalier: General Earl Van Dorn, C.S.A.* (Knoxville: University of Tennessee Press, 1999), 120–121; "The War in the Southwest," New York *Times*, November 16, 1862.

3. Grant, *Personal Memoirs*, 287.

4. Carter, 112–114.

5. "News from Cairo," [Washington, D. C.] *Daily National Republican*, November 29, 1862; *ORA*, series I, vol. 17, part II, 360. A few days after the Confederate raid on Henderson, General Sullivan reported to Grant that he had assessed citizens living near the railroad "a sum sufficient to pay all damages" and had raised $8000. He wanted to use the surplus as a secret service fund "having employed several citizens as scouts." It was also called to Grant's attention that several of Henderson's ladies had turned out with water buckets to "extinguish a fire which had been kindled by these lawless persons, threatening a railroad bridge important to the Government." They had saved the M&O RR bridge and Grant directed that they would be rewarded. He instructed Sullivan "that they be protected in their property and the quiet of their homes, and also that rations be issued to them from time to time free of charge if necessity requires it, and that every facility be given them to purchase every article of necessity for the use of themselves and families" (*ORA* 17, series I, vol. 17, part II, 360, 574; vol. 17, part I, 526).

6. *ORA*, series I, vol. 17, part I, 505.

7. *Ibid.*, 473; Grant, *Personal Memoirs*, 288–289.

8. *ORA*, series I, vol. 17, part II, 388; Hartje, 253; Carter, 123. Sherman led his advance against Vicksburg from Memphis, unaware that Grant had ended his advance and was dug in at Oxford. Uncle Billy's part of the campaign ended in defeat at Chickasaw Bayou.

9. Robert George Hartje, "Van Dorn Conducts a Raid on Holly Springs and Enters Tennessee," *Tennessee Historical Quarterly*, June 1959, 124.

10. *ORA*, series I, vol. 17, part II, 410; *ORA*, series I, vol. 17, part I, 497; Sylvanus Cadwallader, *Three Years With Grant* (Lincoln: University of Nebraska Press, 1996),

32. Coonewar Station should actually be Coonewah, which is the name of a local creek. The Federals often had difficulty spelling southern place names.

11. *ORA*, series I, vol. 17, part I, 498.

12. *Ibid.*; Cadwallader, 35.

13. *ORA*, series I, vol. 17, part I, 499.

14. Ronald C. White, *American Ulysses: A Life of Ulysses S. Grant* (New York: Random House, 2016), 249; Hartje, 123; Dan Lee, *General Hylan B. Lyon: A Kentucky Confederate and the War in the West* (Knoxville: University of Tennessee Press, 2019), 76; *ORA*, series I, vol. 17, part I, 503.

15. Hartje, 129; James W. Rabb, *Confederate General Lloyd Tilghman: A Biography* (Jefferson, N.C.: McFarland, 2006), 141.

16. *ORA*, series I, vol. 17, part I, 478; Grant, *Personal Memoirs*, 290–291.

17. "Twenty Days' Reign of Terror," Memphis *Daily Appeal*, February 10, 1863.

18. W.H. Whitsitt, "A Year With Forrest," *Confederate Veteran* (August 1917), 358; Dabney H. Maury, *Recollections of a Virginian in the Mexican, Indian, and Civil Wars* (New York: Charles Scribner's Sons, 1894), 204; McPherson, *Battle Cry of Freedom*, 402.

19. Thomas Jordon and J.P. Pryor, *The Campaigns of Lieut.-Gen. N. B. Forrest, and of Forrest's Cavalry* (New Orleans: Blelock & Company, 1868) 194; Brian Steel Wills, *A Battle from the Start: The Life of Nathan Bedford Forrest* (New York: HarperCollins, 1992), 85; John Allan Wyeth, *That Devil Forrest: Life of General Nathan Bedford Forrest* (Baton Rouge: Louisiana State University Press, 1989), 94; "Forrest's West Tennessee Expedition," Memphis *Daily Appeal*, January 27, 1863.

20. Jordan and Pryor, 196–197; *ORA*, series I, vol. 17, part I, 598.

21. Jordan and Pryor, 200; *ORA*, series, I, vol. 17, part I, 561, 593.

22. Jordan and Pryor, 201; *ORA*, series I, vol. 17, part I, 561, 593.

23. Shelby Foote, *The Civil War, A Narrative: Fredericksburg to Meridian* (New York: Random House, 1986), 67; Jordan and Pryor, 202, 203; *ORA*, series I, vol. 17, part I, 562, 593.

24. Jordan and Pryor, 203; *ORA*, series I, vol. 17, part I, 594; "The War in the Southwest," New York *Times*, December 22, 1862.

25. Jordan and Pryor, 204; *ORA*, series I, vol. 17, part I, 594.

26. Jordon and Pryor, 205.

27. "From the 72nd Illinois Regiment," Chicago *Daily Tribune*, November 21, 1862; "Important from Tennessee," [Washington, D.C.] *Evening Star*, December 22, 1862; *ORA*, series I, vol. 17, part II, 447, 454.

28. Foote, *Fredericksburg to Meridian*, 67; *ORA*, series I, vol. 17, part II, 479.

29. *ORA*, series I, vol. 17, part II, 493–494.

30. *Ibid.*, 508, 520, 521; Wyeth, 102; Jordan and Pryor, 221.

31. Wyeth, 105.

32. ORA, series I, vol. 17, part I, 596, 598.

33. *Ibid.*, 596.

34. *Ibid.*: Wyeth, 111.

35. ORA, series I, vol. 17, part I, 596; Wills, 95; Foote, *Fredericksburg to Meridian*, 68.

36. *ORA*, series I, vol. 17, part I, 552–553.

37. *ORA*, series I, vol. 17, part I, 597.

38. Jordan and Pryor, 220.

39. ORA, series I, vol. 17, part I, 597.

40. *Ibid.*

41. Bruce Catton, *Grant Moves South* (Boston: Little, Brown & Company, 1960), 342. Van Dorn, a libertine and an incorrigible philanderer, was shot to death by a wronged husband on May 7, 1863, in Spring Hill, Tennessee.

Chapter Seven

1. Milton Brown, President's Report, Fifteenth Annual Meeting of the Stockholders of the Mobile and Ohio Railroad Company, April 21, 1863, 1. From the archives of the Norfolk Southern Corporation, Norfolk, Virginia.

2. *Ibid.*, 3; "Railroad Collisions," New York *Times*, August 16, 1862.

3. Milton Brown, President's Report, Fifteenth Annual Meeting. The six percent dividend was paid as recommended.

4. L.J. Fleming, Engineer's Report, Fifteenth Annual Meeting of the Stockholders of the Mobile and Ohio Railroad Company, April 21, 1863, 6. From the archives of the Norfolk Southern Corporation, Norfolk, Virginia.

5. *Ibid.*

6. *Ibid.*

7. *Ibid.*

8. Arndt Stickles, *Simon Bolivar Buckner: Borderland Knight* (Chapel Hill: University of North Carolina Press, 2001), 211.

9. "The Question in a Nutshell," Memphis *Daily Appeal*, February 11, 1863; *ORA* 15, 937.

10. *ORA*, series I, vol. 15, 937.

11. *Ibid.*, 937–938.

12. *Ibid.*, 938.

13. *Ibid.*

14. "An Interesting Batch of Telegrams," *Confederate Veteran* (April 1894), 110 .

15. *ORA*, series I, vol. 24, part III, 625.

16. *Ibid.*, 1068–1069.

17. *Ibid.*, 1069.

18. Bergeron, 101.

19. *ORN*, series I, vol. 1, 464.

20. Chester G. Hearn, *Gray Raiders of the Sea: How Eight Confederate Warships Destroyed the Union's High Seas Commerce* (Camden, Maine: International Marine Publishing, 1992) 67; *ORN*, series I, vol. 1, 768.

21. "Mrs. Ella Palmer as Nurse," *Confederate Veteran* (March 1910), 74.

22. *ORA*, series I, vol. 24, part III, 12.

23. Grant, *Memoirs*, 308. The raiding party under Grierson that Grant sent out to distract attention from his landing on the Mississippi shore below Vicksburg ran the length of Mississippi, but it barely touched the M&O.

24. *ORA*, series I, vol. 52, part II, 471.

25. *ORA*, series I, vol. 24, part III, 902–903.

26. *Ibid.*, 323, 338.

27. *Ibid.*, 968; *ORA*, series I, vol. 23, part II, 817.

28. *ORA*, series I, vol. 24, part III, 325.

29. Sherman, *Memoirs*, 356–357; Earl J. Hess, *Civil War Logistics: A Study of Military Transportation* (Baton Rouge: Louisiana State University Press, 2017), 238; William T. Sherman, letter to David Dixon Porter, July 19, 1863, *Sherman's Civil War: Selected Correspondence of William T. Sherman, 1860–1865*, edited by Brooks D. Simpson and Jean V. Berlin (Chapel Hill: University of North Carolina Press, 1999), 505.

30. *ORA*, series I, vol. 52, part II, 508.

31. "Provisions," Memphis *Daily Appeal*, July 22, 1863; *ORA* 26, part II, 120.

32. "Provisions," Memphis *Daily Appeal*, July 22, 1863.

33. *ORA*, series I, vol. 26, part II, 111–112.

34. *Ibid.*, 128, 130.

35. *ORA*, series I, vol. 24, part III, 528; Ron Chernow, *Grant* (New York: Penguin Books, 2017), 327; Grant, *Personal Memoirs*, 388.

36. Bruce Catton, *Grant Takes Command* (Boston: Little, Brown & Co. 1969), 13; Grant, *Personal Memoirs*, 388; *ORA* 26, part I, 666.

37. Catton, *Grant Takes Command*, 14; John Hay, *Lincoln and the Civil War in the Diaries and Letters of John Hay* (New York: Dodd, Mead & Company, 1939), 77; Abraham Lincoln, letter to U.S. Grant, August 9, 1863. *The Collected Works of Abraham Lincoln*, edited by Roy P. Basler (New Brunswick, N.J.: Rutgers University Press, 1953–1955), Vol. 6, 375.

38. Grant, *Personal Memoirs*, 389. Lincoln's reference to "Western" Texas is perplexing, for the Texas coast was the Union's natural point of entry to the Lone Star State, and it was there that the XIII Corps landed after it was detached from Grant. As for General Banks, he led the Red River Expedition in the spring of 1864 and took Farragut's gunboat fleet along to protect his flanks. It was an ambitious adventure, but ill-fated, and it ended as one of the most notable defeats of the war.

39. *ORA*, series I, vol. 24, part III, 1022.

40. J.F. Gilmer, letter to Joseph E. Johnston, August 14, 1863. Bright, Mobile and Ohio Railroad, csa-railroads.com. The name of the Commissioner for the Removal of Railroad Iron in the late summer of 1863 was Colonel C.F.M. Garnett.

41. Andrew Smith, *Starving the South: How the North Won the Civil War* (New York: St. Martin's Press, 2011, 62; "Terrible Bread Riot in Mobile," Nashville *Daily Union*, October 7, 1863; "Another Bread Riot," *Harper's Weekly*, October 10, 1863.

42. Smith, *Starving the South*, 62; Nashville *Daily Union*, October 7, 1863; Bergeron, 102.

43. Foote, *Fredericksburg to Meridian*, 819; *ORA*, series I, vol. 26, part I, 891.

44. Foote, *Fredericksburg to Meridian*, 820; William Edward Dodd, *Jefferson Davis* (Philadelphia: George W. Jacobs & Company, 1907), 315; J.T. Scharf, "The

Sinking of the Housatonic," *Confederate Veteran* (June 1916), 281.

45. Foote, *Fredericksburg to Meridian*, 820.

46. Sherman, *Memoirs*, 363.

Chapter Eight

1. "Interesting from West Tennessee," Memphis *Daily Appeal*, July 25, 1863.

2. *Ibid.*

3. Mercer Otey, "Story of Our Great War," *Confederate Veteran* (March 1901), 107; *ORA*, series I, vol. 31, part III, 374.

4. Wills, 152–153.

5. *Ibid.*, 155, 156.

6. Horn, 361, 365.

7. *ORA*, series I, vol. 32, part II, 689; Victoria Bynum, "Newt Knight and the Free State of Jones: Myth, Memory, and Imagination," *Journal of Mississippi History*, Winter, 2013, 28.

8. Maury, *Recollections of a Virginian*, 248; Victoria Bynum, *The Free State of Jones: Mississippi's Longest Civil War* (Chapel Hill: University of North Carolina Press, 2003), 116.

9. *ORA*, series I, vol. 32, part II, 75.

10. *Ibid.*, 100–101; Sherman, *Memoirs*, 418.

11. Sherman, *Memoirs*, 418.

12. *ORA*, series I, vol. 32, part I, 182.

13. *Ibid.*, 175; William T. Sherman, letter to wife, February 7, 1864, *Sherman's Civil War*, 602.

14. Buck T. Foster, *Sherman's Mississippi Campaign* (Tuscaloosa: University of Alabama Press, 2006), 32; *ORA*, series I, vol. 32, part I, 175, 210–211, 358; Jim Woodrick, "Successful in an Eminent Degree: Sherman's 1864 Meridian Expedition," *Journal of Mississippi History*, Winter 2013, 74.

15. Horn, 367; *ORA*, series I, vol. 32, part I, 366; *ORN*, series I, vol. 21, 63. A third diversion was a Yazoo River expedition led by Lieutenant Commander Elias K. Owen. His gunboats set out on February 1 accompanied by an infantry complement on shore.

16. *ORA*, series I, vol. 32, part II, 751.

17. Foster, 100–101; *ORA*, series I, vol. 32, part II, 724; ORA series I, vol. 32, part I, 361.

18. *ORA*, series I, vol. 32, part I, 175.

19. Peter J. Lamb, *Railroads of Meridian* (Bloomington: Indiana University Press, 2012), 8; Timothy B. Smith, *Mississippi in the Civil War: The Home Front* (Jackson: University Press of Mississippi, 2010), 82.

20. Lamb, 11.

21. Foote, *Fredericksburg to Meridian*, 925; "Yankee Occupation of Meridian Described by a Rebel Lady," Nashville *Daily Union*, March 20, 1864.

22. Horn, 376; Foster, 101; *ORA*, series, I, vol. 32, part I, 367.

23. Foster, 113; *ORA*, series I, vol. 32, part I, 217.

24. Foster, 106, 109; Sherman, *Memoirs*, 420.

25. Foster, 106, 152; Lamb, 11.

26. *ORA*, series I, vol. 32, part I, 256.

27. *Ibid.*, *ORA*, series I, vol. 32, part II, 317.

28. Sherman, *Memoirs*, 452–453.

29. *ORA*, series I, vol. 32, part I, 252; George E. Waring, Jr., "The Sooy Smith Expedition (February 1864)," in *Battles and Leaders of the Civil War: Retreat with Honor*, edited by Robert Underwood Johnson and Clarence Clough Buel (Edison, N.J.: Castle Books, 1995), 416.

30. *ORA*, series I, vol. 32, part I, 252; Foote, *Fredericksburg to Meridian*, 928. By an order dated February 14, Lee was assigned "command of all cavalry west of Alabama" (*ORA*, series I, vol. 32, part II, 738).

31. Foster, 133; *ORA*, series I, vol. 32, part I, 252.

32. Benjamin H. Grierson, *A Just and Righteous Cause: Benjamin H. Grierson's Civil War Memoir*, edited by Bruce J. Dinges and Shirley A. Leckie (Carbondale: Southern Illinois University Press, 2008), 217, 220; *ORA*, series I, vol. 32, part I, 252, 257.

33. Grant, *Personal Memoirs*, 464; Waring, "The Sooy Smith Expedition," 417; *ORA*, series I, vol. 32, part I, 353; Foster, 138.

34. *ORA*, series I, vol. 32, part I, 353; Waring, "The Sooy Smith Expedition," 417.

35. Richard R. Hancock, *Hancock's Diary: Or, A History of the Second Tennessee Confederate Cavalry* (Nashville: Brandon Publishing Co., 1887), 322.

36. Wills, 164; George, 72; *ORA*, series I, vol. 32, part I, 353; Waring, "The Sooy Smith Expedition," 417; Hancock, 323.

37. *ORA*, series I, vol. 32, part I, 354; Hancock, 325, 327.

38. *ORA*, series I, vol. 32, part I, 354; Waring, "The Sooy Smith Expedition," 418.

39. "The Opening of the Campaign of '64," *Harper's Weekly*, March 19, 1864.

40. "The Expedition of Gen. Sherman," Nashville *Daily Union*, March 8, 1864; "Progress of Sherman's Operations," New York *Times*, February 20, 1864.

41. Foote, *Fredericksburg to Meridian*, 936–937; Foster, 169; *ORA*, series I, vol. 32, part I, 338, 342, 346.

42. Foster, 105; Jim Woodrick, "Success in an Eminent Degree: Sherman's 1864 Meridian Expedition," *Journal of Mississippi History*, Winter 2013; 78.

43. *ORA*, series I, vol. 32, part I, 173; *ORA*, series I, vol. 32, part II, 498.

44. *ORA* series I, vol. 32, part I, 175.

45. *ORA*, series I, vol. 32, part I, 341, 345.

46. L.J. Fleming, Engineer's Report, Sixteenth Annual Meeting of the Stockholders of the Mobile and Ohio Railroad Company, April 19, 1864, 4. From the archives of the Norfolk Southern Corporation, Norfolk, Virginia.

47. *Ibid.*, 3; George Whitfield, letter to F.W. Sims, March 19, 1864. Bright, Mobile & Ohio, csa-railroads.com.

48. L.J. Fleming, Engineer's Report, Sixteenth Annual Meeting., 7. The guilty Confederate officers were operating in the delirium of destruction that affects the military mind at war. Herman Hattaway and Archer Jones explain the value of railroad destruction by its own defenders in their book *How the North Won*. They say, "The railroad tended to favor strategic maneuver by the defender. Though its logistical impact strengthened the invader by immensely facilitating the supply of invading armies, the railroad could confer strategic advantage upon the defender; *if the defender destroyed the railroad as he retreated*, he could deprive the advancing army of the advantage of railways while at the same time he himself could continue to enjoy their strategic use for defensive concentrations" (emphasis added). But, Fleming's point was equally valid when he charged that the retreating Confederates'

recklessly extravagant destruction of railroad was unnecessary and ultimately self-defeating (Herman Hattaway and Archer Jones, *How the North Won: A Military History of the Civil War* [Urbana: University of Illinois Press, 1991], 158).

49. *Ibid.*, 6, 7.

Chapter Nine

1. *ORA*, series I, vol. 32, part II, 552.
2. *Ibid.*, 565–566.
3. *Ibid.*, 552–553; 566.
4. "Southern News," New York *Times*, March 5, 1864.
5. "From the South," New York *Times*, February 23, 1864.
6. *ORN*, series I, vol. 21, 96–97, 101–102.
7. *Ibid.*, 96–97.
8. *Ibid.*, 97.
9. Special Orders No. 56, February 25, 1864. Bright, Mobile & Ohio, csa-railroads.com; Leonidas Polk, letter to L.J. Fleming, February 26, 1864. Bright, Mobile & Ohio, csa-railroads.com; *ORA*, series I, vol. 32, part I, 339.
10. *ORA*, series I, vol. 32, part I, 343.
11. "Mobile and Ohio Railroad," Memphis *Daily Appeal*, March 30, 1864.
12. "From Corinth," Chicago *Daily Tribune*, January 30, 1864; Leonidas Polk, letters to L.J. Fleming, April 1, 1864 and April 29, 1864. Bright, Mobile & Ohio, csa-railroads.com.
13. "Forrest's Command—Rebuilding Railroads, Etc.," Memphis *Daily Appeal*, May 18, 1864; *ORA*, series I, vol. 32, part III, 34, 429.
14. *ORA*, series I, vol. 32, part III, 782.
15. George, 76.
16. *ORA*, series I, vol. 38, part IV, 655; *ORA*, series I, vol. 32, part II, 833; Leonidas Polk, letter to Nathan Bedford Forrest, May 7, 1864. Bright, Mobile & Ohio, csa-railroads.com.
17. *ORA*, series I, vol. 39, part II, 591.
18. *Ibid.*, 41–42.
19. *ORA*, series I, vol. 39, part I, 85, 217–218.
20. *Ibid.*, 85.
21. *Ibid.*, 91, 128.
22. *Ibid.*, 91; Grierson, 240.
23. *ORA*, series I, vol. 39, part I, 91.
24. *Ibid.*, 222.
25. *Ibid.*, 222–223; James Dinkins, "The Battle of Brice's Crossroads," *Confederate Veteran* (October 1925), 380.
26. *ORA*, series I, vol. 39, part I, 223.
27. *Ibid.*, 92, 129.
28. Dan Lee, *General Hylan B. Lyon*, 112; *ORA*, series I, vol. 39, part I, 92.
29. George, 89; *ORA*, series I, vol. 39, part I, 223.
30. *ORA*, series I, vol. 39, part I, 92, 119; Grierson, 246.
31. Edwin C. Bearss, "The Battle of Brice's Crossroads," *Blue & Gray*, August 1999, 44.
32. *ORA*, series I, vol. 3, part I, 93, 125; Grierson, 249.
33. Bearss, "The Battle of Brice's Crossroads," 47; Grierson, 250; *ORA*, series I, vol. 39, part I, 224.
34. *ORA*, series I, vol. 39, part I, 125, 126.
35. *Ibid.*, 108; Bearss, "The Battle of Brice's Crossroads," 48–49.
36. *ORA*, series I, vol. 39, part I, 89, 110.
37. *ORA*, series I, vol. 39, part II, 122; Grierson, 256.
38. *ORA*, series I, vol. 39, part I, 229.
39. *Ibid.*, 330.

Chapter Ten

1. *ORA*, series I, vol. 38, part IV, 480.
2. *ORA*, series I, vol. 39, part II, 122, 123.
3. *Ibid.*, 696; John Watson Morton, *The Artillery of Nathan Bedford Forrest's Cavalry* (Nashville: Printing House of the M.E. Church, South, 1909), 202.
4. *ORA*, series I, vol. 39, part I, 307; David W. Reed, *Campaigns and Battles of the Twelfth Regiment Iowa Veteran Volunteer Infantry* (Evanston, IL: by the author, 1903), 151. Serving in the 7th Kansas Cavalry was a young trooper named William F. Cody, a Kansan who was learning that campaigning as a regular under General A.J. Smith was something different than raiding as a jayhawker along the Missouri border. Cody, of course, later became known world-wide as Buffalo Bill, hunter, scout, and showman. When his Wild West and Congress of Rough Riders visited Tupelo in 1911, Cody went with a group of citizens out to the battlefield, and he walked them through the battle from the perspective of a Federal soldier.

5. *ORA*, series I, vol. 39, part I, 321.

6. Paul Ashdown and Edward Caudill, *The Myth of Nathan Bedford Forrest* (Lanham, MD: Rowman & Littlefield, 2005), 43; Thomas E. Parson, "The Battle of Tupelo (or Harrisburg)," *Blue & Gray*, Vol. XXX, No. 6, 23.

7. *ORA*, series I, vol. 39, part I, 301.

8. *Ibid.*, 301; Parson, 23.

9. *ORA*, series I, vol. 39, part I, 321.

10. *Ibid.*, 251; Jordan and Pryor, 502; W.H. Tucker, *The Fourteenth Wisconsin Vet. Vol. Infantry (Gen. A. J. Smith's Command) in the Expedition and Battle of Tupelo* (Indianapolis: F.E. Engle & Son, 1892), 8; Parson, 23.

11. *ORA*, series I, vol. 39, part I, 330; Lee, *General Hylan B. Lyon*, 126.

12. "The Tupelo Victories," New York *Times*, August 1, 1864.

13. Nathaniel C. Hughes, Jr. *Brigadier General Tyree H. Bell, C.S.A.* (Knoxville: University of Tennessee Press, 2004), 248.

14. Maury, *Recollections of a Virginian*, 206, 213; Parson, 43; Hancock, 422.

15. *ORA*, series I, vol. 39, part I, 280.

16. *Ibid.*, 252, 337.

17. *Ibid.*, 252; "Gen. Smith's Battle Near Tupelo," [St. Paul, MN] *Weekly Pioneer and Democrat*, August 5, 1864.

18. *ORA*, series I, vol. 39, part I, 252; "The Death of Colonel Wilkin," St. Cloud *Democrat*, August 4, 1864; "Col. Alexander Wilson," St. Paul *Weekly Pioneer and Democrat*, August 29, 1864.

19. *ORA*, series I, vol. 39, part I, 322, 336; Herman Hattaway, *General Stephen D. Lee* (Oxford: University Press of Mississippi, 1988), 123.

20. *ORA*, series I, vol. 39, part I, 326.

21. Parson, 46.

22. *ORA*, series I, vol. 39, part I, 331; Morton, 207–208.

23. Wyeth, 388–389.

24. "Gen. Smith's Battle Near Tupelo," St. Paul *Weekly Pioneer and Democrat*, August 5, 1864; "The Tupelo Victories," New York *Times*, August 1, 1864.

25. *ORA*, series I, vol. 39, part I, 280, 363.

26. Andrew Nelson Lytle, *Bedford Forrest and His Critter Company* (Nashville: J.S. Sanders & Company, 1992), 314–315.

27. *ORA*, series I, vol. 39, part I, 323, 332.

28. *Ibid.*, 252; Stephen D. Lee, "The Battle of Tupelo, or Harrisburg, July 14, 1864," *Publications of the Mississippi Historical Society, Vol. VI*, edited by Franklin L. Riley (Oxford: by the Society, 1902), 50; Shelby Foote, *The Civil War, A Narrative: Red River to Appomattox* (New York: Random House, 1986), 512.

29. Parson, 49

30. *Ibid.*.

31. *ORA*, series I, vol. 39, part I, 323; Robert M. Browning, Jr., *Forrest: The Confederacy's Restless Warrior* (Washington, D. C.: Potomac Books, 2004), 70.

32. *ORA*, series I, vol. 39, part I, 324, 328.

33. Edwin C. Bearss, *Forrest at Brice's Crossroads and in North Mississippi in 1864* (Dayton: Press of Morningside Bookshop, 1979), 232.

34. *ORA*, series I, vol. 39, part I, 253.

35. Hattaway, 124; Lee, "The Battle of Tupelo, or Harrisburg," 51–52.

36. Parson, 49.

37. ORA, series I, vol. 39, part II, 204.

38. *Ibid.*, 796.

Chapter Eleven

1. Sherman, *Memoirs*, 621. There was no implied censure of General Maury when Richard Taylor succeeded him in command of the department. Maury's had been an interim assignment between General Stephen D. Lee and whoever came next, and he had known for weeks that a new commander had been selected and was on his way.

2. *ORA*, series I, vol. 32, part III, 868; *ORA*, series I, vol. 32, part II, 772; *ORN*, series I, vol. 21, 719.

3. John Bell Hood, *Advance and Retreat: Personal Experiences in the United States and Confederate States Armies* (New Orleans: Hood Orphan Memorial Fund, 1880), 271–272; Charles Todd Quintard, *Doctor Quintard: Chaplain C. S. A. and Second Bishop of Tennessee; Being His Story of the War (1861–1865)* (Sewanee, TN: The University Press, 1905), 104. Quintard was the bishop who officiated at the funeral of General Polk in Atlanta.

4. "Emancipation In The Border States," New York *Times*, July 19, 1862.

5. Hood, 272.

6. L.J. Fleming, letter to F.W. Sims, July

25, 1864. Bright, Mobile & Ohio, csa-rail-roads.com.

7. Hood, 272; *ORA*, series I, vol. 39, part III, 877.

8. *ORA*, series I, vol. 45, part I, 1243.

9. *ORA*, series I, vol. 52, part II, 776; *ORA*, series I, vol. 45, part II, 55, 306; *ORA*, series I, vol. 41, part IV, 782.

10. Grierson, 302.

11. *Ibid.*, *ORA*, series I, vol. 45, part I, 845.

12. Grierson, 303; *ORA*, series I, vol. 45, part I, 845, 848.

13. Grierson, 304; *ORA*, series I, vol. 45, part I, 845.

14. *ORA*, series I, vol. 45, part I, 863.

15. *Ibid.*, 848; Grierson, 304; "Grierson's Great Raid Through Mississippi," Chicago *Tribune*, February 2, 1865.

16. *ORA*, series I, vol. 45, part I, 849.

17. "Grierson's Great Raid Through Mississippi," Chicago *Tribune*, February 2, 1865.

18. *ORA*, series I, vol. 45, part I, 857.

19. Grierson, 306; "Gen. Grierson's Last Raid," Chicago *Tribune*, January 14, 1865. General Gholson lived until 1883.

20. ORA, series I, vol. 45, part I, 867, 870.

21. *Ibid.*, 846, 871; Ballard, 267.

22. *ORA*, series I, vol. 45, part I, 872.

23. *Ibid.*, 871–872.

24. *Ibid.*, 846–847; 852.

25. "News By Telegraph," Chicago *Tribune*, January 10, 1865; "Gen. Grierson's Last Raid," Chicago *Tribune*, January 14, 1865; "Grierson's Last Raid," New York *Times*, January 13, 1865. A second expedition against the M&O went out in December. General John W. Davidson set out from Baton Rouge with four thousand men to strike the southern end of the railroad, but he failed. He reported, "The bad weather and horrible condition of the roads impeded our march so as to destroy one of the essential elements of our success, celerity." Davidson's men repeatedly had to rebuild bridges and corduroy roads, and their slow rate of progress enabled the enemy to know where they were at all times. In the end, General Canby had to report to Halleck, "General Davidson did not succeed in cutting the Mobile and Ohio Railroad." Davidson's failure made Grierson's success look even greater by comparison (*ORA*, series I, vol. 45, part I, 788; *ORA*, series I, vol. 4, part IV, 869).

26. ORA, series I, vol. 45, part II 740.

27. "Mrs. Ella Palmer as Nurse," *Confederate Veteran* (March 1910), 115; James L. Cooper, "Service with the Twentieth Tennessee," *Confederate Veteran* (June 1925), 223. When the Confederates marched out of Corinth on January 19, they burned the Tishomingo Hotel, inflicting a final indignity on the lodging that, though a witness to so much suffering, had been built only six years earlier, when Corinth was the crossroads of the South.

28. *ORA*, series I, vol. 45, part II, 443; Cooper, 223; R.N. Rea, "Mississippi Soldier of the Confederacy," *Confederate Veteran* (August 1922), 288.

29. Foote, *Red River to Appomattox*, 758; Taylor, 265–266.

30. Rea, 289; Smith Powell, "A Boy Soldier of Alabama," *Confederate Veteran* (January 1921), 22.

31. Statement of the Board of Directors, 1864; "Eighteenth Annual Meeting of the Stockholders of the Mobile & Ohio Railroad Co.," 11. Both from the archives of the Norfolk Southern Corporation, Norfolk, Virginia. Just before the end of the year, the M&O had increased its passenger rates from ten to fifteen cents per mile. The Macon [Georgia] *Telegraph* said, "This is rather a high toll on citizen passengers, but we suppose it is justified by the peculiar circumstances of the times" (Macon *Telegraph*, December 13, 1864).

Chapter Twelve

1. *ORA*, series I, vol. 49, part I, 613.

2. *Ibid.*, 327. The trains did run, but Thomas would not allow Confederate guards to accompany them, as Forrest proposed. He did guarantee that his soldiers would not molest trains run for the stated purpose and under a white flag of truce, "provided none of your soldiers are on board" (*ORA* 49, part I, 735).

3. *ORA*, series I, vol. 45, part I, 779.

4. Milton Brown, letter to C.S.A. Quartermaster General, January 21, 1865. Bright, Mobile & Ohio, csa-railroads.com.

5. *Ibid.*

6. *ORA*, series I, vol. 41, part IV, 684.

7. *ORA*, series I, vol. 39, part I, 429.

8. John Coddington Kinney, "Farragut at Mobile Bay," in *Battles and Leaders of*

the Civil War: Retreat with Honor, edited by Robert Underwood Johnson and Clarence Clough Buel (Edison, N.J.: Castle Books, 1995), 381; Oliver A. Batcheller, "The Battle of Mobile Bay, August 5, 1864," in War Papers: Read Before the Commandery of the State of Maine, Military Order of the Loyal Legion of the United States, Volume I. Portland: The Thurston Print, 1898, 59.

9. ORN, series I, vol. 21, 416–417. Captain Miles D. McAlester explained the reason for lashing the ships together. He said, "The object in lashing by twos was to diminish the chances of sinking or abandonment—one of the couple being struck, for example, so as to sink her, the other would float her up, or if her machinery were disabled, her consort would take her through" (ORA 39: 1, 406).

10. ORN, series I, vol. 21, 405, 417; Paul Calore, Naval Campaigns of the Civil War (Jefferson, N.C.: McFarland, 2015), 190; Kinney, 389, 391.

11. ORN, series I, vol. 21, 417. Farragut was tied to his observation post not only because of the danger of being flung to the deck from the vibrations and concussions of battle, but also because he suffered from vertigo.

12. Ibid., 418.

13. ORA, series I, vol. 39, part I, 408; ORN, series I, vol. 21, 418.

14. ORN, series I, vol. 21, 580.

15. Ibid.

16. ORA, series I, vol. 39, part I, 418.

17. Ibid., 403.

18. ORA, series I, vol. 39, part I, 403; 439

19. Ibid., 440; ORN, series I, vol. 21, 535.

20. ORA series I, vol. 39, part I, 419; ORN, series I, vol. 21, 538.

21. ORA, series I, vol. 39, part II, 796.

22. Ibid., 306.

23. Cox, "Mobile in the War Between the States," 210.

24. ORN, series I, vol. 21, 721; Grant, Personal Memoirs, 679, 758.

25. Grierson, 327; ORA, series I, vol. 49, part I, 81–82.

26. ORA, series I, vol. 49, part I, 92. The spelling of Fort Blakeley presents a problem. It is often spelled Blakely, without the final "e." This is incorrect. The author has used the proper spelling, but when those he quotes have spelled it in the other manner, he has retained it.

27. Ibid., 93, 141; David J. Eicher, The Longest Night: A Military History of the Civil War (New York: Simon & Schuster, 2001), 839.

28. ORA, series I, vol. 49, part I, 93; Eicher, 839; C.C. Andrews, History of the Campaign of Mobile (New York: D. Van Nostrand, 1867), 48–49.

29. ORA, series I, vol. 49, part I, 142, 229.

30. William Lochiel Cameron, "The Battles Opposite Mobile," Confederate Veteran (July 1915), 305; Stephenson, Civil War Memoirs, 361.

31. Andrews, 66, 68.

32. Ibid., 132–133; ORN, series I, vol. 22, 70, 87–88.

33. Stephenson, Civil War Memoirs, 361; Andrews, 88.

34. Noah André Trudeau, Like Men of War: Black Troops in the Civil War, 1862–1865 (Edison, N.J.: Castle Books, 2002), 396, 398.

35. Trudeau, 401, 402; ORA 49, part I, 287; Andrews, 135, 136.

36. Andrews, 141.

37. ORA, series I, vol. 49, part I, 96.

38. Ibid. 96, 132, 229, 283.

39. Ibid., 97.

40. ORA, series I, vol. 49, part I, 9; Eicher, 839.

41. ORA, series I, vol. 49, part I, 230.

42. ORN, series I, vol. 22, 101.

43. Ibid., 101–102.

44. Cameron, 306.

45. Ibid., 306; Trudeau, 406–407; Andrews 201.

46. ORN, series I, vol. 22, 93–94.

47. ORA, series I, vol. 49, part II, 340; "By Telegraph," Nashville Daily Union, March 21, 1865.

48. Dabney H. Maury, "The Defense of Mobile in 1865," Southern Historical Society Papers, Vol. III (Richmond: Southern Historical Society, 1877), 8; "By Telegraph," Nashville Daily Union, March 21, 1865.

49. Maury, "The Defense of Mobile in 1865," 1–2; Richard Taylor, dispatch to Dabney H. Maury, April 11, 1865. Bright, Mobile & Ohio, csa-railroads.com; Taylor, 272.

50. Maury, "The Defense of Mobile in 1865," 3: ORA, series I, vol. 49, part II, 1225.

51. Maury, "The Defense of Mobile

in 1865," 8; *ORA*, series I, vol. 49, part II, 1227, 1231.

52. *ORA*, series I, vol. 49, part II, 459; R.C. Beckett, "The Last Man Killed in the War," *Confederate Veteran* (November 1903), 513.

53. Taylor, 274.

54. *Ibid.*, 276, 277.

55. "Department of the Gulf," New York *Times*, May 16, 1865; *ORA*, series I, vol. 49, part II, 624; Maury, *Recollections of a Virginian*, 131.

56. "But One Army Left to the Rebels," Nashville *Daily Union*, May 10, 1865.

Epilogue

1. *ORA*, series I, vol. 49, part I, 624; Andrew Johnson, *The Papers of Andrew Johnson, Volume 8, May–Aug. 1865*, ed. Paul H. Bergeron (Knoxville: University of Tennessee Press, 1967), 425. *ORA*, Series III, vol. 5, 471–472.

2. *ORA*, Series III, vol. 5, 471–472.

3. Milton Brown, President's Report, Eighteenth Annual Meeting of the Stockholders of the Mobile and Ohio Railroad Company, April 17, 1866, 3. From the archives of the Norfolk Southern Corporation, Norfolk, Virginia.

4. L.J. Fleming, Engineer's Report, Eighteenth Annual Meeting of the Stockholders of the Mobile and Ohio Railroad Company, April 17, 1866, 17–18. From the archives of the Norfolk Southern Corporation, Norfolk, Virginia.

5. *Ibid.*, 25.

Bibliography

Allen, Hall. *Center of Conflict: A Factual Story of the War Between the States in Western Kentucky and Tennessee.* Paducah: The Paducah Sun-Democrat, 1961.

Ambrose, D. Leib. *History of the Seventh Regiment Illinois Volunteer Infantry.* Springfield: Illinois Journal Company, 1868.

Anderson, Charles W. "My Last Meeting With Gen. Forrest." *Confederate Veteran* (Nov. 1896).

Andrews, C.C. *History of the Campaign of Mobile.* New York: D. Van Nostrand, 1867.

Ashdown, Paul, and Edward Caudill. *The Myth of Nathan Bedford Forrest.* Lanham, MD: Rowman & Littlefield, 2005.

Askew, Samuel L., III. "An Analysis of Unit Cohesion in the 42nd Alabama Infantry." Master's Thesis, U.S. Army Command and General Staff College, Fort Leavenworth, KS, 2003. https://apps.dtic.mil/dtic/tr/fulltext/u2/a416140.pdf. Accessed September 21, 2019.

Austill, Hurieosco. "Fort Morgan in the Confederacy: Letter by Hurieosco Austill." *Alabama Historical Quarterly* (Summer 1945).

Ballard, Michael B. *The Civil War in Mississippi: Major Campaigns and Battles.* Jackson: University Press of Mississippi, 2011.

Banta, R.E. *The Ohio.* New York: Rinehart & Company, 1940.

Barry, Robert L. "The Lookout Battery." *Confederate Veteran* (Oct. 1922).

Batcheller, Oliver A. "The Battle of Mobile Bay, August 5, 1864." In *War Papers: Read Before the Commandery of the State of Maine, Military Order of the Loyal Legion of the United States, Volume I.* Portland: The Thurston Print, 1898.

Bearss, Edwin C. *Forrest at Brice's Crossroads and in North Mississippi in 1864.* Dayton: Press of Morningside Bookshop, 1979.

Beauregard, G.T. "The Campaign of Shiloh." In *Battles and Leaders of the Civil War: The Opening Battles.* Edited by Robert Underwood Johnson and Clarence Clough Buel. Edison, N.J.: Castle Books, 1995.

Bennett, Stewart. "From Brice's Crossroads to Grierson's Raid: The Struggle for North Mississippi." *Journal of Mississippi History* (Winter 2013).

Bergeron, Arthur W., Jr. *Confederate Mobile.* Baton Rouge: Louisiana State University Press, 2000.

Bielski, Mark F. "A Mortal Blow to the Confederacy." *North and South* (Sept. 2020).

Black, Robert C. *The Railroads of the Confederacy.* Chapel Hill: University of North Carolina Press, 1998.

Briant, Charles C. *History of the Sixth Regiment Indiana Volunteer Infantry.* Indianapolis: Wm. B. Burford, Printer and Binder, 1891.

Bright, David L., compiler. "M&O." http://www.csa-railroads.com/Mobile_and_Ohio.htm.

Brooks, Addie Lou. "The Building of the Trunk Line Railroads in West Tennessee, 1852–1861." *Tennessee Historical Quarterly,* June 1942.

Brown, Milton. President's Reports, Annual Meetings of the Stockholders of the Mobile and Ohio Railroad Company. From the archives of the Norfolk Southern Corporation, Norfolk, Virginia.

Browning, Robert M., Jr. *Forrest: The Confederacy's Restless Warrior*. Washington, D.C.: Potomac Books, 2004.

Browning, Robert M., Jr. "Go Ahead, Go Ahead." *Naval History Magazine*, December 2009.

Busbee, Westley F., Jr. *Mississippi: A History*. Malden, MA: John Wiley & Sons, 2015.

Byers, S. H. M. *With Fire and Sword*. New York: The Neal Publishing Company, 1911.

Bynum, Victoria E. *The Free State of Jones: Mississippi's Longest Civil War*. Chapel Hill: University of North Carolina Press, 2003.

Bynum, Victoria E. "Newt Knight and the Free State of Jones: Myth, Memory, and Imagination." *Journal of Mississippi History* (Winter 2013).

Cadwallader, Sylvanus. *Three Years With Grant*. Lincoln: University of Nebraska Press, 1996.

Calbert, Jack. "The Jackson Purchase and the End of the Neutrality Policy in Kentucky." *Filson Club History Quarterly* (July 1964).

Calore, Paul. *Naval Campaigns of the Civil War*. Jefferson, N.C.: McFarland, 2015.

Cameron, William Lochiel. "The Battles Opposite Mobile." *Confederate Veteran* (July 1915).

Carter, Arthur B. *The Tarnished Cavalier: General Earl Van Dorn, C. S. A*. Knoxville: University of Tennessee Press, 1999.

Cartmell, J.M. "Witness to the Battle of Belmont." *Confederate Veteran* (Apr. 1908).

Catton, Bruce. *Grant Moves South*. Boston: Little, Brown, 1960.

Catton, Bruce. *Grant Takes Command*. Boston: Little, Brown, 1969.

Chernow, Ron. *Grant*. New York: Penguin, 2017.

Chetlain, Augustus L. "The Battle of Corinth, October 3 and 4, 1862." In *War Papers Read before the Michigan Commandery of the Military Order of the Loyal Legion of the United States, Volume 2*. Detroit: James H. Stones & Co., Printers, 1898.

Chetlain, Augustus L. *Recollections of Seventy Years*. Galena, IL: The Gazette Publishing Company, 1895.

Civil Engineer. *Mobile & Ohio Railroad, Diary Dec. 14, 1853—Dec. 31, 1854*. Alabama Department of Archives and History, Montgomery, Alabama.

Clark, John E. *Railroads in the Civil War: The Impact of Management on Victory and Defeat*. Baton Rouge: Louisiana State University Press, 2004.

Collins, Richard H. "Civil War Annals of Kentucky (1861–1865)." Edited by Hambleton Tapp. *Filson Club History Quarterly* (July 1961).

Collins, Steven Gedson. "Organizing the *South: Railroads, Plantations, and War." PhD diss. Louisiana State University, 1999. www.digitalcommons.lus.edu/cgi/viewcontent.cgi?article=8074&content=gradschool_disstheses. Accessed August 11, 2019.

Commonwealth of Kentucky. *Acts of the General Assembly of the Commonwealth of Kentucky: Passed at the December Session, 1847*. Frankfort: A.G. Hodges & Co., State Printers, 1848.

Commonwealth of Kentucky. *Journal of the Senate of the Commonwealth of Kentucky* [Dec. 31 1847–Mar. 1, 1848]. Frankfort: A. G. Hodges, State Printer, 1847.

Cook, V.Y. "Scouting Expedition of Forrest's Men." *Confederate Veteran* (Jan.1909).

Cooper, James L. "Service With the Twentieth Tennessee." Edited by Deering J. Roberts. *Confederate Veteran* (June 1925).

Coulter, E. Merton. *The Civil War and Readjustment in Kentucky*. Gloucester, MA: Peter Smith, 1966.

Cox, Benjamin B. "Mobile in the War Between the States." *Confederate Veteran* (May 1916).

Cozzens, Peter. *The Darkest Days of the War: The Battles of Iuka and Corinth*. Chapel Hill: University of North Carolina Press, 1997.

Craig, Berry F. "Northern Conquerors and Southern Deliverers: The Civil War Comes to the Jackson Purchase." *Register of the Kentucky Historical Society* (Jan. 1975).

Cunningham, O. Edward. *Shiloh and the Western Campaign of 1862*. Eds. Gary D. Joiner and Timothy B. Smith. New York: Savas Beatie, 2007.

Davidson, N.P. Untitled. *Confederate Veteran* (Apr. 1908).

De Bow, J.D.B. "Direct Trade of Southern States With Europe." *The Commercial Review of the South and West*, Volume IV, 1847.

Dinkins, James. "The Battle of Brice's Crossroads." *Confederate Veteran* (Oct. 1925).

Dinkins, James. "The Last Campaign of Forrest's Cavalry." *Confederate Veteran* (Apr. 1927).

Dinkins, James. *Personal Recollections and Experiences in the Confederate Army*. Cincinnati: The Robert Clarke Company, 1897.

Dodd, William Edward. *Jefferson Davis*. Philadelphia: George W. Jacobs & Company, 1907.

Duncan, Thomas D. *Recollections of Thomas D. Duncan: A Confederate Soldier*. Nashville: McQuiddy Printing Company, 1922.

Eaton, Clement. *The Growth of Southern Civilization, 1790–1860*. New York: Harper Torchbooks, 1961.

Eicher, David J. *The Longest Night: A Military History of the Civil War*. New York: Simon & Schuster, 2002.

Farley, James W. *Forgotten Valor: The First Missouri Cavalry Regiment, C.S.A.* Shawnee Mission, KS: Two Trails Publishing, 1996.

Fisher, Charles E. "The U. S. Military Railroads." *The Railway and Locomotive Historical Society Bulletin*, October 1942.

Fleming, L.J. Chief Engineer's Reports, Annual Meetings of the Stockholders of the Mobile and Ohio Railroad Company. From the archives of the Norfolk Southern Corporation, Norfolk, Virginia.

Foote, Shelby. *The Civil War, a Narrative: Fort Sumter to Perryville*. New York: Random House, 1986.

Foote, Shelby. *The Civil War, a Narrative: Fredericksburg to Meridian*. New York: Random House, 1986.

Foote, Shelby. *The Civil War, a Narrative: Red River to Appomattox*. New York: Random House, 1986.

Forbes, Stephen A. *Grierson's Cavalry Raid*. Springfield: Illinois State Historical Society, 1907.

Forrester, Rebel. "A Note on Obion County." *Tennessee Historical Quarterly*, Winter 1978.

Forsyth, Michael J. *The Red River Campaign of 1864 and the Loss by the Confederacy of the Civil War*. Jefferson, NC: McFarland, 2002.

Fort, W. B. "First Submarine in the Confederate Navy." *Confederate Veteran* (Oct. 1918).

Foster, Buck T. *Sherman's Mississippi Campaign*. Tuscaloosa: University of Alabama Press, 2006.

Frémont, John C. "In Command in Missouri." In *Battles and Leaders of the Civil War: The Opening Battles*. Edited by Robert Underwood Johnson and Clarence Clough Buel. Edison, N.J.: Castle Books, 1995.

George, Henry. *History of the 3d, 7th, 8th and 12th Kentucky C. S. A.* Lyndon, KY: Mull Wathen Historic Press, 1970.

Grant, Ulysses S. "Chattanooga." In *Battles and Leaders of the Civil War: The Tide Shifts*. Edited by Robert Underwood Johnson and Clarence Clough Buel. Edison, N.J.: Castle Books, 1995.

Grant, Ulysses S. *Personal Memoirs of U.S. Grant*. New York: Library of America, 1990.

Grierson, Benjamin H. *A Just and Righteous Cause: Benjamin H. Grierson's Civil War Memoir*. Edited by Bruce J. Dinges and Shirley A. Leckie. Carbondale: Southern Illinois University Press, 2008.

Hamilton, Charles S. "Hamilton's Division at Corinth." In *Battles and Leaders of the Civil War: The Struggle Intensifies*. Edited by Robert Underwood Johnson and Clarence Clough Buel. Edison, N.J.: Castle Books, 1995.

Hancock, Richard R. *Hancock's Diary: Or, A History of the Second Tennessee Confederate Cavalry*. Nashville: Brandon Printing Co., 1887.

Harrison, Lowell H., and James C. Klotter. *A New History of Kentucky*. Lexington: University Press of Kentucky, 1997.

Hartje, Robert George. "Van Dorn Conducts a Raid on Holly Springs and Enters Tennessee." *Tennessee Historical Quarterly*, June 1959.

Hartje, Robert George. *Van Dorn: The Life and Times of a Confederate General*. Nashville: Vanderbilt University Press, 1967.

Hattaway, Herman. *General Stephen D. Lee.* Jackson: University Press of Mississippi, 1988.

Hattaway, Herman, and Archer Jones. *How the North Won: A Military History of the Civil War.* Urbana: University of Illinois Press, 1991.

Hay, John. *Lincoln and the Civil War in the Diaries and Letters of John Hay.* New York: Dodd, Mead, 1939.

Headley, Joel. *Farragut, and Our Naval Commanders.* New York: E.B. Treat & Co., Publishers, 1867.

Hearn, Chester G. *Gray Raiders of the Sea: How Eight Confederate Warships Destroyed the Union's High Seas Commerce.* Camden, ME: International Marine Publishing, 1992.

Hearn, Chester G. *Mobile Bay and the Mobile Campaign: The Last Great Battles of the Civil War.* Jefferson, N.C.: McFarland, 2010.

Helm, W. P. "Close Fighting at Iuka, Miss." *Confederate Veteran* (Apr. 1911).

Hess, Earl J. *Civil War Logistics: A Study of Military Transportation.* Baton Rouge: Louisiana State University Press, 2017.

Holmes, W.C. "The Battle of Corinth." *Confederate Veteran* (Aug. 1919).

Hood, John Bell. *Advance and Retreat: Personal Experiences in the United States and Confederate States Armies.* New Orleans: Hood Orphan Memorial Fund, 1880.

Horn, Huston. *Leonidas Polk: Warrior Bishop of the Confederacy.* Lawrence: University Press of Kansas, 2019.

Hubbard, George H. "In the Battle of Belmont." *Confederate Veteran* (Dec. 1925).

Hubbard, John Milton. *Notes of a Private.* Memphis: E.H. Clarke & Brother, 1909.

Hughes, Nathaniel Cheairs, and Roy P. Stonesifer. *The Life and Wars of Gideon J. Pillow.* Chapel Hill: University of North Carolina Press, 1993.

Hughes, Nathaniel Cheairs, Jr. *The Battle of Belmont: Grant Strikes South.* Chapel Hill: University of North Carolina Press, 1991.

Hughes, Nathaniel Cheairs, Jr. *Brigadier General Tyree H. Bell, C. S. A.* Knoxville: University of Tennessee Press, 2004.

Inge, Mrs. F.A. "Corinth, Miss., in Early War Days." *Confederate Veteran* (Sept. 1909).

Irwin, Richard B. "Land Operations Against Mobile." In *Battles and Leaders of the Civil War: Retreat with Honor.* Edited by Robert Underwood Johnson and Clarence Clough Buel. Edison, N.J.: Castle Books, 1995.

Jackson, Oscar L. *The Colonel's Diary: Journals Kept Before and During the Civil War by the Late Colonel Oscar L. Jackson; Sometime Commander of the 63rd Regiment O.V.I.* Edited by David Prentice Jackson. Sharon, PA: by the editor, 1922.

Jodon, F.D. "Concerning the Battle of Belmont." *Confederate Veteran* (Jan. 1901).

Johnson, Andrew. *The Papers of Andrew Johnson, Vol. 8, May—Aug 1865.* Edited by Paul H. Bergeron. Knoxville: University of Tennessee Press, 1967.

Johnston, James D. "The Ram 'Tennessee' at Mobile Bay." In *Battles and Leaders of the Civil War: Retreat with Honor.* Edited by Robert Underwood Johnson and Clarence Clough Buel. Edison, N.J.: Castle Books, 1995.

Johnston, Joseph E. "Jefferson Davis and the Mississippi Campaign." In *Battles and Leaders of the Civil War: The Tide Shifts.* Edited by Robert Underwood Johnson and Clarence Clough Buel. Edison, N.J.: Castle Books, 1995.

Johnston, William Preston. "Albert Sidney Johnston at Shiloh." In *Battles and Leaders of the Civil War: The Opening Battles.* Edited by Robert Underwood Johnson and Clarence Clough Buel. Edison, N.J.: Castle Books, 1995.

Jordon, Thomas, and J.P. Pryor. *The Campaigns of Lieut.-Gen. N. B. Forrest, and of Forrest's Cavalry.* New Orleans: Blelock & Company, 1868.

Keegan, John. *The American Civil War: A Military History.* New York: Vintage, 2009.

Kinney, John Coddington. "Farragut at Mobile Bay." In *Battles and Leaders of the Civil War: Retreat with Honor.* Edited by Robert Underwood Johnson and Clarence Clough Buel. Edison, N.J.: Castle Books, 1995.

Kornweibel, Theodore, Jr. "Railroads and Slavery." *Railroad History* (Fall-Winter 2003).

Kurtz, William B. "Old Rosy Reconsidered." *The Civil War Monitor* (Summer 2019).

Lamb, J. Peter. *Railroads of Meridian.* Bloomington: Indiana University Press, 2012.

Lamb, Justin. "The South Carolina of Kentucky: The Jackson Purchase Secession

Movement" B.A. thesis, Murray State University, Murray, KY, 2017 https://digitalcommons.murraystate.edu/bis437/108. Accessed August 16, 2019.

Lang, Andrew F. "The Perils of Occupation." *The Civil War Monitor* (Summer 2019).

"The Last Man Killed in the War." *Confederate Veteran* (Nov. 1903).

Lee, Dan. *The Civil War in the Jackson Purchase, 1861–1862.* Jefferson, N.C.: McFarland, 2014.

Lee, Dan. *General Hylan B. Lyon: A Kentucky Confederate and the War in the West.* Knoxville: University of Tennessee Press, 2019.

Lee, Stephen D. "The Battle of Tupelo, or Harrisburg, July 14, 1864." *Publications of the Mississippi Historical Society, Vol. VI.* Edited by Franklin L. Riley. Oxford: by the Society, 1902.

Lincoln, Abraham. *The Collected Works of Abraham Lincoln.* Edited by Roy P. Basler. New Brunswick, N.J.: Rutgers University Press, 1953–1955, Vol. 6.

Love, W.A. "Company Records." *Confederate Veteran* (Feb. 1925).

Love, W.A. "Mississippi Comrades." *Confederate Veteran* (Aug. 1921).

Lyon, Hylan B. "Memoirs of Hylan B. Lyon." Edited by Edward M. Coffman, *Tennessee Historical Quarterly,* May 1959.

Lytle, Andrew Nelson. *Bedford Forrest and His Critter Company.* Nashville: J.S. Sanders & Company, 1993.

Marrs, Aaron W. *Railroads in the Old South: Pursuing Progress in a Slave Society.* Baltimore: JHU Press, 2009.

Marthon, Joseph. "The Lashing of Admiral Farragut in the Rigging, II." In *Battles and Leaders of the Civil War: Retreat with Honor.* Edited by Robert Underwood Johnson and Clarence Clough Buel. Edison, N.J.: Castle Books, 1995.

Maury, Dabney H. "The Defense of Mobile in 1865." *Southern Historical Society Papers, Vol. III.* Richmond: Southern Historical Society, 1877.

Maury, Dabney H. *Recollections of a Virginian in the Mexican, Indian, and Civil Wars.* New York: Charles Scribner's Sons, 1894.

McClay, J.H. "Defense of Robinette." In *Civil War Sketches and Incidents: Papers Read by Companions of the Commandery of the State of Nebraska, Military Order of the Loyal Legion of the United States, Volume I.* Omaha: by the Commandery, 1902.

McCord, William B. "Battle of Corinth, The Campaigns Preceding and Leading Up to This Battle, and Its Results." In *Glimpses of the Nation's Struggle, Fourth Series: Papers Read Before the Minnesota Commandery of the Military Order of the Loyal Legion of the United States, 1892–1897.* Saint Paul: H. L. Collins Co., 1898.

McFeely, William S. *Grant: A Biography.* New York: W.W. Norton, 1982.

McKinstry, J.A. "With Col. Rogers When He Fell: Thrilling Recollections of Fort Robinette." *Confederate Veteran* (July 1896).

McPherson, James M. *Battle Cry of Freedom: The Civil War Era.* New York: Oxford University Press, 1988.

Miller, M.A. "Another Account." *Confederate Veteran* (June 1904).

Miller, Nathan. *The U. S. Navy: A History.* Annapolis: Naval Institute Press, 1997.

Milner, W.J. "Lieutenant General William Joseph Hardee." *Confederate Veteran* (Aug. 1914).

Montgomery, Frank A. *Reminiscences of a Mississippian in Peace and War.* Cincinnati: The Robert Clarke Company Press, 1901.

Morgan, George H. "Experiences in the Enemy's Lines." *Confederate Veteran* (May 1909).

Morton, John Watson. *The Artillery of Nathan Bedford Forrest's Cavalry.* Nashville: Printing House of the M. E. Church, South, 1909.

"Mrs. Ella Palmer as Nurse." *Confederate Veteran* (Mar. 1910).

"Mrs. Ella Palmer: Reminiscences of Her Service in Hospitals." *Confederate Veteran* (Feb. 1910).

Mullen, Jay Carlton. "The Turning of Columbus." *Register of the Kentucky Historical Society* (July 1966).

Munday, Jessie. "The Railroads of Kentucky 1861–1865." Master's Thesis, University of Louisville, 1925. https://doi.org/10.18297/etd/1026. Accessed July 26, 2019.

Osborne, Thomas D. "Kentucky's Gifts to the Confederacy." *Confederate Veteran* (May 1905).

Otey, Mercer. "Story of Our Great War." *Confederate Veteran* (Mar. 1901).

Page, Richard L. "The Defense of Fort Morgan." In *Battles and Leaders of the Civil War: Retreat with Honor.* Edited by Robert Underwood Johnson and Clarence Clough Buel. Edison, N.J.: Castle Books, 1995.

Parson, Thomas E. "The Battle of Tupelo (or Harrisburg)." *Blue & Gray*, Vol. XXX, No. 6.

Payne, James E. "The Sixth Missouri at Corinth." *Confederate Veteran* (Dec. 1928).

Perkins, J.R. "Gen. Sterling Price." *Confederate Veteran* (Jan. 1904).

Phillips, Ulrich B. *A History of Transportation in the Eastern Cotton Belt to 1860.* New York: Columbia University Press, 1908.

Pickett, William D. "The Bursting of the Lady Polk." *Confederate Veteran* (June 1904).

Polk, William M. "General Polk and the Battle of Belmont." In *Battles and Leaders of the Civil War: The Opening Battles.* Edited by Robert Underwood Johnson and Clarence Clough Buel. Edison, N.J.: Castle Books, 1995.

Powell, Smith. "A Boy Soldier of Alabama." *Confederate Veteran* (Jan. 1921).

Quintard, Charles Todd. *Doctor Quintard: Chaplain C. S. A. and Second Bishop of Tennessee; Being His Story of the War (1861–1865).* Sewanee, TN: The University Press, 1905.

Rabb, James W. *Confederate General Lloyd Tilghman: A Biography.* Jefferson, N.C.: McFarland, 2006.

Randall, G.M. "A Mitred Major-General." *The Church Monthly,* June 1861.

Rawley, James A. *Turning Points of the Civil War.* Lincoln: University of Nebraska Press, 1989.

Rea, R.N. "Mississippi Soldier of the Confederacy." *Confederate Veteran* (Aug. 1922).

Reed, David W. *Campaigns and Battle of the Twelfth Regiment Iowa Veteran Volunteer Infantry.* Evanston, IL: by the author, 1903.

Rosecrans, William S. "The Battle of Corinth." In *Battles and Leaders of the Civil War: The Struggle Intensifies.* Edited by Robert Underwood Johnson and Clarence Clough Buel. Edison, N.J.: Castle Books, 1995.

Russell, William Howard. *My Diary North and South.* Boston: T.O.H.P. Burnham, 1863.

Scharf, J. T. "The Sinking of the Housatonic." *Confederate Veteran* (June 1916).

Seaton, John. "The Battle of Belmont." In *War Talks in Kansas: A Series of Papers Read Before the Kansas Commandery of the Military Order of the Loyal Legion of the United States.* Kansas City: Franklin Hudson Publishing Company, 1906.

Sherman, William T. "The Grand Strategy of the Last Year of the War." In *Battles and Leaders of the Civil War: Retreat with Honor.* Edited by Robert Underwood Johnson and Clarence Clough Buel. Edison, N.J.: Castle Books, 1995.

Sherman, William T. *Memoirs of General W.T. Sherman.* New York: Library of America, 1990.

Sherman, William T. *Sherman's Civil War: Selected Correspondence of William T. Sherman, 1860–1865.* Edited by Brooks D. Simpson and Jean V. Berlin. Chapel Hill: University of North Carolina Press, 1999.

Singletary, Don. "The Battle of Belmont." *Confederate Veteran* (Nov. 1915).

Smith, Albert E. "A Few Days with the Eighth Regiment, Wisconsin Volunteers at Iuka and Corinth." In *War Papers Read before the Commandery of the State of Wisconsin, Military Order of the Loyal Legion of the United States, Volume IV.* Milwaukee: Burdick & Allen, 1914.

Smith, Andrew F. *Starving the South: How the North Won the Civil War.* New York: St. Martin's Press, 2011.

Smith, Timothy B. "'How Does It All Sum Up?': The Significance of the Iuka—Corinth Campaign." *Journal of Mississippi History* (Winter 2013).

Smith, Timothy B. *Mississippi in the Civil War: The Home Front.* Jackson: University Press of Mississippi, 2010.

Snead, Thomas L. "With Price East of the Mississippi." In *Battles and Leaders of the Civil War: The Struggle Intensifies.* Edited by Robert Underwood Johnson and Clarence Clough Buel. Edison, N.J.: Castle Books, 1995.

Spence, Philip B. "Services in the Confederacy." *Confederate Veteran* (Nov. 1900).

Stanley, David S. "The Battle of Corinth." In *Personal Recollections of the War of the Rebellion: Addresses Delivered Before the Commandery of the State of New York, Military Order of the Loyal Legion of the United States, Volume II.* Edited by A. Noel Blakeman. New York: G.P. Putnam's Sons, 1897.

Stanley, Henry Morton. *The Autobiography of Sir Henry Morton Stanley.* Boston: Houghton Mifflin, 1909.

State of Tennessee. *Journal of the House of Representatives of the State of Tennessee at the Twenty-Seventh General Assembly, Held at Nashville, 1847–1848.* Knoxville: Jas. C. & Jno. L. Moses, 1848.

Stephenson, P. D. "Defense of Spanish Fort on Mobile Bay." *Southern Historical Society Papers.* Richmond: Wm. Ellis Jones' Sons, Printers, 1914.

Stephenson, Philip Daingerfield. *Civil War Memoir of Philip Daingerfield Stephenson, D.D.* Edited by Nathaniel Cheairs Huges, Jr. Baton Rouge: Louisiana State University Press, 1998.

Stickles, Arndt. *Simon Bolivar Buckner: Borderland Knight.* Chapel Hill: University of North Carolina Press, 2001.

Stiles, John C., compiler. "In the Years of War: Confederates at Corinth. *Confederate Veteran* (Mar. 1918).

Stuart, C.B. *A Biographical Sketch of John Childe, Civil Engineer.* New York: Charles B. Norton, 1861.

Sun Tzu. *The Art of War.* Translated by Lionel Giles. New York: Cosimo Classics, 2010.

Surby, R. W. *Grierson's Raids and Hatch's Sixty-Four Days March.* Chicago: Rounds and James, Steam Books and Job Printer, 1865.

Tarrant, E.W. "Siege and Capture of Fort Blakely." *Confederate Veteran* (Oct. 1915).

Taylor, John M. *Confederate Raiders: Raphael Semmes of the Alabama.* Washington, D.C.: Brassey's, 1994.

Taylor, Richard. *Destruction and Reconstruction.* Edited by Richard Harwell. New York: Longmans, Green and Co., 1955.

Thomas, William G. *The Iron Way: Railroads, the Civil War, and the Making of Modern America.* New Haven: Yale University Press, 2011.

Trefousse, Hans L. *Andrew Johnson: A Biography.* New York: W.W., 1989.

Trudeau, Noah André. *Like Men of War: Black Troops in the Civil War, 1862–1865.* Edison, N.J.: Castle Books, 2002.

Tucker, W. H. *The Fourteenth Wisconsin Vet. Vol. Infantry (Gen. A. J. Smith's Command) in the Expedition and Battle of Tupelo.* Indianapolis: F.E. Engle & Son, 1892.

Twain, Mark. *Life on the Mississippi.* New York: Harper and Brothers, 1917.

United States Congress. *Biographical Directory of the United States Congress, 1774–1989, Bicentennial Edition.* Washington, D.C.: Government Printing Office, 1989.

United States Naval Records Office. *Official Records of the Union and Confederate Navies in the War of the Rebellion, Series I.* 27 Volumes. Washington, D.C.: Government Printing Office, 1894–1917.

United States War Department. *The War of the Rebellion: A Compilation of the Official Records of the Union and Confederate Armies.* 129 Volumes. Washington, D.C.: Government Printing Office, 1880–1901.

"Vivid War Experiences at Ripley, Miss." *Confederate Veteran* (June 1905).

Walke, Henry. "The Gun-Boats at Belmont and Fort Henry." In *Battles and Leaders of the Civil War: The Opening Battles.* Edited by Robert Underwood Johnson and Clarence Clough Buel. Edison, N.J.: Castle Books, 1995.

Walke, Henry. *Naval Scenes and Reminiscences of the Civil War.* New York: F.R. Reed, 1877.

Ward, John A. "A New Look at Antebellum Southern Railroad Development." *Journal of Southern History* (Aug. 1973).

Wardner, Horace. "Reminiscences of a Surgeon." In *Military Essays and Recollections: Papers Read Before the Commandery of the State of Illinois, Military Order of the Loyal Legion of the United States, Volume III.* Chicago: The Dial Press, 1899.

Waring, George E., Jr. "The Sooy Smith Expedition (February 1864)." In *Battles and Leaders of the Civil War: Retreat with Honor.* Edited by Robert Underwood Johnson and Clarence Clough Buel. Edison, N.J.: Castle Books, 1995.

Warner, Ezra J. *Generals in Blue*. Baton Rouge: Louisiana State University Press, 2006.

Warner, Ezra J. *Generals in Gray*. Baton Rouge: Louisiana State University Press, 2008.

Waterman, George S. "Afloat—Afield—Afloat." *Confederate Veteran* (Jan. 1898).

Waterman, George S. "Afloat—Afield—Afloat." *Confederate Veteran* (Jan. 1901).

Watkins, Sam. *Company Aytch*. Edited by M. Thomas Inge. New York: Plume Books, 1999.

Watson, J. Crittenden. "The Lashing of Admiral Farragut in the Rigging, I." In *Battles and Leaders of the Civil War: Retreat with Honor*. Edited by Robert Underwood Johnson and Clarence Clough Buel. Edison, N.J.: Castle Books, 1995.

"The Weight They Carried." *The Civil War Monitor* (Summer 2019).

White, Ronald C. *American Ulysses: A Life of Ulysses S. Grant*. New York: Random House, 2016.

Whitsitt, W.H. "A Year With Forrest." *Confederate Veteran* (Aug. 1917).

Wills, Brian Steel. *A Battle from the Start: The Life of Nathan Bedford Forrest*. New York: HarperCollins, 1992.

Wolcott, Laurens W. "The Battle of Corinth." In *War Papers Read before the Michigan Commandery of the Military Order of the Loyal Legion of the United States, Volume 2*. Detroit: James H. Stone & Company, Printers, 1898.

Wood, W.J. *Civil War Generalship: The Art of Command*. Cambridge, MA: Da Capo Press, 1997.

Woodrick, Jim. "Successful in an Eminent Degree: Sherman's 1864 Meridian Expedition." *Journal of Mississippi History* (Winter 2013).

Woodworth, Steven E. *Jefferson Davis and His Generals: The Failure of Confederate Command in the West*. Lawrence: University Press of Kansas, 1990.

Woodworth, Steven E. *Nothing But Victory: The Army of the Tennessee, 1861–1865*. New York: Alfred A. Knopf, 2005.

Wright, Marcus J. "Personal Recollections of General Grant." *Confederate Veteran* (Aug. 1909).

Wyeth, John Allan. *That Devil Forrest: Life of General Nathan Bedford Forrest*. Baton Rouge: Louisiana State University Press, 1989.

Wynne, Ben. *Mississippi's Civil War: A Narrative History*. Macon: Mercer University Press, 2006.

Index

Numbers in **bold italics** indicate pages with illustrations